The Daily Economist

A chronicle of contemporary subjects showing the scope and originality of economic research and its application to real-world issues.

Edited by

HARRY G. JOHNSON

*The University of Chicago
and
The London School of Economics*

and

BURTON A. WEISBROD

The University of Wisconsin

PRENTICE-HALL, INC., Englewood Cliffs, N. J.

Library of Congress Cataloging in Publication Data

JOHNSON, HARRY GORDON,   comp.
    The daily economist.

    1. Economics—Addresses, essays, lectures.
I. Weisbrod, Burton Allen,   joint comp.
II. Title.
HB34.J62   330   72-8473
ISBN 0-13-196717-7

Printed in the United States of America

10   9   8   7   6   5   4   3   2   1

PRENTICE-HALL INTERNATIONAL, INC., *London*
PRENTICE-HALL OF AUSTRALIA, PTY. LTD., *Sydney*
PRENTICE-HALL OF CANADA, LTD., *Toronto*
PRENTICE-HALL OF INDIA PRIVATE LIMITED, *New Delhi*
PRENTICE-HALL OF JAPAN, INC., *Tokyo*

ACKNOWLEDGMENTS

*The editors wish to acknowledge their indebtedness to
the following for permission to reprint the articles
appearing in this book.*

American Economic Review: "The Marine Fisheries: A
Problem in International Cooperation," by James Crutchfield, May 1964, 207-218; "The Economic Effects of
Malaria Eradication," by Robin Barlow, May 1967,
130-148, (appendix deleted); "Economics of the University," by Allan M. Cartter, May 1965, 481-494;
"On the Performing Arts: The Anatomy of Their Economic Problems," by W. J. Baumol and W. G. Bowen,
May 1965, 495-502; "The Economics of Broadcasting
and Advertising—The Economics of Broadcasting and
Government Policy," by R. H. Coase, May 1966, 440-
447; "The Pricing of Textbooks and the Remuneration
of Authors," by Paul M. Horvitz, May 1966, 412-420;
"The Pope and the Price of Fish," by Frederick W.
Bell, December 1968, 1346-1350.

Basic Research and National Goals: "Federal Support
of Basic Research: Some Economic Issues," by Harry G.
Johnson, from a report to the Committee on Science and
Astronautics, U.S. House of Representatives, by the
National Academy of Sciences (Washington, D.C.:
Government Printing Office, March 1965), 127-141.

The Cambridge Journal: "The Economics of Undertaking," by Harry G. Johnson, 1950-1951, *4*, 240-244.

Journal of Human Resources: "Investing in Human
Capital," by Burton A. Weisbrod, Summer 1966, 5-21;
"The Distribution of Costs and Direct Benefits of
Public Higher Education: The Case of California," by
W. Lee Hansen and Burton A. Weisbrod, Spring 1969,
176-191.

The Journal of Law and Economics: "Price Discrimination in Medicine," by Reuben A. Kessel, 1958, 20-53,
(excluding footnotes, original enumeration 1-5, 7, 8, 11,
14, 15, 17, 19-34, 38, 39, 42-45, 47-77, 79-84, and
deleting text, original pagination 26, 37, 38-41, 42).

Journal of Political Economy: "The Baseball Players'
Labor Market," by Simon Rottenberg, © 1956 by The
University of Chicago Press, June 1956, 242-258;
"The Clandestine Distribution of Heroin, Its Discovery
and Suppression," by Simon Rottenberg, © 1968 by
The University of Chicago Press, January-February 1968,
78-90; "An Economic Theory of Political Action in a
Democracy," by Anthony Downs, © 1957 by The Uni-
versity of Chicago Press, April 1957, 135-150; "The
Economy of Patronage," by James Q. Wilson, © 1961
by The University of Chicago Press, August 1961, 369-
380; "Castro and Economic Man, or What Is a
Prisoner Worth," by Burton A. Weisbrod, © 1963 by
The University of Chicago Press, April 1963, 172;
"Are You Worth Your Weight in Gold," by Harry G.
Johnson, © 1967 by The University of Chicago Press,
April 1967, 205-207.

The Macmillan Company: "Economics of The Brain
Drain: An 'Internationalist' Model," by Harry G. Johnson, reprinted with permission of The Macmillan Company from *The Brain Drain* by Walter Adams, copyright © 1968 by Walter Adams.

New Society: "The Economics of Student Protest," by
Harry G. Johnson, November 1968, 673-675.

Quarterly Journal of Economics: "The Wizard Who
Oversimplified: A Fable," by Robert N. Anthony [Harold
Peterson], May 1965, 209-211; "The Peculiar Eco-
nomics of Professional Sports," by Walter C. Neale,
February 1964, 1-14.

Western Economic Journal: "The Economics of Recreation: Progress and Problems," by Omer L. Carey,
Spring 1965, *3*, 172-181.

The Daily Economist

TABLE OF CONTENTS

The Daily Economist

PREFACE

The daily newspaper chronicles contemporary events in a wide variety of forms. Every reader has become accustomed to reading, or at least turning past, the "economic" news—of Wall Street, taxation, interest rates, balance-of-payments, unemployment, and inflation. Yet this distinction between economic news and other news is actually quite artificial, for economists have been turning their attention to an ever-widening array of current social issues.

This book has been planned from the onset to show the great scope and originality of recent applications of economics to real-world problems. The articles reprinted here have been organized according to the sections of a newspaper, not in an attempt to be different, but to document our view that the tools of economic analysis can be—and indeed are being—used to advantage in understanding problems ranging from the Arts to Zoology.

We do not for a moment suggest that important social problems can be fully understood, let alone solved, by economists. Yet how many people realize that economists are in fact investigating not only the traditional economic issues but also such matters as the prospects for theaters and ballets (Baumol and Bowen); the reasons why professional sports teams organize into groups competing for broader and broader championships (Neale); the effect on commercial fishermen of the Papal decision to permit Catholics to eat meat on Fridays (Bell); the "desirability" of eradicating malaria in underdeveloped countries (Barlow); the ways that narcotics pushers react to antidrug laws (Rottenberg); the functioning of the political voting mechanism (Downs); the effects of schooling on job opportunities and income (Weisbrod); and the wisdom of national political concerns about the brain drain (Johnson).

Every one of the articles referred to above was written since 1964—a testimonial to the growing willingness of economists to explore new, exciting and important issues, whether conventional or not.

We hope that this book will serve to convince the reader that economics has more to say than he previously thought it could about ordinary issues of everyday life.

Finally, we should like to thank Donna Beutel for her help in monitoring our judgments as to which articles to include. We are very grateful for her valuable advice.

EDITORIALS

THE WIZARD WHO OVERSIMPLIFIED: A FABLE

An education in checkers does not prepare one for a life of chess.

By **HAROLD PETERSON**

In a certain kingdom, there was a school for the education of princes approaching manhood. Since the king and his court spent much of their time playing chess—indeed, chess was called the sport of kings—it was decided that the subject called "games" should be added to the curriculum of this school. A wizard was engaged to develop the course.

Never having played chess himself, the wizard was a little uncertain about what to teach in this course. (Only a *little* uncertain because his ignorance of chess was outweighed by his strong confidence in his general ability.) He sought the advice of a colleague in another kingdom and from him received the following communication:

"Above all else, a course in games should be rigorous and intellectually challenging. We wizards long ago concluded that chess, as actually played, is so complicated that it is impossible to formulate a body of principles and decision rules; these are essential to the rigorous analysis of any subject. We have therefore introduced a few simplifying assumptions. For example, in chess, the pieces move in a bewildering fashion —some forward, some on the diagonal, and some even at a right angle; we have tidied up this confusion by assuming that all pieces move according to the same rule. With such assumptions, we have been able, albeit with great difficulty, to develop a model, a set of principles, and decision rules which are teachable, and intellectually challenging. A 700-page treatise describing these is enclosed."

The wizard was much impressed by the 700-page treatise, and used it in his course. He found that it was teachable, and that the task of learning this model and solving problems with the decision rules was indeed rigorous and intellectually challenging, as proved by the fact that good students did well on their examinations, while poor students failed them.

The wizard maintained an active correspondence with wizards in other kingdoms about the model and its decision rules. In this correspondence, the game was referred to as "chess" although this was solely for convenience of expression; it was taken for granted that everyone knew that their game was not quite like chess as played in the real world. Eventually, some of this correspondence came to the king's attention. Although he didn't understand the formulas and the jargon, he did notice that the word "chess" was mentioned, so he commanded the wizard to appear before him.

At this audience, the wizard asked, "How can I serve you, O King?"

And the king replied "I understand that you are teaching the princes how to play chess. I wish to improve my own game. Can you help me?"

"What we call chess may not be exactly like your game, your majesty. So before answering your question, I must analyze the problem. Please describe chess as you play it."

So the king explained the game of chess. As he did so, the wizard noted that it had the same physical layout, the same number of pieces, and apparently the same objective as the game he taught in school. It seemed clear therefore that the solution was simply to apply the decision rules for this game, although he of course did not immediately reveal this fact to the king for he wanted to preserve his reputation for wizardry. Instead, he said thoughtfully: "I will study the problem and return in ninety days."

At the appointed time, the wizard appeared agan, carrying a crimson pillow on which lay a spiral-bound report with a Plexiglas cover. It was a paraphrase of the 700-page manuscript. "Follow the rules in this report, your majesty, and you will become the best chess player in the world," he said.

The king avidly studied the report, but soon ran into difficulty. He summoned the wizard again. "I see reference to kings, and men, and

squares, which are familiar terms to me; but what is all this about 'jumping,' and 'double jumping,' and 'countervailing force,' 'suboptimization'; and where do you mention queens, rooks, bishops, and knights?"

"But your majesty, as I have clearly explained in the introduction, it was necessary to simplify the environment a trifle. I doubt that these simplifications lessen the practical usefulness of what I have written, however."

"Have you by chance watched some chess players to find out?" asked the king.

"Oh, no, your gracious majesty, but I do carry on an extensive correspondence with other wizards. This is better than observing actual practice because it is generally agreed that wizards are smarter than chess players."

"And your princes. Are they equipped to play chess in the real world because of what they have learned in your course?"

"No offense intended, sir, but we wizards do not believe this to be a proper question. The purpose of our course is to teach princes to think, not to prepare them for a mere vocation."

At this point, the king lost his patience, but since he was a kindly king, he sent the wizard back to his school room rather than to a dungeon.

Moral for economics professors: An education in checkers does not prepare one for a life of chess.

Moral for operations researchers: Half a loaf is not necessarily better than no bread; it may be only chaff.

Moral for businessmen: A consultant who wants to play his own game rather than yours is worthless.

THE ECONOMICS OF STUDENT PROTEST

*Students get low grants; they get little market-type
choice of activities. Their time (and staff time) is
not treated as having its true economic value*

By HARRY G. JOHNSON

University student unrest and protest with violence are endemic in some countries, common enough in others, and were characteristic of some periods in the history of the European universities. Yet the widespread outbreak of student protest in British and continental universities in the past two academic years, and especially last spring, surprised many people, and not least the academic community itself.

The bunching together of these protests can largely be explained by the facts that similarly placed social groups tend towards imitation, and that technology has made possible the rapid communication of ideas and the fast, cheap transport of people. The communications media also tend to induce demonstrations of protest by providing publicity and a large audience for them. The timing of the protests in the later 1960s, and the increasing resort to physical violence, may have a lot to do with the fact that this is the first generation of students for over half a century to mature with neither the memory of a past major war to awe it, nor a prospective or actual major war to engage it in legitimised and socially controlled violence.

The purpose of this article, however, is to suggest that underlying the student protest are some deep-seated economic factors which both generate and maintain the dissatisfaction. They point protest in the direction of demonstrations which are aimed primarily at increasing student control over the universities, and secondarily at increasing the influence of student opinion on governments. These economic factors go with the democratisation of university education, the assumption of governmental responsibility for providing most of the cost of university education, the bureaucratic character of the university as an institution, and the increasing affluence of contemporary society, especially the rising value of people's time.

Since the second world war, in most countries, there has been a rapid increase in the proportion of young people going to university. But this "democratisation" is in some ways illusory and self-defeating. The traditional function of a university education was to prepare students for membership in the country's political, social and economic elite. Correspondingly, university teachers could esteem themselves as an important section of the elite, and consecrate themselves to their teaching functions. Democratisation has, on the one hand, reduced the value to the student of his university degree, because it has become increasingly a hunting licence rather than a meal ticket in the competition for elite jobs. On the other hand, it has reduced the social incentives to university teachers to concentrate their efforts on teaching rather than on research and consulting. (Scholarly quality and experience have also been inevitably diluted, as in the rapid expansion of any type of employment.)

None of these results is *necessarily* socially bad in itself; nor would they create any problems if they were fully understood by university teachers and students. But because they are not understood, they cause chronic tension between the two sides of the teaching process. Each side expects of the other more than it can deliver. In technical economic terms, there is a "dynamic disequilibrium" between expectations and realisations. The dynamic disequilibrium is reflected in the students' efforts to use political power to force the university staff to deliver more, and in the staff's response that students are getting at least as much as they are entitled to.

The disequilibrium is reinforced by the economic implications of governmental responsibility for the finance of education, and by the bureaucratic character of the university, especially in its British and European form. Governments respond to political demands for the provision of more education; but they are also sensitive to the taxpayers' wish for lower taxes and governmental economy. So governments are under pressure to provide higher education "on the cheap"—by close control of student grants, stretching university facilities, and holding down university salaries. They are also under pressure to distribute the available funds in an egalitarian way.

Cheeseparing on student grants makes a student even more conscious of the private cost to him of his university education. This cost is the difference between his grant and the earnings he could obtain from normal commercial employment. This private element in the cost of educational investment is rarely recognised by the academic community, let alone by politicians and the public. The line usually is that, since education is being provided "free," students have no right to criticise whatever educational offering is paid for by the public and administered by the government and university bureaucracies. In fact, the contrary is true. This cheeseparing increases the cost of education to the student in another way. It obliges him to substitute his time for money he has not got—notably, in the larger urban universities, by travelling long distances to and from university in order to save on rent. Finally, cheeseparing on grants leads the student to identify emotionally with the poorer classes of the community—a great help to sincere protesting—in spite of the fact that, if you look at lifetime prospects, university students are an upper income group.

The stretching of existing facilities obviously reduces the quality of a student's university experience, even if it does not necessarily reduce the quality of his instruction. But the effort to hold down staff salaries does affect instruction, in two ways. Insofar as it holds down the real wages paid for a given teaching commitment, it reduces the quality of those willing to teach—i.e., the quality of people that universities have to accept to fill their teaching posts. But the more important effect is to reduce the amount of time and effort that teachers consider a legitimate exchange for the salary received. Universities traditionally give teachers a lot of discretion about how much time and energy they devote to "outside" research, writing and consulting. Universities would generally rather have less of the time of a good scholar than more of the time of a poor one. Thus the amount of work supplied in return for a university salary gradually gets adjusted downwards to keep the pay per unit of work in line with the value of academic time in competing uses.

The pressure for an egalitarian distribution of funds makes the decline in the quality of university education universal. This in turn makes worse the dynamic disequlibrium of expectations. Except at privileged institutions like Oxford and Cambridge, staff can expect the quality of students to be a random variable. And in *all* institutions the students can expect the quality of the staff and the instruction to be a random variable. Contrast this with the situation in the United States. There, private competitive universities are free to charge high fees, and to use the proceeds and their endowment income to hire good staff and good students—in order to attract other good staff and good students, which lets them charge still higher fees, etcetera, etcetera. So American students and staff have fairly reliable knowledge of the educational status of the different colleges and universities.

The dismal impact of egalitarianism is reinforced by (and reinforces) how bureaucratic British universities are. I mean specifically the common pay scales, with seniority increments for academic staff, and the early grant of academic life-tenure. These practices have two effects, both of which make it hard to keep up academic quality when the pay scales are low and more and more staff are needed.

First, tenure and automatic increments are strong incentives for teachers to minimise academic effort and to maximise outside earnings, especially for those not overendowed with scholarly or scientific ambitions.

Secondly for those who have such ambitions, the rewards come not from financial recognition within the institution—i.e., higher pay for the better chaps in the same grade-and-age group, for either better teaching or better scholarship—but from promotion to a higher rank, generally in another institution. This system of advancement scatters the talented among universities like "currants in the duff," according to the accidents of vacant appointments. It breaks up any unusually effective team of senior, middle and junior men soon after its effectiveness is recognised. More seriously, from the standpoint of university unrest, it puts a heavy premium on research and publication rather than on good teaching as an academic activity. It is virtually impossible for an outstanding teacher, who does not publish, to win promotion to a professorial chair, even in his own university. Yet that university has no alternative way by which to reward him financially—other perhaps than by transferring him to administrative duties.

Pay and promotion policies are only one aspect of the bureaucratic nature of universities. It is more directly relevant to the university unrest—among both students and staff—that, as bureaucracies, universities take decisions by bureaucratic methods. That means decision-taking by committees of more or less senior people, seeking to arrive at reasonable conclusions and compromises that can be embodied in administrative procedures and operations. These decisions are subject to budgets laid down or controlled by higher authority. They are not subject to any direct market test of success or failure or, in the absence of such a test, based on extensive cost-benefit and cost-effectiveness analysis.

For the university, this means failures of entrepreneurship in some directions and runaway empire-building in others. For the staff, it means frustration and resentment over the apparent arbitrariness of decisions and over the allocation of university resources among rival claimants. For the student, it means that, while the decisions may vitally affect his present welfare and his future prospects, he has little or no voice in taking them. He can influence them only through whatever provision is made for student consultation and representation. These methods of influencing a bureaucracy are both slow and uncertain, and require sustained efforts behind the scenes. Individual students are rarely committed deeply or long enough to their university to warrant making such sustained efforts, so they naturally resort to protest, demonstration and violence when their dissatisfaction becomes acute. Because rank and seniority in the university correlate strongly with power in its governing bureaucracy, junior staff identify with the students rather than with the staff side on these occasions.

In Britain and on the continent, people usually accept that the bureaucratic method suits university management. The method is necessary anyway because of the government role in providing finance. Bureaucracy is usually justified educationally by the assumption that the university should be in loco parentis in relation to its students. This assumption is appropriate to an elitist educational system but not to a democratic one.

Politically, it brings painful conflicts of loyalties on both sides in any staff-student dispute. Economically, it increases university unrest by obliging the portion of the country's economic adults who go to university to submit to a bureaucratic decision-taking process that extensively affects their lives—a process which is not forced on older people or on those who do not attend university, unless they choose voluntarily to join the armed forces.

Because students are deprived of the economic liberty and freedom of choice available to other adults, universities are freed of the competitive pressures to satisfy their customers that freedom of choice imposes on commercial enterprises. If universities were compelled, like commercial firms, to compete for the custom of students who had their own money to spend, their decision-taking would probably remain largely bureaucratic; but they would have to make far more effort both to adapt the characteristics of their product to the customer's reasoned taste, and to persuade the community at large that their product was worth its cost.

The tensions created by bureaucratic decision-taking, in an environment where there is generally competition and free consumer choice, becomes more acute as the economy gets richer and the average real income (and therefore the value of

⅞⅞⅞⅞⅞⅞⅞

human time) rises. The bureaucratic process does not allow the real value of student and staff time to exercise pressure for appropriate changes in teaching programmes and instructional methods. Change would generally mean capital-intensive, rather than labour-intensive, methods. Instead, it is assumed that students and staff must both spend a budget of time which was fixed by conventions developed when intelligent human time was far less valuable than it is now. The assumption is perpetuated by bureaucratic concepts of how to allot manpower.

Two minor observations on the economics of student protest in conclusion.

First, the rhythm of the academic year is a feudal survival, geared inversely to the rhythm of agricultural production. It concentrates instruction in the first two terms and examination at the end of the third.

This produces a maximum of anxiety and a minimum of organised effort about the end of the second and the beginning of the third term. It is especially conducive to demonstrations and protests in the spring of the year. Examinations at the end of each term would increase the economic cost of student protest and reduce the psychological incentives.

Secondly, the geography of universities frequently reduces the cost of protest to the students, by channelling academic traffic through restricted areas which can be blocked by a small number of students. (The main entrance to the London School of Economics, for example, can be blocked by less than 100 sitting students.) If student protest becomes a regular part of university life, universities should invest in opening more doorways in university buildings and in laying more and wider pathways among them.

ARTS

ON THE PERFORMING ARTS: THE ANATOMY OF THEIR ECONOMIC PROBLEMS

Can performing arts continue their present role in cultural life of this country? Increased support from new sources deemed necessary.

By W. J. BAUMOL and W. G. BOWEN*

I. THE SETTING

Romanticism long ago fixed in our minds the idea that there is something inevitable about the association between artistic achievement and poverty. The starving artist has become a stereotype among whose overtones is the notion that squalor and misery are noble and inspiring. It is one of the happier attributes of our time that we have generally been disabused of this type of absurdity. We readily recognize that poverty is demeaning rather than inspiring—that instead of stimulating the artist it deprives him of the energy, time, or even the equipment with which to create or perform.

While we have come to accept the idea that artists are often impecunious, even a cursory encounter with the facts of the matter usually proves surprising. One may or may not see something shocking in the fact that the median total income in 1959 of males classified by the census as actors was $5,640; that for musicians and music teachers the comparable figure was $4,757; and that for dancers and dancing teachers, $3,483.[1] But one must recognize that these figures include income from all sources, some of them (e.g., truck driving, lobster fishing, waiting on

* This paper is based on a study being prepared by the authors for the Twentieth Century Fund, through the administrative channel of Mathematica. The study is still in progress and this paper is nothing more than a brief introduction and a statement of certain theoretical ideas. The Fund has facilitated our work, not only by making generous financial provision for the extensive job of data collection and analysis which has been necessary, but also by helping to secure the cooperation of organizations and individuals and by allowing us full freedom to proceed as we wish. In the volume which will emerge from this study, we shall acknowledge our debt to the many people whose patient assistance has been essential to our work.

[1] U.S. Bureau of the Census, U.S. Census of Population: 1960, Subject Reports, *Occupational Characteristics*, Final Report PC(2)–7A, Table 25.

tables) rather unrelated to the performer's art.[2]

A detailed and specific investigation of economic conditions in the performing arts was conducted by Senate and House Committees in 1961 and 1962, and the volumes of *Hearings* which resulted are very revealing.[3] At that time the minimum weekly salary for Off-Broadway actors was $45 per week (it is currently $60); and what makes this figure significant is that most Off-Broadway actors are at the minimum. In such circumstances it is not difficult to see why Joseph Papp, producer of the New York Shakespeare Festival, was able to report that "Banks and landlords consider him [the actor] a credit risk without visible means of support."[4]

Mrs. Helen Thompson, of the American Symphony Orchestra League, presented figures indicating that in 1961–62 the average salary paid to musicians in the twenty-six

major orchestras in this country was $4,512; if the four highest-paying orchestras are excluded, the average for the remaining twenty-two major orchestras (again as of 1961–62) falls to $3,500.[5]

Dancers are in even worse financial circumstances, as illustrated by the case of a leading modern dance company whose members normally receive $25 after a trip which frequently includes four days of travel, a day of rehearsals, and a public performance.

In the main, performing artists are employed by organizations—by orchestras, opera and dance companies, producers and impresarios, resident theater companies—and the underlying economic pressures which manifest themselves in low performer salaries are transmitted through these organizations. Inadequate financial flows to these groups can threaten not only the welfare of individual performers but also the very existence of the institutions serving the entrepreneurial and managerial functions in the field of the performing arts. And, notwithstanding the publicity that has been given to the alleged "cultural boom" in America, we continue to hear frequently of theatrical groups which collapse, of opera houses whose seasons are in danger, and performing arts organizations of all kinds for whom financial emergency seems to have become a way of life. It is this situation and the threat that it poses for the cultural prospects of our society which constitutes the setting for the study we have undertaken.

The first objective of our study is to explain the strained economic cir-

---

[2] As the Department of Labor's career guidance publication stresses: "Many performers ... supplement their incomes by teaching, and thousands of others have to work much of the time in other occupations." (U.S. Dept. of Labor, Bureau of Labor Statistics, "Employment Outlook in the Performing Arts," Bulletin No. 1300–65, 1961, p. 214.) The BLS goes on to warn: "... the difficulty of earning a living as a performer is one of the facts young people should bear in mind in considering an artistic career" (*loc. cit.*).

[3] U.S. House of Representatives, *Hearings Before the Select Subcommittee on Education of the Committee on Education and Labor*, "Economic Conditions in the Performing Arts," 87th Cong., 1st and 2nd Sess., 1962 (cited hereafter as "House *Hearings*"). U.S. Senate, *Hearings Before a Special Sub-Committee of the Committee on Labor and Public Welfare*, "Government and the Arts," 87th Cong., 2nd Sess., 1962.

[4] House *Hearings*, p. 111.

[5] House *Hearings*, p. 47.

cumstances which beset performing companies, to determine whether they are attributable mainly to fortuitous historical circumstances, to mismanagement or poor institutional arrangements, or whether there is something fundamental in the economic order which accounts for these difficulties. On the basis of our analysis we hope to produce some conditional forecasts of the financial future of the performing arts, the prospective costs, the operating revenues likely to be associated with various levels of activity, and the proportion of the resultant financial gaps which one can expect to be met from current sources of contributed income.

This session is intended to deal with theoretical matters and, while much of our work has been empirical, we welcome this opportunity to try to describe the basic economic relationships which seem to us to underlie the financial problems of the performing arts.

II. BASIC ECONOMIC CHARACTERISTICS OF NONPROFIT ORGANIZATIONS

Before we turn to the special economic properties of the performing arts, it is useful to devote some discussion to the economics of nonprofit-making organizations in general, for only in this way can the difficulties which beset the performing arts be seen in perspective.

Nonprofit organizations as a group share at least two characteristics: (1) they earn no pecuniary return on invested capital and (2) they claim to fulfill some social purpose. These two features are not wholly independent. Any group which sought to fulfill no social purpose and earned no financial return would presumably disappear from the landscape. Moreover, its goals themselves often help explain why no money is earned by such an organization. While an automobile producer may take pride in the quality of his cars, he is much less likely to regard product quality per se as an ultimate objective of the enterprise than is the head of a nonprofit organization. Nor is the auto producer likely to be nearly as concerned about the social composition of his clientele.

The significant point is that the objectives of the typical nonprofit organization are by their very nature designed to keep it constantly on the brink of financial catastrophe, for to such a group the quality of the services which it provides becomes an end in itself. Better research, more adequate hospital facilities, more generous rehearsal time, better training for those engaged in these activities—all these are not merely incidental desiderata. They are fundamental goals in themselves, and with objectives such as these, the likelihood of surplus funds is slim indeed. These goals constitute bottomless receptacles into which limitless funds can be poured. As soon as more money becomes available to a nonprofit organization, corresponding new uses can easily be found, and still other uses for which no financing has been provided will inevitably arise to take their place. Any lively nonprofit organization always has a group of projects which it cannot afford to undertake and for whose realization it looks hopefully to the future. Once this fundamental fact is grasped, it is hardly surprising that such groups feel themselves constantly strapped. It becomes clear that they are simply built that way.[6]

Nor is it just through its quality aspirations that the social goals of the nonprofit enterprise contribute to its financial difficulties. The concern of the typical nonprofit organization for the size and composition of its clientele often causes operating revenue to be lower than would be the case if services were priced to satisfy a simple profit-maximization goal. Since such a group normally considers itself to be a supplier of virtue, it is natural that it should seek to distribute its bounty as widely and as equitably as possible. The group is usually determined to prevent income and wealth alone from deciding who is to have priority in the consumption of its services. It wishes to offer its products to the needy and the deserving—to students, to the impecunious, to those initially not interested in consuming them, and to a variety of others to whom high prices would serve as an effective deterrent to consumption. In short, a low price for the product of a nonprofit group is normally an inevitable consequence of its objectives, and indeed sometimes becomes an article of faith. The ancient doc-

trine of "just price" is imbedded in the operations of these groups and carries with it all the difficulties which inevitably accompany an attempt to put it into practice.

The desire to provide a product of as high a quality as possible and to distribute the product in a manner other than that which maximizes revenue combine to produce a situation which is unusual in yet another respect. For such an enterprise a substantial increase in the demand for its product may well worsen the organization's financial health! Marginal costs may well exceed marginal revenues over the relevant interval. An increased number of student applications, an increased number of hospital patients, an increased number of orchestral performances may well increase the size of the contributions required for solvency. More generally, it follows that, contrary to widespread impressions, the much publicized cultural and educational "booms," whatever their composition, may in many cases prove a very mixed financial blessing.

Yet even in such circumstances the organizations cannot simply refuse to expand their activities in response to an increase in demand. By such a refusal the organization would renege on its fundamental objectives, and, incidentally, it might even produce a loss in private and community support.

---

[6] The fact that any nonprofit organization can always find uses for a temporary excess of funds—and indeed may be embarrassed to report to its contributors that it has some money left at the end of the year—makes it very difficult to determine its cost functions. If an auto producer finds that a sudden increase in demand has swollen his receipts, he is only too happy to report higher profits; a nonprofit enterprise, however, may well use the extra revenue in a way which, in effect, deliberately raises it costs.

III. THE PERFORMING ARTS IN PARTICULAR

It is apparent that all of the standard problems of nonprofit organizations which have just been discussed beset the performing arts. It is not surprising, therefore, that the survival of the great majority of its organizations requires a constant flow of contributions. We can then easily understand why the arts find themselves in their present unhappy financial circumstances. But, up to this point, our discussion has offered no portents for the future. Here we don the inherited mantle of the dismal scientist and argue that one can read the prospects of the arts tomorrow in the economic structure which characterizes them today. The evidence will suggest that the prospects offer no grounds for complacency— that there are fundamental reasons to expect the financial strains which beset the performing arts organizations to increase, chronically, with the passage of time.

To understand the prospective developments on the cost side, it is necessary to digress briefly and consider in general terms the implications of differential rates of growth in productivity within the economy for the relative costs of its various outputs.[7] Let us think of an economy -divided into two sectors: one in which productivity is rising and another where productivity is stable. As an illustration, let us suppose that where technological improvements are possible they lead to an increase in output per man-hour of 4 percent per annum, but that output per man-hour remains absolutely constant in the stable productivity sector. If these sectors are assigned

equal weights in the construction of an economy-wide productivity index, the aggregate rate of increase in output per man-hour will be 2 percent per annum. For the moment let us assume that there is only one grade of labor, that labor is free to move back and forth between sectors, and that the real wage rate rises *pari passu* with the aggregate rate of change of productivity, at 2 percent per annum. Finally, let us suppose that the money supply and the level of aggregate demand are controlled in such a way that the price level is kept stable. Assuming that there are no changes in the shares of capital and labor, this means that money wages will also increase at the rate of 2 percent a year.

The implications of this simple model for costs in the two sectors are straightforward. In the rising productivity sector, output per man hour increases more rapidly than the money wage rate and labor costs per unit must therefore decline. However, in the sector where productivity is stable, there is no offsetting improvement in output per man-hour, and so every increase in money wages is translated automatically into an equivalent increase in unit labor costs—2 percent per annum in our example. It should be noted that the extent of the increase in costs in the stable productivity sector varies directly with the economy-wide rate of increase in output per man-hour. The faster the general pace of technological advance, the greater will be the increase in the overall wage level and the greater the upward pressure on costs in those industries which do not enjoy increased productivity. Faster technological progress is no blessing for the laggards, at

---

[7] There is, of course, nothing new in the following observations on the effects of differential rates of productivity change on costs and prices. See, e.g., Tibor and Ann Scitovsky, "What Price Economic Progress?" *Yale Review*, Autumn, 1959. Only its application to the state of the arts is novel.

least as far as their costs are concerned.

It is apparent that the live performing arts belong to the stable productivity sector of our economy. The legitimate theater, the symphony orchestra, the chamber group, the opera, the dance—all can serve as textbook illustrations of activities offering little opportunity for major technological change. The output per man-hour of the violinist playing a Schubert quartet in a standard concert hall is relatively fixed, and it is fairly difficult to reduce the number of actors necessary for a performance of *Henry IV*, Part II.

Moreover, from the standpoint of long-term developments, the essence of the matter is not absolute or relative levels of productivity at a given date but the rates of change in productivity over time. This means that even if the arts could somehow manage to effect technological economies, they would not solve their long-term cost problem if such savings were once-and-for-all in nature. In order to join the ranks of the rising productivity industries, the arts would somehow have to learn not only to increase output per man-hour but to continue to do so into the indefinite future. Otherwise, they must at some juncture fall behind the technologically progressive industries and experience increases in costs which stem not from their own decisions but from the inexorable march of technological change in other parts of the economy.

True, some inefficiencies of operation are to be found in the field, and their elimination can help matters somewhat. Moreover, performing arts organizations can reduce the rate of increase in their unit costs by permitting some deterioration in the quality of their product—by fewer rehearsals, the use of more poorly trained performers, shoddy costumes and scenery. But such a course is never popular with organizations dedicated to quality, and, furthermore, it may lead to loss of audience and community support. Nevertheless, it is not an uncommon "temporary" expedient, imposed by the realization that the cutting of corners may be the only alternative to abandonment of the enterprise.

There is one other important avenue for cost saving open to the performing arts which has so far not been considered. We refer to wages paid performers. In the simple model sketched above, we postulated a situation in which a single, market-clearing wage was paid to all persons regardless of the industry in which they were employed. In actual fact, the live performing arts constitute a rather special labor market—a market in which the need for great native ability and extensive training limits the supply, but in which the psychic returns to those who meet these tests often offers a very substantial inducement to remain in the field. For these reasons, the performing arts are relatively insensitive to general wage trends, especially in the short run. It is largely for this reason that performing arts organizations in financial difficulty have often managed to shift part of their financial burden back to the performers—and to the managements, who also are generally very poorly paid by commercial standards. The level of the incomes in this general field must be considered remarkably low by any standards, and particularly so in light of the heavy investment that has often been made by the artists in their education, training, and equipment. And it is surely explained at least in part by the willingness of those who work in these fields to sacrifice money income for the less material pleasures of their participation in the arts.

However, there are limits to the financial sacrifices society can extract from the performers in exchange for psychic returns. One may reasonably expect that rising incomes in other sectors will ultimately produce untoward effects on the supply of talent. At what point this will occur depends partly on the income elasticity of the demand for psychic income. As the general level of real income rises, it may well be possible to persuade performers to accept a lower relative position in the income hierarchy. However, there are symptoms which suggest that, in some specialized areas, effects involving both quantity and quality are already being felt, though, overall, excess supply continues to be one of the market's most notable characteristics.

In sum, the cost structure of the performing arts organizations promises them no easier future. One might anticipate, therefore, that this structural problem would produce discernible effects on pricing policy. Certainly, in most of the industries in which productivity is stable, we would expect the price of the product or service to rise relative to the general price level. And there is a widespread impression that the arts have indeed behaved in accord with this anticipation—that ticket prices have been soaring. Yet our prelimi-

nary evidence suggests strongly that this view is incorrect and is largely a product of money illusion. Indeed, our preliminary data indicate that the rate of increase of ticket prices has barely managed to keep up with the price level and has lagged substantially behind increases in costs.

One might undertake to account for the surprisingly modest rate of increase in ticket prices in terms of a revenue maximization model—on the hypothesis that arts organizations believe the demand for their product to be highly elastic. We suspect, however, that a more valid explanation is the role of a doctrine of just price in the objectives of these organizations.

The tendency for increases in prices to lag behind increases in costs means simply that arts organizations have had to raise larger and larger sums from their contributors—and our analysis leads us to expect this trend to continue. Thus our analysis has offered us not only an explanation for the current state of affairs; it has also provided us with a basis for speculation about the future. What it has shown will not, we are afraid, be reassuring to those to whom ready availability of the arts constitutes an important objective of society. If our model is valid, and if, as may be suspected, there are limits to the amounts that can be obtained from private contributors, increased support from other sources will have to be found if the performing arts are to continue their present role in the cultural life of this country and especially if it is intended that they will expand their role and flourish.

THE ECONOMICS OF BROADCASTING, ADVERTISING, AND GOVERNMENT POLICY

Does broadcasting give the public what it wants?
Broadcasting industry and FCC fall short in safe-
guarding best interests of public.

By R. H. COASE

The broadcasting industry, with its various methods of finance, its intricate organization and its close, and peculiar, relations with the government offers a rich field for study by the economist. But I will not dwell on those aspects of the industry which would mainly be of interest to students of industrial organization. I wish to consider a more general question. I want to examine the part the economics of broadcasting has played in the formulation of government policy and to consider what conclusions we should draw from this in making our own policy recommendations and in the conduct of our researches.

We must first note that economic factors are taken into account in a world in which ignorance, prejudice, and mental confusion, encouraged rather than dispelled by the political organization, exert a strong influence on policy making. I will illustrate this by a quotation from the Canadian Royal Commission on Broadcasting of 1957 (the Fowler Commission). The Commission was discussing the proposal to finance the broadcasting service by means of an annual license fee for set-owners. This is what they said:

This certainly seems a logical way for a group of people to make a joint purchase of a service they want. It is not strictly equitable as presumably a flat fee would be charged and all licencees would not make the same use of the service; but it seems much more equitable than the ear-marking of a particular tax paid both by those with radio and television sets and by those who hope never to have one in the house. The yield from the licence fee is reasonably predictable and the support required or desired to be given can easily be adjusted upwards or downwards, by changing the amount of the individual licence fee.

But the Commission concluded:

The flaw in this approach to the problem is that virtually nobody favours it, and many people feel quite strongly in their opposition. The arguments against it range from the inefficiency and excessive cost of collection, through the likelihood of evasion and difficulty of enforcement, to the simple claim that a licence fee is a nuisance tax and generally unpopular.

Thus we see that a method of finance which was considered "logical," "more equitable" than the alternatives, which could be "easily adjusted" to meet the changing requirements of the service, was politically impossible because it would be "generally unpopular."[1] The main reason

---

[1] See the *Report of the Royal Commission on Broadcasting* (1957), 274–75.

for this unpopularity, heightened in Canada, as always, by describing the hardship a license fee would impose on the old-age pensioner, is an objection to paying for anything. This is, of course, bad economics. It is our duty to point this out, but at the same time we can hardly ignore, in deciding whether or not to advocate particular government policies, the extent to which political considerations will prevent the execution of those policies in a manner which is economically efficient. In Britain the BBC is financed by the proceeds of a license fee, but the BBC has not usually been allowed by the Treasury to receive the total proceeds, while the level of the fee has not always been as high as officials of the BBC desired. If the withholding of part of the license fee and the reluctance to raise it were due to political considerations unconnected with the needs of the service and if most licensees would have been willing to pay a higher fee to secure the additional service that this could have made possible, a reason for the introduction of commercial television is provided which would have been absent if one assumed that the license fee was fixed at an "optimum" level, however that may be defined.

Of course we may hope that, over time, the influence of the economics profession will be such as to make it more difficult to gain political advantage by the propagation of bad economics. But there are other features of the system which I think we must regard as permanent. The first is that the businessmen in the broadcasting industry will try to make as much money as possible. I know that there are some economists who would argue that businessmen merely seek a reasonable return on their capital. But consider the facts. We know from recent figures that the profits of television stations in the first fifty TV markets represented, on an average, 36 percent of gross revenue and that the rate of return on capital for some stations was 200 or 300 percent per annum (after taxes). One wonders what an unreasonable rate of return would be. I personnally believe that the only reason the rate is not 500 percent per annum (after taxes) is that the businessmen have not yet discovered how to achieve this. If one reads the trade press about changes in programming, it is apparent that the aim is almost invariably to gain audience (which facilitates the sale of time) and that the adjustments in rates which occur are designed to increase the receipts of the stations. I do not wish to moralize. As has been said, a man is seldom more innocently employed than when he is making money.

So much for the first permanent feature. The second is that we cannot expect a regulatory commission to act in the public interest, particularly if we have regard to its actions over the long period. I am not primarily thinking of the fact that commissions in the United States tend to be responsive to the wishes of Congress or committees of Congress or that, appointed and reappointed by the executive, their views are liable to be in tune with those who have political power. What I have in mind is a feature which, with the best will in the world, it seems to me very difficult to eliminate. However fluid an organization may be in its beginning, it must inevitably adopt certain policies and organizational forms which condition its thinking and limit the range of its policies. Within limits, the regulatory commission may search for what is in the public interest, but it is not likely to find acceptable any solutions which imply fundamental changes in its settled policies. The observation that a regulatory commission tends to be captured by the industry it regulates is I think a reflection of this, rather than, in general, the result of sinister influences. It is difficult to operate closely with an industry without coming to look at its problems in industry terms. The result is that the commission, although thinking of itself as apart from and with different aims from the industry, will nonetheless be incapable of conceiving of or bringing about any radical changes in industry practices or structure. In fact, the regulation of the broadcasting industry by the Federal Communications Commission resembles a professional wrestling match. The grunts and groans resound through the land, but no permanent injury seems to result.

It is of course wholly proper that public discussion of broadcasting policy should have centered on programming, since public policy must be appraised by considering its effects on the programs. But the discussion, particularly in Britain but also in the United States, has taken on a somewhat peculiar character and has tended to confuse rather than clarify the basic issues. Perhaps the best example is to be found in the Pilkington Report of 1962.

The report examines the question of whether it is desirable "to give the public what it wants." It states that at first sight this aim seems to be "unexceptionable" but adds that, "when applied to broadcasting it is difficult to analyse." The reason is that not everyone wants the same things. It is somewhat surprising that the Committee should have thought this peculiar to broadcasting. Had they realized that this was a general problem that every economic system has to solve in dealing with every product or service and that, in most Western countries, it is solved with the aid of a pricing system, I think the Committee would have been led to a more useful discussion of the question. I would not wish to imply that we fully understand the logic of a pricing system or that special institutional arrangements are not necessary for its tolerable performance. But an understanding of the pricing system does lay bare the nature of the problem. As it is, what follows in the report is a discussion of an economic problem without benefit of economics.

I can give you the flavor of the argument by quoting some passages, the character of which will not be altogether unfamiliar to those of you who know only the American literature:

No one can say he is giving the public what it wants, unless the public knows the whole range of possibilities which television can offer and, from this range, chooses what it wants to see. For a choice is only free if the field of choice is not unnecessarily restricted. The subject matter of television is to be found in the whole scope and variety of human awareness and experience. If viewers—the public—are thought of as "the mass audience," or "the majority," they will be offered only the average of common experience and awareness; the "ordinary"; the commonplace—for what all know and do is, by definition, commonplace. They will be kept unaware of what lies beyond the average of experience; their field of choice will be limited. In time they may come to like only what they know. But it will always be true that, had they been offered a wider range from which to choose, they might and often would have chosen otherwise, and with greater enjoyment.... "[T]o give the public what it wants" is a misleading phrase: misleading because as commonly used it has the appearance of an appeal to democratic principle but the appearance is deceptive. It is in fact patronising and arrogant, in that it claims to know what the public is, but defines it as no more than the mass audience; and in that it claims to know what it wants, but limits its choice to the average of experience. In this sense we reject it utterly. If there is a sense in which it should be used, it is this: what the public wants and what it has the right to get is the freedom to choose from the widest possible range of programme matter. Anything less than that is deprivation. . . .

It is I think apparent that these passages, full of sound and fury, do not give us any criteria by which to decide whether any particular program should be transmitted. It is easy to talk about "the widest possible range of programme matter" but there is surely some point at which, as more and more resources are devoted to increasing the supply of programs, the gain from additional broadcast programs is of less value than the loss in output elsewhere. And if the resources devoted to broadcasting are limited in this way, it follows that the provision of programs which are liked by one group will have deprived some other group of programs that they would have liked. According to what principles is it to be decided which demands

are to be satisfied? The Committee never tells us this. But later they tell us how this problem should be solved. I will quote another passage:

The broadcast authorities have certainly a duty to keep sensitively aware of the public's tastes and attitudes as they now are and in all their variety; and to care about them. But if they do more than that, this is not to give the public "what someone thinks is good for it." It is to respect the public's right to choose from the widest possible range of subject matter and so to enlarge worthwhile experience.

Up to now we have heard of respect for the public's right to choose and of need for the widest possible choice. It is at this point that the trap closes. They continue:

Because, in principle, the possible range of subject matter is inexhaustible, all of it can never be presented, nor can the public know what the range is. So, the broadcaster must explore it, and choose from it first. This might be called "giving a lead": but it is not the lead of the autocratic or arrogant. It is the proper exercise of responsibility by public authorities duly constituted as trustees for the public interest.

Thus the committee avoids the question of how it should be decided which programs to transmit and for the phrase "what the public wants," they substitute another and better, "what the public authority wants." What the public authority should want, how it would get the information which would enable it to do what it should, and how in practice it would be likely to act are questions which all disappear in a cloud of pious platitudes.[2]

In the United States it is improbable that many would seriously suggest that a public authority such as the Federal Communications Commission should be given the power to determine in detail what programs should be broadcast, and while sentiments similar to those found in the Pilkington Report will no doubt continue to be expressed in the United States, there is no likelihood that they will lead to the establishment of a broadcasting system operated by some organ of the government (leaving aside the question of whether this would be held constitutional by the Supreme Court). The broadcasting system in the United States is likely to continue as a decentralized system, operated in the main by private enterprise. What programs will be broadcast will therefore be determined by the economics of the industry. Put shortly, the programs that will be broadcast will be those that it is most profitable to broadcast. I would not wish to argue that all the businessmen consider is money. A television station operator earning 200 percent per annum (after taxes), if he had been grasping and less aware of the finer things, might no doubt have earned 210 percent per annum. I do not doubt that some programs will be broadcast which reduce the profits of the station, but I am quite certain that the broad pattern of programming will be determined by profitability. My view is that we should not bewail

the fact that businessmen maximize profits. We should accept it and use it. The task which faces us (and the task of good government policy) is to devise institutional arrangements which will lead the businessman, as it were by an invisible hand, to do what is desirable (by making it profitable for him to do so).

I would emphasize that belief in the invisible hand does not imply that the government has no part to play in the economic system. Quite the contrary. If it is in general true that men, following their own self-interest, act in a way that is of benefit to society, it is, to quote Edwin Cannan, "because human institutions are arranged so as to compel self-interest to work in directions in which it will be beneficial."[3] Our task as economists is to help in the devising and improving of those institutions. In doing this, we should not ignore the noble side of human nature when this can be brought into play. But we should never forget the words of Alfred Marshall to which Robertson has drawn our attention: "progress chiefly depends on the extent to which the *strongest* and not merely the *highest* forces of human nature can be utilized for the increase of social good."[4]

I think we should ponder these words of Cannan and Marshall when we contemplate the institutional framework within which the broadcasting industry operates in the United States. It is obviously incredibly bad. But how should it be im-

[2] These quotations will be found in the *Report of the Committee on Broadcasting*, 1960 (Cmnd. 1753, June, 1962), 16–18.

[3] See the *Economic Review*, July, 1913, p. 333.

[4] See A. C. Pigou, ed., *Memorials of Alfred Marshall*, p. 310.

proved? The allocation of the major resource used in the industry, the radio frequency spectrum, is carried out by a method which is inefficient, inequitable, and inflexible. I have explained my grounds for holding this view on other occasions and there is no need for me to spend much time going over them now, particularly as there is really no dispute about the correctness of my position. If I may quote Dr. Goldin when he was with the FCC, but giving, I need hardly say, his personal views, the present procedure for choosing among competing applicants for the radio frequency spectrum is "ritualistic, formalistic, wasteful and inefficient."[5] I have proposed that radio frequencies should be disposed of to the highest bidder because it would avoid the costs of the present procedure, would tend to allocate these frequencies to those who could use them most efficiently, would prevent the unjustifiable enrichment of those (commonly wealthy) private individuals who obtain these grants from the FCC, and would facilitate changes in the use of radio frequencies when this seemed to be called for.

I would not argue that there should be no government regulation of the broadcasting industry. But such regulation is not inconsistent with use of the pricing system. There is no industry which is not in some way regulated. What is extraordinary if we contemplate the allocation of the radio frequency spectrum is that it makes no use at all of the pricing system. Of course there would be difficulties in introducing a pricing scheme. Dr. Goldin has said that

"after the initial shock of rationally considering the use of the pricing mechanism in frequency allocations, the virtually unanimous view of communications specialists" would be that these practical difficulties were too great and he adds that until I, or a friendly ally, make a study of how such a system would actually operate, my suggestion will not get into "the mainstream."[6] I think that this is right. The FCC is rather like a whale stranded on the seashore, waiting while the local inhabitants, ignorant of whale anatomy, try to show it the direction in which it should swim. If we are to get sensible government policy in this area, it will, I am afraid, have to come from the work of economists outside the government service (and, for that matter, outside the industry).

The position is the same if we think of another fundamental question: the finance of the industry. With commercial broadcasting, the person who pays for the broadcast of a program is the advertiser. It follows that the programs broadcast are those which maximize the profits to be derived from advertising. The market for broadcast programs is one from which the consumer is barred: what he would pay plays no part in the determination of programs. The result is that some sectors of the public feel that they are not being catered for. The FCC is uneasily aware that all is not well. And so it has exhorted the businessmen to act in the public interest and, incidentally, against their own. It seems clear that in this case the highest motive was not the strongest.

The obvious way of dealing with

---

[5] *Land Economics*, May, 1965, p. 168.

[6] *Ibid.*

this problem is to introduce some form of pay-television. If this were done, consumers who were willing to pay more for resources used in the broadcasting industry than were the advertisers could secure the kind of programs they wanted. This proposal has been strongly opposed by the broadcasting industry. This opposition comes, as Dr. Frank Stanton of CBS has told us, not because the industry has any "economic axe to grind," but because it would not be in the best interests of the public.[7] It is I think a universal rule that businessmen never act from higher motives than when they are engaged in restricting potential competition. Of course, the opposition has been successful. Proposals for pay-television were first made in the late 1940's, but in spite of determined attempts to secure the approval of the Federal Communications Commission, all that has been granted is authorization for experimental pay-television services operating under restrictive conditions which make it impossible for pay-television to realize its potentialities. So far only one such service has been started, that in Hartford, Connecticut. I do not know what the future will be. But there are no signs that the Federal

Communications Commission intends to change its policy of support for the commercial broadcasting system.

What should be done? The task of charting a sensible future for the broadcasting industry is not one which can be left to the industry, which has its own interests to protect. It cannot be left to the Federal Communications Commission, which cannot conceive of any future which is not essentially a repetition of the past. Who, therefore, is to perform this task? I suggest that it has to be assumed by academic economists. You may recall what Adam Smith said about university education: "The parts of education which are commonly taught in universities, it may, perhaps, be said are not very well taught. But had it not been for those institutions, they would not have been commonly taught at all; and both the individual and the public would have suffered a good deal from the want of those important parts of education."[8] The position seems to me similar in the present case. I would not argue that academic economists are technically the best qualified to investigate what government policy should be towards the broadcasting industry. But unless they do it, no one else will.

---

[7] CBS Statement on Pay-Television by Dr. Frank Stanton, President of Columbia Broadcasting System, May 19, 1955.

[8] Adam Smith, *Wealth of Nations* (Modern Library edition), p. 721.

BUSINESS AND FINANCE

THE PRICING OF TEXTBOOKS
AND THE REMUNERATION OF AUTHORS

*Most textbook writing not profitable use of econo-
mists' time. Can publisher/author conflict be
ameliorated?*

By **PAUL M. HORVITZ**

The textbook industry is one of particular interest to economists, as economists are active both as consumers and as producers of the industry's output. Despite the time economists spend with the products of the industry, relatively little research has been done on some of the basic economic problems of the industry.

College enrollment will continue to rise in the future and so will sales of textbooks. Many new textbooks will be published in the next several years, and economists will write their share of them. Textbook publishers have benefited from increased enrollments and the trend toward larger per student expenditures on textbooks. Their earnings have increased at a rapid rate. While it is clear that textbook publishing is a profitable business, it is not so clear that textbook writing is generally profitable. This paper examines two questions of concern to authors and publishers. First, how are authors paid for their effort and, second, a related question on which economic analysis should shed light: how are textbooks priced. The focus in this paper is on college textbooks. The study is based on a questionnaire sent to authors of recent economics textbooks and on consideration of some elementary aspects of price theory.

PRICING TEXTBOOKS

The process by which publishers determine prices is somewhat mysterious. Most publishers have formulas that, while differing in details, are roughly similar in concept and yield similar results. Generally the formula starts with an estimate of first-year sales. An estimate is made of the direct costs of a first printing equal to estimated sales. This cost can be estimated quite accurately. While per-unit costs could be lowered somewhat by a printing run larger than estimated sales, there is a strong aversion to carrying inventories. This is not irrational. Inventory-carrying costs can easily outweigh the modest savings from larger printings. The resulting cost figure is then multiplied by some number to determine list price. This number varies from publisher to publisher and from book to book, but is generally around 3½ to 5.[1] This provides the margin for overhead, royalties, advertising, and retailer profit.

If the resulting price is roughly in line with prices of competing books, the book will be published at that price.[2] If the formula-determined price turns out to be substantially higher than the going price, some reconsideration is in order. If the reason for the high price is inadequate volume, one alternative is a decision not to publish. Another alternative is to price the book on the basis of a printing of more than one year's sales, though this necessitates carrying heavier inventories than desired.[3] The book could be priced on the basis of a "split-run," that is, pricing on the basis of more than one printing, but this would violate what appears to be almost an article of faith in the industry that each printing (including the first) should pay its own way.

If the formula price turns out to be too high because of unusually high costs (a book with a large number of tables, illustrations, or complex mathematical symbols), an attempt may be made to reduce costs by cutting material (if the author is willing) or by setting type for the book in England or Japan where production costs are lower. One author responding to the questionnaire faced this problem and, reluctant to cut material, resolved it by agreeing to forego royalties on the first 500 copies sold.

It is not immediately obvious whether this procedure maximizes profit. Publishers tend to view the situation as one of a kinked demand curve—an increase in price above the prevailing level will result in a substantial reduction in sales, but a price cut will not significantly increase sales. The fact that there is some dispersion in textbook prices tends to cast doubt upon the applicability of the kinked demand curve approach to the textbook field.

My guess would be that neither a higher nor a lower average level of prices for his textbooks would increase a publisher's profits. This does not necessarily mean, however, that profits are being maximized. I have suggested that profit maximization might require relating book prices to the age of the book on the grounds that the profit maximizing price for a new book is necessarily higher than the profit maximizing price of that same book when there are used copies available.[4] This approach does not necessarily imply any change in the average level of prices.[5]

---

[1] A higher multiplier is generally used for trade books, primarily because of the larger retailer markup on trade books. These comments are based upon discussions with several publishers and review of the very limited literature on the subject. The best discussion of pricing is in Sir Stanley Unwin's *The Truth About Publishing* (Macmillan Co., 1960).

[2] The figure may be rounded up. A book will probably be priced at, say, $7.95 rather than $7.60, or $7.50 rather than $7.10.

[3] Occasionally inventory costs can be reduced by printing more than one year's sales but binding only a portion of those copies printed.

[4] Cf. *American Economic Review*, Sept., 1965, p. 844.

[5] One further question of profit maximization and textbook pricing has been frequently raised. Is it consistent with profit maximization for best-selling and poor-selling textbooks to carry the same price? Does profit maximization require that McGraw-Hill charge a higher price for Samuelson than for McConnell? It has been argued

PAYING THE AUTHOR

While estimating profit is difficult, publishing firms are able to estimate costs quite accurately. The cost item of particular interest to economists is the author's remuneration. There are several ways in which an author conceivably could be paid. He could sell his manuscript outright to a publisher for a fixed sum. If the book is more successful than anticipated, the publisher reaps the benefit; if less successful, the publisher takes the loss. This is a rational manner in which to handle the uncertainty associated with forecasting sales of a new book. The publisher is generally better able to bear this risk than the author and simply on the basis of numbers is better able to insure

that the fact that these books are priced roughly the same indicates that the publisher is not maximizing profits on the book for which demand is greater. In fact, assuming constant marginal costs (a reasonable assumption in this range of sales), the same price for the two books is consistent with profit maximization if the elasticity of demand is the same for the two books at all prices. For example, if demand for Samuelson were twice that for McConnell at all prices, profit maximization would require that both books be sold at the same price. Thus, in the diagram D_1 is twice D_2 at all prices, and the profit maximizing price, P, is the same for both.

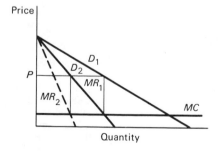

against the danger of disastrous failure. The number of firms bidding for manuscripts would assure the author of a competitive return.

This procedure could be carried back a step or two further. Publishers could contract with authors before the manuscript is completed or even before it is started. This would reduce the risk to the author of putting time and effort into a product which is not marketable. It is a small step from this procedure for the publisher to hire the potential author, putting him on the publisher's payroll while he is working on the book. In fact, in the very high risk (from the author's point of view) field of elementary school texts, many publishers do this.

Despite the potential advantages of this system of remuneration, I have been unable to discover any recent college economics text which was bought outright by the publisher. Of course, contracts involving a large advance and a relatively low royalty rate approach this system, since publishers do not seem to attempt to recover any excess advance from authors. In fact, the practice of guaranteeing a specified level of sales, common in trade publishing, is now being used in the text field.

The general procedure, of course, is for authors to be paid on a royalty basis; that is, the author receives a specified percentage of the sales price of the book. The range of royalty rates is fairly wide—running from 10 to 16 percent of list price—but there is a strong central tendency. Most recent economics texts carry royalty agreements of 15 percent.

There is another means of remunerating authors that, while now quite uncommon, is of increasing importance. A few recent books have been published on a profit-sharing basis; that is, author and publisher share, on an agreed-upon basis, in the sales revenue remaining after costs are deducted. The usual arrangement apparently is for publisher and author to share equally in the net receipts (total revenue less certain costs). One obvious difficulty is specifying how costs are to be calculated. This system, of course, adds to the risk of the author. If the book is a poor seller, he will receive no income under this system, while under a royalty arrangement he receives income from the first sales. On the other hand, a very successful book will give the author a greater return than he would have received under the most favorable royalty arrangement. The profit-sharing plan is of analytical importance because it overcomes some author-publisher conflicts that are inherent in the royalty arrangement.

CONFLICTS IN PRICING

It is inherent in the royalty arrangement that pricing results in a conflict between the interests of author and publisher;[6] that is, the price which maximizes profit for the publisher is higher than the price which maximizes royalty payments for the author. Profit is maximized where marginal revenue equals marginal cost. Since the author is paid a percentage of total revenue, the optimal price from his point of view

is where marginal revenue is zero. With negatively inclined demand curves and positive marginal costs, $MR = MC$ at a higher price than that at which $MR = 0$. (See Figure 1.) In other words, the publisher obviously must consider the cost of any additional books that will be sold as a result of lower prices, but the author, paid a fixed percentage of the price, is not concerned with costs.

Publishers have long been aware that their authors frequently argue for a lower price. Unwin concludes that authors do so because they tend to overestimate the elasticity of demand and underestimate costs of production. This analysis, of course, misses the point that costs are irrelevant to the author and that the only assumption about elasticity necessary to justify a lower price from the author's point of view is that it be greater than one.[7]

OTHER CONFLICTS

There are other conflicts between author and publisher that result from the royalty arrangement. Advertising is perhaps the most important. Publishers frequently complain that authors ask for exorbitant advertising expenditures.[8] Authors complain that publishers fail to advertise their book adequately. Of course, under the royalty arrangement, a $1,000 additional advertising outlay

---

[6] The first exposition of this point is found in Arnold Plant, "The Economic Aspects of Copyright in Books," *Economica*, May, 1934, p. 185.

[7] And obviously it must be greater than one at the price the publisher has selected. If not, marginal revenue would necessarily be negative and he could earn more by raising the price, thus increasing revenue and decreasing costs.

[8] This problem is perhaps more serious in trade than in textbooks.

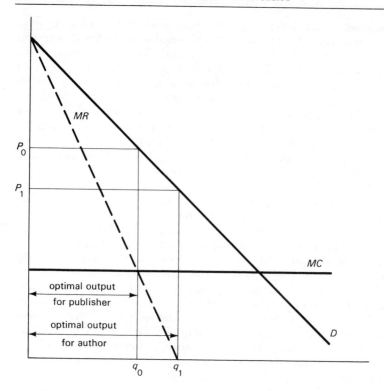

FIGURE 1

that produces $100 in additional sales is advantageous to the author. Publishers do not seem aware of this conflict and in discussing advertising with authors stress the fact that sales are not very sensitive to advertising.[9]

Distribution of complimentary copies is a special case of the advertising conflict. Neither author nor publisher want to give a book to someone who would otherwise buy it. However, the author wants free copies distributed as long as there is some chance that additional adoptions will result. He is interested in distributing an extra hundred free copies if the result is an additional ten copies sold. Obviously, the publisher, who must pay for the hundred, would not consider this a profitable transaction.

A more significant distortion of optimum decision making resulting from the royalty system is found in the production process. Publishers may be inhibited from using higher-cost production techniques by the need to pay the author on the basis of the higher price that results. Suppose, for example, that the publisher estimates that using color in a text-

[9] It may be stressed that, particularly in the case of textbooks, profit may not be the only concern to the author. The author's reputation (and hence his value in the academic market) may be favorably affected by wide knowledge of his authorship. In some cases advertising may fail to sell more books but may succeed in selling the author.

book will increase costs by $5,000 and revenue by $5,500. There would seem to be a net gain by use of color. However, under his contract, the author may be entitled to, say, 10 percent of this additional revenue. In such a case the publisher will not find it desirable to use color. This situation arises, not only with respect to use of color, but also with regard to charts, illustrations, mathematical symbols and perhaps even pages (the publishers' preference for shorter textbooks may be based on the view that shorter books sell better but it may result from the fact that they cost less to manufacture). As Unwin puts it:[10] "If an author gets 10 percent royalty on a 7s 6d *cloth* book, and it seems advisable to do a *leather* edition at 10s 6d, ought he to expect 10 percent on the increased cost of the leather binding?"

A more basic conflict between interests of author and publisher lies in the differences in risks taken and investments made in publication of a new textbook. Publishers are constantly in search of new manuscripts for textbooks. A high percentage of the time of publishers' college salesmen is spent in attempting to unearth manuscripts under way and to encourage professors to write textbooks. Contracts are typically offered at a fairly early stage in the writing process. This is virtually costless to the publisher since, while the contract binds the author to the publisher, it does not commit the publisher to publish the manuscript. The publisher does not have to make any substantial investment until the completed manuscript is in hand and

the decision to go ahead is made. It thus costs the publisher little to encourage authors to write books and to offer contracts without making any careful analysis of the quality of the manuscript or its chances of success.[11] Obviously the policies of publishers differ greatly in regard to the quality of their precontract investigation.

As a result, an author may be encouraged to put effort equivalent to more than a year's full-time work into a book which will not be published or which will yield him an insignificant return on his investment. It is possible, and perhaps is the general result, for a textbook to yield a satisfactory return to the publisher but an inadequate return to the author. Of course, the author in most cases has other than purely financial objectives in writing a textbook. Desire for prestige, desire to expound a new approach, and response to a "publish or perish" policy lead to some textbook writing in which the prospects for financial success are not important considerations. Even if profit seeking is not the primary motive for writing most textbooks, however, it is desirable that the potential author be aware of the potential conflicts between his interests and those of his publisher.

---

[10] *The Truth About Publishing,* p. 50.

[11] The only significant cost to the publisher in signing a contract is the advance that may be necessary. Advances run around $1,000 and hence are no great barrier to casual signing of contracts. There are also costs associated with editorial time spent on the manuscript and payments for reviews. It should be pointed out, however, that many publishers bend over backwards to be fair to their authors and may make an unprofitably great effort to salvage a poor or marginal manuscript.

SURVEY RESULTS

In order to determine the extent to which economist-authors are aware of these potential conflicts and to learn something of the income derived from textbook authorship, a questionnaire was sent to ninety-eight authors of textbooks advertised in recent economics journals. Response was excellent, with seventy-one questionnaires returned.

All publishers and most authors seem to believe that there is no inherent conflict of interest between author and publisher in regard to pricing. Most authors assume that since they are sharing the revenue with the publisher, what is best for the publisher is best for them. While we should not be surprised at this attitude if held by authors of English or physics texts, it is somewhat surprising how many economists have been willing to leave the pricing decision completely to the publisher. Only seven of the authors queried in my survey participated to any extent in the pricing of their book. Several indicated that it was quite naïve of me to suggest that the author (even an economist) should participate. As one author put it: "They know more about pricing the merchandise than I do."

When asked if they were satisfied with the pricing of their book, nearly all said they were. It is interesting to note, however, that of the five who indicated dissatisfaction, all would have preferred a lower price.[12]

The conflict was somewhat sharper in the matter of advertising. Less than half of the respondents to my survey felt that their publisher had adequately advertised their book. One fairly frequent criticism of advertising should be mentioned. Several authors complained that the publisher did not adequately promote their textbook in trade channels. Books in banking, investments, real estate, etc., have a potential market among practitioners that authors felt was not adequately exploited.

The potential conflict between publisher and author with regard to distribution of free copies of the book failed to materialize. Only three authors indicated that their publisher failed to distribute an adequate number of free copies.[13]

The questionnaire asked about payment arrangements. All but one of the respondents were on a royalty basis. As noted above, 15 percent is the most common royalty percentage. In some cases the royalty is expressed in terms of list price and in others is based on net price, but since the relationship between list price and net price is fairly standard (list = 125 percent net), it is easy to convert these to standard basis. For example, 15 percent of net price equals 12 percent of list price. Many contracts are on a variable basis with the royalty changing with sales. A fairly common arrangement is 10 percent on the first 5,000 copies, 12.5 percent on the next 5,000, and 15 percent on all

---

[12] Moreover, three of those who indicated satisfaction said they would have preferred a lower price. No author indicated a preference for a higher price for his book.

[13] However, six did indicate they felt that wider free distribution would have increased sales. This willingness to see things from the publisher's point of view is also evidenced in the advertising question. Many authors who felt that the publisher spent enough on advertising also felt that more advertising would have increased sales.

in excess of that. These royalty rates are comparable with those paid on nontextbooks.[14]

The strong central tendency in royalty agreements is rather strange in view of the very wide distribution in sales of textbooks. A few books sell over 30,000 copies per year, while many sell less than 3,000. Of the forty-three replies to my questionnaire giving information on first year sales, twenty-six reported sales of 3,000 copies or less. Only three sold more than 9,000 copies.

There does not seem to be any correlation between royalty percentage and sales. Publishers appear willing to make the same royalty arrangement for an advanced book with small potential sales as for an elementary book with much greater probable sales. Several publishers apparently have a standard royalty agreement which is offered to all (or nearly all) authors without any attempt to discriminate on the basis of probable sales.

It seems clear from these data that most textbook writing is not likely to be a profitable use of an economist's time, particularly in view of the increasingly attractive alterna-tives available to economists.[15] Publishers, however, will continue to seek to persuade potential authors to write. Some of the conflicts between the interests of publisher and author obviously are ameliorated under a profit-sharing agreement. Profit-sharing agreements are not a solution to all problems, however. Allocations of costs would become a source of difficulty. It would still be difficult to determine the profit maximizing price or amount of advertising expenditures. It would not completely resolve the fact that the author is often interested in wide distribution of his book even at a cost of some reduction in profit. Furthermore, most authors do better under a royalty arrangement than they would on a profit-sharing basis. For these authors, however, it is likely that the direct income derived from their books will not be sufficient incentive to write. For those who feel compelled to write and who are confident that they have a good product, the profit-sharing arrangement does appear to have real advantages over the traditional royalty contract.

---

[14] See *Publisher's Weekly*, Mar. 1, 1965, p. 54.

[15] I refer here only to royalty income. Promotions, pay raises, etc., that may be immediate by-products of authorship may make the venture profitable.

ARE YOU WORTH YOUR WEIGHT IN GOLD?

*Old-fashioned measure of individual worth found
lacking. Gold standard falls short again.*

By HARRY G. JOHNSON

When a person is extraordinarily effective in performing his responsibilities, so much so that he appears indispensable to the organization that employs him, he is frequently said to be "worth his weight in gold." The implication is that he is extremely valuable to the organization, far more valuable than any remuneration he may receive. But inflation has been gradually eroding the real value (purchasing power) of gold, while rising educational levels and technical progress have been gradually increasing the value of human beings. In consequence, a significant number of people in our society have become worth far more than their weight in gold. For these people, to say that they are worth their weight in gold is not to praise them but to belittle them, since it implies that they are grossly overpaid.

Gold is currently priced at $35.00 an ounce. This, however, is a Troy ounce, not the avoirdupois ounce used in weighing people. It takes 14.58333 Troy ounces to make a pound avoirdupois. Hence a pound of gold, in terms of the system of measurement of human weight, is worth $510.41 $\frac{2}{3}$; an ounce of gold, in terms of the same measurement system, is worth $31.90; and a hundredweight of gold is worth $51,041.66 $\frac{2}{3}$. Hence a person who weighed 125 pounds would have to be worth $63,802.08, a person who weighed 150 pounds would have to be worth $76,562.50, a person who weighed 175 pounds would have to be worth $89,322.92, and a 200 pounder would have to be worth $102,083.33, to be worth his weight in gold.

People's weights vary with their age, height, and sex, and it is these variations that are of interest to insurance companies, public health authorities, and others interested in compiling statistics of average weights. Hence it is difficult to find average figures for the typical American male or female adult. Margaret Reid has, however, provided me with the following figures: the average American adult male weighs 168.5 pounds, the average American adult female weighs 139.1 pounds, and the average American adult weighs 153.5 pounds.[1] To be worth their weight in gold, therefore, the average American male adult would have to be worth $86,000, the average American female adult $71,000, and the average American adult $78,300 (all figures rounded to the nearest $100).

How much is a person worth? Colloquially, this question refers to the value of a person's holdings of property, that is, to his wealth. The notion of a person's being "worth his

---

[1] Weights are for adults aged twenty through fifty-nine; the average for males and females is based on the 1960 population (Agricultural Research Service, 1960).

weight in gold," however, is usually taken to refer to his value on the job, rather than to his wealth. For the purpose of assessing the value of a person in this sense, economists have invented the concept of "human capital"; that is, they look at the worker or salaried employee as a kind of capital equipment, which contributes a stream of productive services to the economic system and receives in exchange an income that represents the return on the human capital. Like other capital equipment, human capital can be valued in two different ways, useful for different purposes. One way is by the cost of producing it; this is most useful for assessing the value of people who have just completed some stage of their formal education. The other way is by the present value of the stream of income that a particular item of human capital will yield over its probable remaining future lifetime; this is most useful for assessing the value of people already established in a career.

Some estimates of the average investments in human-capital formation involved in the formal education system have been furnished me by Herbert G. Grubel and Anthony D. Scott. According to their figures (which relate to 1956 and include both education costs and foregone earnings) it takes an investment of $2,240 to complete eight years of elementary school, $7,926 to complete four years of high school, $18,722 to complete four years of college (the B.A.), $26,336 to complete two years of graduate school (the M.A.), and $33,950 to complete four years of graduate school (the Ph.D.); all figures relate to total cost cumulated from the beginning of elementary school. These figures, however, seriously understate the amounts of the investments involved, because they make no allowance for the accumulation of interest on the investments between the time they are made and the time of graduation.

A rough calculation of the true value of the investments involved in the various levels of educational attainment, assuming a 5 per cent rate of interest, indicates the following capital values of people at the point of graduation:[2] eight years of elementary school, $2,745; four years of high school, $9,621; four years of college, $23,628; two years of graduate school, $34,046; four years of graduate school, $45,553. To these figures should properly be added whatever values people would have if they had no education whatever; but this can probably safely be regarded as negligible. On the basis of these figures, it appears that—contrary to the expressed belief of some eminent educators—the products of the education system are not worth their weight in gold, except for students who have completed four years of graduate school and weigh 89.2 pounds or less.[3]

---

[2] The calculation assumes that the costs are the same per year within each stage of the educational system and are incurred at the middle of the year.

[3] The use of a higher interest rate would of course increase the capital values and make many more graduates appear to be worth their weight in gold. Using the 8 per cent rate corresponding to the average rate of return on business investment, the values would be as follows: elementary school, $3,095; high school, $10,869; college, $27,425; two years of graduate school, $41,225; four years of graduate school, $57,321. On the basis of these figures, a person who had finished two years of grad-

The alternative method of estimating the capital value of a person is to calculate the present value of his expected future earnings. Burton Weisbrod (1961) has used this method to estimate the values of American males by age ranges from zero to four to seventy to seventy-four years of age. At a 4 per cent discount rate, he finds that a male aged zero to four is worth $27,124—which makes boy babies worth considerably more than their weight in gold—and that the value of a male rises rapidly with age to a peak of $57,494 at ages twenty-five to twenty-nine, declining thereafter to $241 in the age group seventy to seventy-four. In the age group twenty to thirty-four, the average value is $55,836, so that on the average any male in this age group who weighs less than 109.4 pounds is worth more than his weight in gold. Since men in this age group weigh considerably less than older men, it is probable that a significant proportion of them are worth more than their weight in gold.

Weisbrod's figures relate to the average of all males. Gary S. Becker (1964) has produced more detailed estimates of the average age-wealth profiles of male graduates of various levels of education in the year 1939, that is, of the capital values of the future earnings of these men at different ages.[4] According to his estimates, wealth (that is, capital value) peaks at thirty-nine, at which age the graduate of seven or eight years of schooling (elementary school) is worth about $34,000, the graduate of twelve years of schooling (high school) is worth about $49,000, and the graduate of sixteen or more years of schooling (college, or college plus graduate school) is worth about $71,000. Using the typical weight of 168.5 pounds previously selected (value $86,000), it appears that the average elementary school graduate is never worth more than about two-fifths of his weight in gold and a high school graduate never worth more than seven-twelfths of his weight in gold, whereas at his maximum a college graduate is worth about 82.5 per cent of his weight in gold. In fact, the average college graduate of this weight is worth at least 80 per cent of his weight in gold between the ages of thirty-seven and forty-one.

Are you worth your weight in gold? To find out, you must first determine the value of your weight in gold, using the figures previously given of $510.42 per pound and $31.90 per ounce. Then you must determine the present (capital) value of your future earnings.

As a very rough estimate indeed, you might start with the amount of your life insurance, since this is a

---

uate work would be worth his weight in gold if he weighed less than 80.8 pounds, and a person who had completed four years of graduate work would be worth his weight in gold if he weighed less than 112.1 pounds. The 8 per cent rate probably results in a serious overstatement, however, because the educational costs relate to the single year 1956, whereas the costs of educating a person would have been incurred in previous years and would have been lower due to the fact that foregone earnings and education costs increase steadily over time. The 5 per cent rate used in the text can be considered as equivalent to the 8 per cent return on business investment, less a factor of 3 per cent for the secular increase in education costs.

[4] See especially Becker's (1964) Chart 3, p. 146, and subsequently. The estimates allow for the secular upward trend of earnings with increasing productivity and employ an 8 percent discount factor corresponding to the average rate of return on business investment.

capital sum, and its magnitude is related to the premiums you can afford to pay, which in turn is related to your income. To compensate for the probability that your insurance underestimates your value, you should probably reckon your value at double the face value of your insurance. Alternatively, you might reckon your value at four times the value of your house, since mortgage lenders generally follow the principle that you should spend no more than a quarter of your income on housing, so that the value of your house will represent approximately a quarter or less of the capitalized value of your income.

Both of these methods, however, are appropriate only for younger people (say, thirty-nine and under), since for older people insurance and house values reflect past income rather than the capitalized value of future income. If you want to be

really accurate, you will have to estimate your future earnings year by year and determine their present value; and this will require an intricate actuarial calculation. A reasonable rough approximation, however, can be obtained by starting with your present annual earnings, estimating the number of years you expect to be an earner, and multiplying your annual earnings by the present value multipliers contained in Table 1. (These multipliers assume a 5 per cent discount rate for future earnings; for numbers of years between those shown, use an average of the two nearest multipliers.)

To illustrate the use of the table, a man earning $10,000 a year and expecting to work ten years altogether would be worth $81,000—more than his weight in gold provided he weighs less than 158.7 pounds. Similarly, a man earning $5,000 a year and expecting to earn it for twenty years altogether would be worth $65,000—and worth his weight in gold provided he weighed no more than a shade under 127.4 pounds.

Try the calculation yourself. You will probably be surprised to find that you are worth your weight in gold. If you are not, you may be able to derive some consolation from the thought that if you went on a diet and lost a few pounds you might quite easily make it.

TABLE 1

Total No. of Earning Years	Present-Value Multiplier
5	4.5
10	8.1
15	10.9
20	13.1
25	14.8
30	16.1
35	17.2
40	18.2
45	18.7

REFERENCES

Agricultural Research Service. *Home Economics Research Report,* No. 10 (1960).

GARY S. BECKER, *Human Capital: A Theoretical and Empirical Analysis with Special Reference to Education.* New York: Columbia University Press, 1964.

BURTON WEISBROD, "The Valuation of Human Capital," *Journal of Political Economy,* LXIX, No. 5 (October, 1961), 425–36.

COMICS

CASTRO AND ECONOMIC MAN, OR WHAT IS A PRISONER WORTH?

Castro viewed as economic determinist. Do Bay of Pigs prisoners have marginal productivity equal to tractors?

By BURTON A. WEISBROD

In the October, 1961, issue of this *Journal,* my article on "The Valuation of Human Capital" presented estimates of the capitalized values of "expected" lifetime earnings for males at various ages. At a 4 per cent rate of discount, the gross value (without deduction for consumption) of a male, age twenty to twenty-four, was $55,950. Thus, the gross value of 1,113 such men would be $62,272,350, or, rounded off, $62 million. The 1,113 is the number of Cuban prisoners from the Bay of Pigs invasion, and $62 million is the ransom demanded for many weeks by Fidel Castro!

If the value of a man as a labor resource were a relevant component of his ransom value, then, it would seem that the value *net* of his consumption should be used; the $55,950 figure cited above was an estimate of his *gross* value. Thus, perhaps we should not have been surprised when in the final days of the negotiations for the prisoners the $62 million figure was reduced to $53 million. This is equivalent to $47,619 per prisoner, which may be compared with the figure of $47,093 presented in the October, 1961, article as the present value of *net* future earnings for a twenty- to twenty-four-year-old male.

I have no knowledge of the method by which either the $62-million or the $53-million figures were actually derived, except that apparently the former was the value of the tractors originally demanded; but then the question is how the number and types of tractors were obtained. Could it be that these tractors have a combined marginal productivity in the United States equal to that of the prisoners? Is it possible that Castro is more of an economic determinist than he realizes?

THE ECONOMICS OF UNDERTAKING

*Packaging and container industry has built-in re-
straints. Non-recurring aspects create problems
not amenable to price-concessions or selling-
expenditures.*

By HARRY G. JOHNSON   **1735633**

Such an undertaker...needed the power of going to the centre of each practical problem as it arose; concentrating the forces of his mind on it; working out connections between it and outlying considerations; developing practical conclusions with a just sense of proportion; and pursuing resolutely the line of policy thus indicated, but with a mind always alert for new ideas, especially such as were demanded by the changing circumstances and conditions of his problem.[1]

Although sociologists and anthropologists have long been interested in the stimulating effects of interment rites on the efficiency of productive and distributive organization in primitive economies, professional economists have by and large neglected this important problem in economic dynamics. Nor have they attempted any institutional study of the production and marketing problems of the modern undertaking industry, so that the lay economist has had to resort for information to the unfamiliar and non-specialist literature of the popular novel. In the interests of stimulating empirical research, this article attempts a preliminary analysis of the industry's major economic characteristics.

From the standpoint of industrial classification, undertaking presents an interesting problem: on the demand side it is a capital-goods industry, on the supply side it is a service industry. If classified by technological process employed, it constitutes a branch of the packaging and container group: the union affiliation of some of the industry's employees in the United States has in fact been established by this criterion. The difficulty of reconciling the demand and supply characteristics is largely responsible for the modern form of the industry and current trends in its development, particularly the growing importance of public relations and the tendency towards increasing selling-expenditures, product-diversification and full-line forcing.

The demand for undertaking is a demand for a consumers' durable good, differing from the demand for other consumers' durables only in the non-recurring nature of the want —a characteristic which is biologically determined and hence not amenable to modification by price-concessions or selling-expenditures. There are exceptions to this generalization. On the one hand, if demand analysis is conducted in the modern fashion with the household rather than the individual as the utility-maximizing unit, it is possible for the undertaking firm to increase the number of sales to each consumer by the usual techniques of monopolistic

---

[1] Marshall, *Industry and Trade.*

competition; but the decreasing size of the family unit and the increasing mobility of labour in modern times greatly reduce this potential source of elasticity in the firm's demand curve. On the other hand, there are intermittent opportunities for the repetition of a sale arising from exogenous factors such as the posthumous growth of personal prestige and the stimulating effect of wars on the international exchange of cadavers. In general, however, each individual sale exhausts its own market, so that the marketing problem of the undertaker is a dual one of maximizing the cash value of the individual sale and tapping the largest possible number of individual markets. Both are general problems in public relations or salesmanship, but the solution of the former is facilitated by other special features of the demand.

The nature of the product as a consumers' durable good might indicate an analysis of demand as deriving from a probability distribution of expected future services extending through time. Lack of information as to the value of the flow of future services in a society not believing in bodily resurrection, and extreme uncertainty as to the probability distribution of those (unspecified) services in an agnostic and materialistic civilization have, however, so shortened the economic horizon of the purchasers of undertaking that the marginal efficiency of interment has come to depend almost entirely on a conventional evaluation. But the conventional evaluation is itself capable of further economic analysis, since for any given undertaking decision it is related to two economic variables—the personal income of

the decedent, and the general level of past undertaking expenditures. These two parameters set limits to the magnitude of the funeral commitment.

Within these limits, however, the conventional evaluation of the marginal efficiency of interment lends itself readily to manipulation by the undertaker, for two reasons. In the first place, the psychological condition of the purchaser at the time of making an undertaking decision is for obvious reasons far from that required by the rationality assumption of economic maximizing behaviour. Not only is "the rationality of irrationality" strongly advised by the circumstances, but the most favourable conditions exist for the application of the techniques of suggestive as well as informative advertising.

In the second place, since the magnitude of the funeral commitment is generally regarded as an index of socio-economic status, its relationship to the two economic parameters mentioned above may be analysed either as a particular case of "conspicuous consumption" on the lines developed by Veblen, or as one aspect of the continual "criticism of standards" discussed by Knight. On either line of analysis, the outcome is a constant upward pressure on the standard of dying, which creates favourable conditions for the application of skilled marketing techniques.

From a more modern theoretical viewpoint, undertaking may be described in the terminology of microeconomic analysis as an industry subject to "external diseconomies of consumption." It is unfortunate that contemporary economic analysis has concerned itself solely with the unfavourable welfare implications of such cases of interdependent consumers' utility functions, and completely neglected their favourable effect on economic growth. In terms of macro-economic analysis, the interment function displays a "secular upward drift," or, by a more recent formulation, contains a Modigliani-factor. The Modigliani-factor facilitates the manipulation of demand by the undertaker through imparting a strong autocatalytic effect to successful efforts to deepen the market.

The emphasis on advertising indicated by demand analysis is reinforced by considerations on the side of supply. From the funeral director's point of view, undertaking is a service industry: the raw material is supplied by the customer, processed according to the customer's order, and returned to the customer in finished form. While this feature of the industry eliminates the risk involved in production in advance of the market, which is in any case rendered impossible by the nature of the technical processes employed, the necessity of building up a flow of orders large and regular enough to meet fixed costs and yield a reasonable profit on the investment reinforces the dual concern of the undertaker with maximizing both the number and the value of sales. On the other hand, the technically optimum scale of operation would seem to be small relative to the average size of the modern undertaking establishment. Indivisibilities of equipment seem to be relatively unimportant, as the basic necroscopic processes require no very expensive machinery; there is little possibility of economies from by-product utilization; and the departmentalization and division of labour characteristic of the largest and most up-to-date establishments would seem to be a result of successful adaptation to the requirements of the market rather than an independent source of production economies. Similarly, while the growth of vertical and lateral integration has undoubtedly permitted substantial economies of overhead costs, particularly in selling-expenditures, the trend towards combination is itself a reflection of the requirements of the market rather than the result of a search for administrative economies.

The scale of operations of the modern mortuary establishment is therefore not primarily attributable to the engineering problems of funeral direction, which is still fundamentally a handicraft industry. The explanation is rather to be found in the requirements of the market for the undertaker's services, although monopolistic restriction of the supply of master morticians has been a contributory factor.

The marketing problem of the undertaker, as previously analysed, is a dual one, calling for a dual market strategy—an extensive public relations programme designed to increase the number of sales, and an intensive advertising campaign aimed at maximizing the value of the individual transaction. The extensive public relations problem has been solved in the past, and to a large extent in the present, by the creation of monopolies of goodwill based on local or religious identification. Goodwill has in such cases been further fostered by lateral integration with the furniture trade and local government; both of these industries share with undertaking the characteristics of high value of individual transactions and low rate of turnover, and have a corresponding interest in building up goodwill. Such lateral integration not only effects significant economies in the overhead costs of public relations, but spreads the risks of investment over industries subject to somewhat different patterns of seasonal fluctuation.

For the more ambitious undertaking firms, however, local or religious affiliations have proved unduly restrictive of sales volume, and the emphasis has instead been placed on public relations campaigns of the usual commercial type, suitably modified to meet the requirements of public taste. Thus advertising displays have come to stress the quality of the product and the reputability of the firm, while avoiding the grosser appeals characteristic of the soap and deodorant trades.

The development of commercial advertising has had two conflicting influences on the form of business organization in the industry. On the one hand, it has promoted the development of large-scale mortuary establishments capable of exploiting the market by providing a fully-diversified range of undertaking and associated services; the amount of capital required by these establishments tends to encourage corporate organization. On the other hand, large-scale commercial advertising has undoubtedly contributed to the retention of the partnership form of organization as a basis for advertising appeals stressing "the personal touch" in the relationship between the mortician and his clientele.

In addition to an extensive public relations programme, successful undertaking requires an intensive campaign to increase the cash value of individual sales. The possibility of manipulating the conventional evaluation of the marginal efficiency of interment is considerably increased if the funeral director is in a position to offer a wide range of product qualities and auxiliary services—a fact which, in conjunction with the requirements of sales volume, has stimulated considerable expansion in the size of the typical establishment. On the one hand, growing awareness of the advertising value of an attractively turned out product has led to increasing emphasis on details of finishing, evident in the emergence of specialized craftsmen such as the faciologist and cosmetician, and of specialized techniques for coping with what were formerly regarded as closed-coffin cases. On the other hand, the desirability of offering a complete range of funeral services has led to the development of both vertical and lateral integration.

Vertical integration extends backward into the provision of ambulance services, and forward into the provision and maintenance of cemetery plots. Lateral integration comprises the provision of chapels, organ music, and ministerial services for the burial rites, and fleets of saloon cars for the funeral procession. The overhead costs of the saloon cars are sometimes defrayed by part-time employment of them as taxi-cabs. In the United States, the typical funeral director is also prepared to provide an escort of motor-cycle police; such escorts are available to the mortician at a low price, as a by-product of machine government and the patronage system.

The establishment of a fully integrated and diversified undertaking plant capable of satisfying the demands of the market created by effective public relations requires a major capital investment. The necessity of protecting the investment has led to an emphasis on full-line forcing through the provision of "all-inclusive" funerals, and to intensified monopolistic competition between undertakers, one result of which has been the emergence of the "bargain funeral." The larger establishments have also attempted to control substitutes by operating their own crematorial departments.

While the trend towards larger-scale establishments is chiefly attributable to the marketing problems of the industry, a contributory factor has been restriction of the supply of master morticians and funeral parlours. In addition to the inhibitory effect of a low social evaluation of the net advantages of undertaking as an occupation, the supply of master morticians has been restricted by industrial control over apprenticeship regulations and training institutions.

In particular areas monopolistic restrictions on the location of undertaking establishments have been administered by the local trade association and occasionally enforced by agreements with the manufacturers of undertaking supplies. The unstable oligopolistic situation created by monopolistic restriction of entry has stimulated efforts to increase competitive strength by building further flexibility into the productive organization and increasing expenditure on public relations, with effects on the scale of undertaking which have already been analysed. The ploughing back of surplus profits into the firm has probably been further fostered by the family character of many undertaking establishments, and the rural origins and outlook of a number of funeral directors.

This investigation therefore ends where it began—with a sociological problem. It is hoped, however, that the intervening analysis has had the effect of stimulating interest in the economic aspects of a long-neglected industry.

The Daily Economist

RELIGION

THE POPE AND THE PRICE OF FISH

Papal-Bishop decree has far-reaching consequences for faltering industry. U.S. coastal communities to feel the bite.

By FREDERICK W. BELL*

For over one thousand years, the Catholic Church required its members to abstain from meat on Friday in the spirit of penance [6, p. 847]. This obligatory abstinence from meat has helped maintain the sagging U.S. commercial fishing industry. However, Pope Paul VI in February of 1966 issued an apostolic decree, "Poenitemini," relaxing the rules on fasting and abstinence during Lent. As part of the decree, the Pope delegated power to national conferences of local Bishops to decide whether to continue the rule of Friday abstinence. Having this authority, the Catholic Bishops of the United States terminated obligatory meatless Fridays, except during Lent. Starting in December 1966, Catholics were no longer bound to abstain from meat eating on non-Lent Fridays (i.e., approximately 46 Fridays during the year).

The actions of Pope Paul VI and the U.S. Bishops have come in the wake of government efforts to arrest the decline in commercial fishing through the 1964 Fishing Fleet Improvement Act [1, pp. 141–62]. On a broader scale, the reaction of the world's 584 million Roman Catholics may seriously damage commercial fishing in many countries. The purpose of this article is to assess the short-run economic impact of the Papal-Bishop decree.[1] For New England, the test area, it will be demonstrated that during the nine-month period following the P-B decree the demand curve for fish has shifted downward resulting in a 12.5 per cent fall in landing prices.

I. THE DEMAND FUNCTION FOR FISH

To evaluate the impact of the P-B decree on fish prices, all other fac-

* This article was written while the author was on leave from the Federal Reserve Bank of Boston as associate professor of economics, Clark University. Presently, the author is chief of economic research, Bureau of Commercial Fisheries. He would like to thank Linda Kreuger, Ellen Temple, Penny Dyson, and Ted Baker for their assistance as well as Walter Sullivan, Neil Murphy, and Harlan Lampe for their comments on this article. Errors are the responsibility of the author.

[1] Since Pope Paul VI authorized the national Bishops to make the meatless Friday decree, we shall refer to the two decrees as the Papal-Bishop decree. The abbreviation P-B will be used throughout the remainder of this note.

tors which affect prices must be held constant. The following log-linear demand function for the i'th species of fish was specified:

1) $\quad P = KQ^aY^bS^cI^dC^eL^fZ^g(P\text{-}B)^h$

where

$P =$ Ex-vessel or landing price in New England for the i'th species (cents per pound)

$Q =$ Quantity landed of the i'th species in New England (thousands of pounds)

$Y =$ Aggregate personal income in 1957–59 dollars for the Northeastern United States (tenths of millions)[2]

$S =$ Cold storage holdings of the i'th species at the beginning of the month in New England (thousands of pounds)

$I =$ Imports of the i'th species into New England (thousands of pounds)

$C =$ Consumer price index for meat and poultry; 1957–59 $= 100$

$L =$ Lenten demand: 1 for non-Lent months; 10 for Lenten months[3]

$Z =$ Weighted ex-vessel price for competing New England fish products landed (cents per pound)

$(P\text{-}B) =$ P-B decree: 1 for all months prior to the decree; 10 for all months in which decree is in effect.

[2] Northeast is defined as Maine, New Hampshire, Vermont, Massachusetts, Connecticut, Rhode Island, New York, Pennsylvania, and New Jersey. Most of the species landed in New England are marketed as fresh fish in the Northeast [2, 7–8].

[3] When 1 and 10 are converted to common logarithms, the dummy variable becomes 0 and 1 in the log-linear equation.

A log-linear demand function was specified since a substantially better statistical fit was obtained through the use of a logarithmic as compared to a simple linear function and the unexplained residuals were more uniform over the range of independent variables when expressed in percentages rather than absolute terms. Most of the variables included in the demand function are self-explanatory. Of special importance, the quantity landed is functionally related to the movement of fish populations and the weather. There is little attempt by fishermen to influence landing prices by deliberate variation in quantity landed. In the short run, the supply function is completely inelastic and shifts in this function should "trace-out" the demand curve [13]. And, since we are using monthly observations, the period is approximately the short run. Therefore, no identification problem is present since quantity landed is exogenous. Cold storage holdings may have two different effects on price. The first is negative or stock adjustment of inventory effect. The second is positive since buyers may purchase when prices are falling (i.e., in the summer months) and sell (i.e., in the winter months) when prices are rising. This latter speculative behavior has been pointed out by Brennan [3]. (P-B) should have a negative parameter if Catholics switch from fish to meat on Fridays. An estimate of "h" will allow us to compute the percentage shift in the demand curve after the November 1966 P-B decree.

II. STATISTICAL ANALYSIS AND RESULTS

The Northeast United States is an excellent area to analyze the impact

TABLE 1

Regression Results: A Test of the Papal-Bishop Decree Impact, Monthly Data, 1957–67 (Landing Price (P) is Dependent Variable)

Species	Constant	Q	Y	S	I	C	L	Z	(P-B)	N	$\overline{R}^2$	D-W	Percent Change in Price Due to (P-B)
Sea Scallops	1.667 (1.540)	−.653 (−9.888)	.395 (1.874)	−.154 (−6.068)	.014 (.759)	.461 (1.700)	−.004 (−.217)	−.260 (−3.900)	−.082 (−3.019)	123	.696	.709	−17
Yellowtail Flounder	−5.678 (−4.766)	−.436 (−13.732)	.861 (3.090)	.182 (5.179)	−.054[a] (−1.097)	1.749[a] (5.417)	.089 (4.791)	.259 (4.511)	−.064 (−1.961)	123	.789	1.164	−14
Large Haddock	−.237 (−.135)	−.460 (−12.431)	.212 (.816)	−.019 (−.513)	−.001 (−.366)	.878 (3.554)	.010 (.721)	.388 (9.314)	−.108 (−4.650)	123	.853	.781	−21
Small Haddock (Scrod)	−1.748 (−1.517)	−.456 (−12.861)	−.152 (−.542)	.057 (1.845)	.042 (1.047)	2.231 (8.569)	.039 (2.412)	.202 (3.745)	−.009 (−.367)	123	.802	.660	−2
Cod	−2.552 (−2.896)	−.317 (−8.859)	.031 (.155)	.117 (4.232)	.028 (.714)	1.784 (7.081)	.031 (2.060)	.307 (6.477)	−.047 (−2.003)	123	.780	.978	−10
Ocean Perch	.383 (.509)	.004 (.182)	.003 (.018)	−.012 (−.605)	.063 (2.465)	−.076 (−.392)	.013 (1.250)	.176 (3.666)	−.045 (−2.630)	123	.309	.513	−10
Whiting	−9.909 (−5.047)	−.045 (−4.961)	1.442 (3.167)	−.058 (2.189)	−.154 (−2.384)	2.127 (4.296)	.103 (3.665)	.558 (3.360)	−.104 (−2.205)	115	.682	1.352	−20

SOURCE: P, Q, S, I, Z [10]; Y [8]; C [11].

[a] Lagged one month. t valves in parentheses.

RELIGION 43

of the P-B decree on the demand curve for fish. Large quantities of fresh fish are landed at many New England ports and are mainly distributed throughout the Northeast. In addition, the last Census of Religion revealed that 45.1 per cent of the population in the Northeast were Catholics, more than double the percentage in any other U. S. region [7, p. 6]. Seven species of fish were selected for this study (see Table 1). There are two time periods under consideration: (1) a 10-year period (monthly observations) before the P-B decree, January 1957 to November 1966[4] and (2) the period after the decree, December 1966 to August 1957, but excluding February and March. These two months were excluded because Catholics are still obliged to abstain from meat on Lenten Fridays.

After logarithmic transformation, the parameters of equation (1) were estimated using least-squares.[5] The parameters and t-values (in parentheses) are shown in Table 1. Quantity landed displayed a negative sign while income showed a positive sign in six out of seven species. The expansion in aggregate personal income has a positive impact on price,

due, primarily, to population increase. The per capita consumption of most species considered in this study has remained relatively constant over the 1957–67 period [2, pp. 4–8], indicating that fish is not an inferior good. Cold storage holdings seemed to conform to a stock adjustment hypothesis for sea scallops, large haddock, ocean perch, and whiting and to a speculative hypothesis for flounder, scrod, and cod. Imports show a mixture of signs: four positive and three negative.[6] Meat and poultry prices, Lenten demand, and the price of competing fish products have a positive impact on price in six out of seven cases. In general, the parameters seem to conform to a priori theory for all variables except imports.

The (P-B) decree dummy variable exhibited a negative sign for all seven species which is consistent with the hypothesis that the demand curve for fish shifted downward after the

---

[4] The Lenten months for 1966 were excluded from the first period due to the possible influence of the Papal decree alone on these observations.

[5] Two other versions of equation (1) were estimated where the variables were first deflated by the consumer price index for all items and then this index was included in the equation as a separate variable. This procedure yielded approximately the same results as shown in Table 1. However the fact that meat, poultry, and fish prices are contained in the consumer price index for all items introduces an unnecessary bias. Hence, these versions were not used.

[6] There are two possible reasons for the poor showing of imports in explaining variation in domestic landing prices. First, there may be an identification problem. That is, higher imports will depress the price, but a higher price will attract more imports. This two-way flow may explain the half-and-half mixture of positive and negative regression signs. Second, fish imports are almost exclusively frozen while domestic landing prices refer to the fresh fish market. New England landed fish usually are marketed to fresh fish outlets such as restaurants and institutions. Hence, there are really two different fish products (fresh and frozen), each not highly price-sensitive to the other. The second explanation is probably the fundamental reason for the weak relation between domestic landing prices and foreign imports [2, p. 7]. Therefore, the parameters for quantity landed (fresh) and quantity imported (frozen) would markedly differ as indicated in Table 1.

P-B decree. For the seven species combined, prices fell approximately 12.5 per cent when weighted by landings. The decline in monthly prices ranged from approximately 21 per cent for large haddock to 2 per cent for scrod as shown in Table 1.

Unfortunately, little can be concluded about the statistical significance of the parameters of equation (1) due to positive autocorrelation in the residuals as evidenced by the Durbin-Watson statistic. However, the estimates remain unbiased and consistent [4] and also agree in direction of sign with a few surveys made of Catholic reaction to the P-B decree [5] [12]. Equation (1) was converted to first-differences in logarithms and the parameters estimated. This procedure eliminated the autocorrelation. However, first-differencing the (P-B) dummy variable yields only *one* observation which shifts the demand function rather than seven when levels are used (i.e., seven months of the P-B decree). Signs for the (P-B) remained negative for all seven species, but the standard errors were as large as the coefficients. Hence, first-differencing of dummy variables is not a satisfactory procedure even though it reduces autocorrelation.[7]

In light of these results, it would appear that the P-B decree had a negative influence on fish prices and therefore industry revenues. If losses in revenue persist, an attrition of both capital and labor from domestic commercial fishing may be produced since wages and the rate of return on capital are already at low levels [2, p. 96]. This may create economic problems for many small communities along the coastal United States.

---

[7] Under certain circumstances, it might be feasible to posit two regimens, with first performing one way, and yielding one set of coefficients, before the decree, and another, presumably significantly different, thereafter. Unfortunately, the model cannot be applied to the period after the decree due to the lack of degrees of freedom (i.e., at the time of this study seven observations were available after the decree while the demand equation contains seven independent variables).

REFERENCES

[1] F. W. BELL, *The Economics of the New England Fishing Industry: The Role of Technological Change and Government Aid,* Federal Reserve Bank of Boston. Boston, 1966.

[2] F. W. BELL and J. E. HAZLETON, editors, *Recent Developments and Research in Fisheries Economics.* New York, 1967.

[3] M. J. BRENNAN, "The Supply of Cold Storage," *American Economic Review,* March 1958, *48,* 50–72.

[4] J. JOHNSON, *Econometric Methods.* New York, 1963.

[5] W. F. LOMASNEY, "The Fish Market: Can It Survive the Loss of Its Bail-Out Factor, the Friday Meat Ban?" *Canner and Packer,* June 1967, 21–23.

[6] *New Catholic Encyclopedia,* V. New York, 1967.

[7] U. S. DEPARTMENT OF COMMERCE, Current Population Reports: *Population Characteristics: Religion Reported by the Civilian Population of the U.S.* Washington, 1957.

[8] ———, OFFICE OF BUSINESS ECONOMICS, Unpublished data on regional personal income, Washington, 1957–67.

[9] ——, *Survey of Current Business.* Washington, 1958–67.

[10] U. S. BUREAU OF COMMERCIAL FISHERIES, MARKET NEWS SERVICE, *New England Fisheries—Monthly Summary.* Boston, 1957–67.

[11] U. S. DEPARTMENT OF LABOR, BUREAU OF LABOR STATISTICS, Unpublished price indices for meat and poultry. Washington, 1947–67.

[12] *Why Catholics Eat Fish.* Chicago, 1966.

[13] E. J. WORKING, "What Do 'Statistical Demand Curves' Show?" *Quarterly Journal of Economics,* Feb. 1927, *41*, 212–35.

The Daily Economist

SPORTS

THE PECULIAR ECONOMICS OF PROFESSIONAL SPORTS

A contribution to the theory of the firm in sporting competition and in market competition.

By WALTER C. NEALE*

Professional sport promoters and owners of professional teams have long claimed a special position in respect to the monopoly laws and the constitutional prohibition against slave labor, and recently they have been deservedly successful in appeals to Congress. This paper presents the results of serious thought about the problem, serious thought engaged in *after* choosing sides on the issue. I submit that the "firm" in professional sports is indeed in a peculiar position vis-à-vis our accepted way of looking at the firm in a competitive market. The basic proposition can be called the

* For the original stimulus to this paper I am indebted to Mr. Charles Conerly of Mara University and to Coach Ore Pro of Falstaff University.

LOUIS-SCHMELLING PARADOX

If we ignore for the moment the legal reasons in the United States for avoiding a monopoly position, it is clear that the ideal market position of a firm is that of monopoly, whether to maximize profits or to maximize the comfort of life. If we consider the monopoly laws, the ideal position is as close to monopoly as the antitrust division will permit without prosecution. In brief, a firm is better off the smaller or less important the competition, and it will try to attain a situation in which it is the sole supplier.

But now consider the position of the heavy-weight champion of the world. He wants to earn more money, to maximize his profits. What does he need in order to do so? Obviously, a contender, and the stronger the contender the larger the profits from fighting him. And, since doubt about the competition is what arouses interest, the demonstration effect will increase the incomes of lesser fighters (lower on the rating scale or lighter on the weighing scales). Pure monopoly is disaster: Joe Louis would have had no one to fight and there-fore no income.

The boxing champion is the strik-ing case, but the problem is equally great for any professional team. Sup-pose the Yankees used their wealth to buy up not only all the good players but also all of the teams in the American League: no games, no gate receipts, no Yankees. When, for a brief period in the late fifties, the Yankees lost the championship and opened the possibility of a non-Yan-kee World Series they found them-selves—anomalously—facing sport-ing disgrace and bigger crowds.[1] If the Yankees, then, do not wish to monopolize their own league, why don't they buy out the National League? The answer is, of course, all those World Series receipts. "Oh Lord, make us good, but not that good," must be their prayer.

Now we must face the question of whether it is possible that there is a business which, contrary to all we have learned about the business world, finds monopoly unprofitable. The answer, economists will be pleased to learn, is no—that a busi-ness monopoly is profitable in the sporting business as well as in the business of life. The first peculiarity of the economics of professional sports is that receipts depend upon competition among the sportors or the teams, not upon business com-petition among the firms running the contenders, for the greater the economic collusion and the more the sporting competition the greater the profits. The paradox appears because the firm in law, as organized in the sporting world, is not the firm of eco-nomic analysis; and the item sold by the sporting firm is not the product of these firms, or not entirely. We have, in fact, the phenomenon of

THE INVERTED JOINT PRODUCT OR THE PRODUCT JOINT[2]

We have long been used to the idea of a firm producing several products from an indivisible process. The sporting firms produce an indi-visible product from the separate processes of two or more firms (in law). But the product itself is a peculiar mixture: it comes divisible into parts, each of which can be and is sold separately, but it is also a joint and multiple yet indivisible product.

To be specific, professional base-ball teams produce a complex prod-uct; or in common parlance several interrelated streams of utility. There is first the saleable unit of the seat in the ball park during the game, the service sold by each firm (Yankees, Senators, and intermediates) and generally regarded as the business of and the utility produced by the sporting firm. Then there is that strange sale of the utility of TV view-ing where we the people enjoy the utility while nonsporting businesses

---

[1] When the San Diego Chargers of the American Football League ran roughshod over their competitors in the fall of 1961 the fans began to stay away.

[2] Since a joint product refers to two prod-ucts technologically resulting from a single process, we need another term for a single product resulting from discrete technologi-cal processes, and following the profession's tradition of jumbling words (value of mar-ginal product, marginal value product) we here invert the words to symbolize single product of two processes.

pay the bill for us.[3] However, there are two other streams of utilities. There is the pennant race enjoyed by all and paid for by none. This we call the

LEAGUE STANDING EFFECT

Of itself there is excitement in the daily changes in the standings or the daily changes in possibilities of changes in standings. The closer the standings, and within any range of standings the more frequently the standings change, the larger will be the gate receipts. Thus the free provision of the *race utility* has a favorable feed-back effect upon gate receipts, and we may treat this effect as a kind of advertising. Note that this advertising is also free to the advertising sporting firms—it has no opportunity cost—and that it too illustrates the Louis-Schmelling Paradox in that the more successful in sporting competition the firm is, the less effective is the advertising feed-back of race utility. The "league standing effect" is not limited to the consumer utility stream and the advertising feed-back because it is also a marketable commodity, but not for the producers. This quirk we may call the

FOURTH ESTATE BENEFIT

Newspapers report the play, the outcomes, and the resulting "league standings" of games, and these reports are a major cause of sales and therefore of direct and advertising revenues to newspapers (and of

course to sports magazines): in fact, a case of economies external to the industry. Two separate sets of activities are needed to produce the game write-up—the game and the reporter-newspaper–printer–distributor complex. The former could occur without the latter, but the latter cannot occur without the former, yet the latter is the financial beneficiary of this product joint from two different economic spheres (although we must allow for the advertising feed-back to gate receipts from press stories).

So far as the argument has carried us we may conclude that the product of professional sporting activity is not merely (1) the match, but also (2) the "league standings" (or championship), the progress towards a championship or changes in the standings, topics of conversation, and press reports. Furthermore, (3) a business firm—Joe Louis or the New York Yankees—cannot produce any of these streams of utilities alone. It must have the cooperation of a second business firm even to produce the game; to produce the other utilities it must have the cooperation of several business firms.[4]

The conclusion, then, is that the business firm as understood in law (and therefore in common discussion) —Louis or the Yankees—is not the firm as understood in economic theory. Rather, the firm is the league, or all professional heavyweights. Once this point is realized, the theo-

---

[3] Which raises an interesting question about whose marginal rates of substitution on what indifference map.

[4] It might be argued that any firm buying inputs from another firm requires the cooperation of the second firm, but this is stretching the meaning. The cooperating firms in sports are not willing buyers and sellers from and to each other but together (and with the press) sell to third parties.

retical conclusion is clear: each professional sport is a natural monopoly. The several joint products which are products joint of legally separate business firms are really the complex joint products of one firm, and this firm is necessarily an all-embracing firm or natural monopoly.

A natural monopoly as commonly understood is an industry in which a single firm can satisfy the market in the declining portion of its long-run average total cost curve. If defined as one in which a single firm can satisfy demand at a lower long-run average total cost than can be achieved if two or more supply the industry's product, it would be possible to have a natural monopoly where long-run costs are constant, if their level varies with the number of firms, or where average costs are rising if the minimum and rising portions are so low that any division of the market between two firms results in higher costs for both on the declining portion of the cost curve because of diseconomies external to the firm although internal to the industry.

In law a firm is regarded as a person, persons, or organization having the right to own property and to contract. In economics a firm may be defined as a "decision-making unit whose major objective is profit" (however Harry Wismer may define the term), but this definition assumes that the "decision-making" and the "profit-taking" units are identical, whereas in professional sports, while the legal firm takes the profits, the league makes the decisions. Professor Robert Dorfman suggests parallels to the league in trade associations, the Eastern Railway Conference, the combination of various firms for construction jobs, and the joint ventures of Gimbel's and Macy's in the United Parcel Service and the bridge connecting the stores, holding that in none of these cases have the business firms merged. But each of these organizations is a firm by the definition, "a decision-making unit whose major objective is profit." The railways make decisions jointly about through-routing and rates, to maximize their profits, and so small a cooperative effort as common billing by a trade association is a joint decision made to reduce costs (i.e., increase profits). In short, although legally separate, in substance the associations and conferences act as would the management of a trust or holding company insofar as they reach joint decisions on marketing and pricing, and therefore can be regarded as merged.

If department stores were to withdraw from all business except the joint ownership of a delivery firm, or if railway companies were to restrict their activities to the joint management of a terminus, one would think of them as merged for any questions of economic substance. Operations such as the cooperative selling to each other and to other buyers by plumbers, carpenters, and builders in the construction industry do parallel sporting firms in that both are

MULTIFIRM PLANTS

Familiarity with the concept of a multiplant firm should not blind us to an occasional reversal of form created largely by the peculiarities of our law of property. The "plant" of the construction trades is the building site. At a minimum one might say that the "plant" of the sporting firms is the playing field, but without the league the playing field is incapable of producing the championship product, so the concept of "plant" must be enlarged to encompass the league. Furthermore, the parallel between the building industry and the sporting firms is not complete, for the sporting firms sell an indivisible product (once divided it is no product at all) to the consumer and *contribute exactly the same inputs.* The parallel should be with two or more plumbing companies joining together to sell their services as a single source of supply. Where there is joint decision-making because it is cheaper to do so, the resulting arrangement may be more easily seen as a monopoly if a (partial) cartel may be considered, as I would, a firm.

As for Gimbel's and Macy's, my mother-in-law assures me that "everyone knows they are in each other's pockets."[5]

An objection may be raised that one can have several leagues, and that these leagues are, or should be, competing firms. As one surveys the history and present state of the sporting trades one must admit the possibility, but one must also recognize that as a matter of observation there appears to be a strong tendency toward a single league, and this for one good reason: only a single league can produce that most useful of all products joint, the World Champion. Analytically we must regard the National League and the American League as one, for they come together each autumn to produce the World Series. Despite the differences in form, the substance of this World Series product is identical with the single league championship in the National Football League arrived at by business collusion in cooperative sporting competition between an "eastern division" and a "western division" team. Hereafter we should therefore refer to the two major leagues in baseball as "divisions" within the larger league-firm.

At the present time the trade of professional football is divided in two in the United States, with a competitor in Canada. There is no meeting on the field of play between the National and the American Football Leagues. The result is an absence of sporting competition, but very strong interfirm competition between the old and new leagues. Do we therefore have oligopoly? Yes, in the short run, in the same way that some American railroads have tried to compete; but in the long run, No, because this is inherently a temporary state of affairs. We witnessed a similar situation just after World War II when the All-America Conference challenged the National Professional Football League. The result in that instance was the demise of the Conference with the older League absorbing some of the teams of the bankrupt Conference. Logically we may distinguish four cases or four possible histories of interleague business competition:

1. The Major League Baseball solution: the joining of economically competing oligopolistic firms into sportingly competitive natural monopolies. [Editors' note: The recent merger of the AFL and the NFL in football illustrates a situation akin to Neale's Major League Baseball solution.]

2. The professional football solution of the forties: bankruptcy for

[5] Mrs. Paul B. Sheldon, New York City, oral communication, March 23, 1963.

one or the other of the economically competing firms.

3. The survival of two or more leagues because they are not economically competitive. This case occurs when the leagues are operating in different geographical areas or are inherently noncompetitive in both the sporting and economic sense, as in the case of boxers of different weights, or, a few years ago, baseball players of different colors.

4. The survival of two or more leagues which are economically competitive and which could be sportingly competitive.

The first two cases have been historically the common ones. The third case is actually rarer than one might expect. Of course, when it is patently ridiculous to compete in sport—to match a heavyweight with a flyweight—two leagues or championships coexist, but where sporting competition is prevented by geographical difference the tendency is to enlarge the area of sporting competition until in fact there is only one league. Thus we find that Australian, West Indian, Indian, Pakistani, and English cricket, separated about as much as is possible (or was possible before Gagarin), merge in that great international cartel, the Test Matches. Again, soccer (mistakenly called football by literally minded foreigners), which is formally organized in teams merged in national leagues, has become a cartel of international matches. Since cartelization is necessary not only to maximization of profits but also, even especially, to maximization of output, the geographical division of the market is an inherently unstable situation usually replaced by a naturally monopolistic firm whose market region is everywhere that the sport is played.[6]

Whether or not two leagues can survive within the market area—our fourth logically possible case—depends on the facts of the matter, or, put more realistically, on the relative shapes and positions of the demand and cost functions. From the sports pages it is difficult to glean solid data to which to fit functions, but one does form the impression from the history of sports that such survival is unlikely. In effect, the argument here depends upon the acceptance of premises for which direct evidence is thin on the grounds that the conclusion reached from the premises is consistent with observation.

The long-run cost curve of seats-at-games for the league-firm is probably flat or almost flat. As one expands the firm the quality of the product is affected by two contrary tendencies. The first is

DIMINISHING QUALITY RETURNS

because the quality of raw materials declines as less efficient inputs are drawn into the sport. One may treat

---

[6] The apparent exceptions of United States and Japanese baseball and of the sportingly independent United States and Canadian football leagues partly reflect difficulties of amalgamation across national boundaries, but more important, both Japanese and Americans agree that the Japanese teams could not win an international World Series and it is thus unnecessary to prove by formal competition that the American winner is the champion. But even here when exhibition games begin to show the American superiority at its own sport is questionable, one should expect cartelization into an international league. Perhaps, too, the pressure for Canadian-United States competition is low because it is not widely believed that the Canadians might win.

this as producing an inferior product for which there is another, lower demand function for lower quality "game seats" (which means a reduction in revenue per game seat).[7] Alternatively one may regard the diminishing quality returns as an increase in the cost of producing the same quality of game seat. In either case there is a limit to the size of the most efficient (least minimum average cost per constant quality game seat) league-firm, given by the cost function. The limit on size applies no matter how few or many leagues there are, so that one large league can provide any quantity of product as cheaply as two or more smaller firms. Thus there is no efficiency argument against monopoly, and there is a likelihood that the first league in the sport—like the first utility in a city—will become a monopoly. But any upward shifts in costs (or downward shift of quality and therefore the substitution of a new demand curve) are counteracted by the

INPUT-ENTHUSIASM EFFECT

Whereas one finds that human abilities in various directions are randomly distributed in any population, one also finds that skillabilities in sports are concentrated regionally. How else can we explain the disproportionate number of first class tennis players and cricket batsmen from Australia, or runners from Australia, England, and Scandinavia, or of passing quarterbacks from Texas, other

than by reference to the public attention and private concentration put into the development of these particular skills? And this input into the inputs is a result of the enthusiasm for the sport in the area, which in turn is both a consequence and a cause of the scale of operations of the sport in the area. In other words, the larger the scale of operations, the higher the quality of inputs and of products, or the lower the cost of a constant quality game seat.

When one shifts one's focus from the use of resources or the quality of product to the money costs it is reasonable to suppose that less perfect inputs (producing lower quality games) will earn a lower return, so that the cost per quality unit will not change as much as the quality changes. Both the "enthusiasm effect" and the lower salaries of lower quality sportsmen will flatten any rising tendency in money costs consequent upon diminishing returns. Enthusiasm simultaneously increases (1) the demand for game admissions and therefore the derived demand for skilled players and hence their salaries, so that the monetary cost of each unit of the larger supply of higher quality players rises; and increases (2) the supply of skilled players. The net effect of the increase in demand on gate receipts and on derived demand will merely tend to shift the curves northeastward without a "squeeze" on profits, while the underlying "enthusiasm effect" will lower the supply schedule of inputs. Larger scale, therefore, does not necessarily increase costs more than revenue.

All this, of course, is in conformity with our economic expectations, but the supply mechanism is not market

---

[7] However, we know by introspection that the reduction will be small since the appeal of the seat depends mostly on the uncertainty of the outcome and on the weather.

pricing. The supply of skilled inputs is developed in the sphere of amateur activity—specifically in the schools—so that the equilibrating mechanism works not through price response but through enthusiastic response and the human desire to conform to standards of group approval.

The net effect of diminishing returns, of the tendency toward constant money costs in quality units of input, and of the "enthusiasm effect" may be constant costs, increasing costs, or decreasing costs. In the absence of information, I guess that the long-run supply curve of the league-firm is roughly constant for output units of games by pairs of teams.

One usually expects a constant cost industry to be competitive, *ceteris paribus*; but *cetera non sunt paria*. Even if professional sports are constant cost industries the "World Champion utility" can only be created by cartelization. Furthermore, there is interdependence between demand and supply. The total size of the industry (in game-seats) is determined by the intersection of demand with supply, and if the long-run supply curve is horizontal, one might say that it is strategically determined by demand. But demand itself is in large part a reaction to the sporting importance of the events, the sporting importance depends upon the "fourth estate effect" and the "public conversation effect," and since these effects in turn depend upon the scale and universality of the championship at stake, the function will move up to the right for a more conclusive championship, and down to the left if the leagues decided to avoid meeting in a play-off. Thus demand and supply tend to

intersect at the point of a single, monopoly championship wherever that intersection may be (the You Don't Say Law).

On the supply side the long-run cost curve is horizontal, but the height of the curve above zero depends on the costs to the business or league-firms. These costs consist mostly of two elements: (1) fixed costs of interest or rent on the stadium capital and the cost of equipment and transportation for the firm, and (2) quasi-rents for the players. The price of any player is partly a function of his willingness to play, for the athlete need not enter the players' market since he has alternative opportunities, but once his minimum supply price is met the team firm is paying for an unreproducible talent, or a quasi-rent. If there are two firms bidding for his talents the quasi-rent will probably be higher than if there is only one bidder who is engaged with the player in bilateral bargaining. Since league firms typically prohibit multiple bidding by their team component firms counterbidding arises only when there are two independent leagues.[8] The existence of economically but not sportingly competing leagues thus raises

---

[8] A variety of liberties and restraints characterize the quasi-rent bargaining process in professional sports. In American football the "player draft" eliminates within-league counterbidding; in baseball the teams must bid against each other to contract with a new player but once the contract is signed the other teams cannot make counteroffers during the following years. Similar arrangements exist in other team sports, but in the sports of individual competition, e.g., boxing, the player and the business firm merge so that the quasi-rent payment to the competitor merges with his windfall profits and his income is undifferentiated.

the money costs to both leagues and so endangers profits. While in logic there is no reason why both leagues cannot continue to enjoy profits, or at least no losses, they are unlikely to do so. The salary of a player has much in common with ground rents, but the analogy must be understood to apply by lot, and is not complete. As in the result only one store actually uses one lot, so only one league employs one player. But whereas several stores can compete in a shopping area when they sell the same products because nonrental costs of and demand for the products of each store are the same, two or more leagues probably will not enjoy identical nonrental costs and demand. Transport to and from Kansas City from other points will not be the same as to and from Houston, while the urge to go to a ball game will differ from city to city (or from the Bronx to Brooklyn). Only in the unlikely event that both leagues field teams in exactly the same cities (and with exactly the same appeal to historic loyalties) will there be a no-profit-no-loss Chamberlinian equilibrium. One therefore expects competitive bidding eventually to raise quasi-rents for one league or the other above the spread between its other costs and its receipts, at which point the fourth solution becomes the second.[9]

Competition exists not between teams or leagues but between sports. Paying fans and newspaper readers prefer one or another sport—I suspect largely because Dad preferred it —but shifts in taste do occur and the leagues, or even the component teams acting independently, can encourage such shifts. Between the wars the New York (football) Giants built a loyal following by selling tickets extremely cheaply to children. Colorful people, youth leaders, immoral people, all can be used to attract attention to a sport. Ice hockey undoubtedly has increased its popularity over what it would otherwise have been by the public notice of brawls during games.

Definite divisions of the sports market seem to be characteristic. First there are the national divisions, marking off American baseball from Commonwealth cricket, American football from international soccer. Second, there are the seasonal divisions, leaving baseball dominant in the spring and summer, football in the autumn, and basketball in the

[9] Professor Benjamin Higgins pointed out that some other trades require competition to succeed. One is law, a single firm needing others to fight in court; another is fashion, the interest arising from the differences between two designers. There are perhaps more for there is no reason to believe that a "peculiar economics" is confined to professional sports alone. However, the two examples, while requiring competition for profits, are not cases on all fours with professional sports. Fashion requires separate, economically as well as aesthetically, competing units and so does not tend to coalesce into a monopoly. Furthermore, the supply of fashionable goods is the product of many factories and stores all over the world, not of the designers themselves. They are more like leading architects than leading coaches. The practice of law also does not tend toward monopolization of the business firms; and unlike both sports and fashion its practice cannot be called inconsequential. The need for competition within the courts stems not from the economics of business, as it does in professional sports, but rather from the adversary structure of our system of justice. Whereas sports require sporting competition and business monopoly, fashion and law require both interfirm business as well as aesthetic and legal competition.

winter. Third, there are divisions among social classes: cricket is upper-class and soccer working-class in England; baseball was the sport of the small town in America while professional football grew up in the industrial cities. Although these divisions may not be immutable they are certainly hard to change. Professional football has crept back into the late baseball season and forward into the basketball-hockey season, but efforts to establish an American soccer league in monopolistic competition with baseball (during June, July, and August) have met with little favor. Within the general framework of a whole-sport monopoly there are some additional peculiarities. We are familiar with the cobweb theorem, which depends upon next period's supply responding to this period's demand. But in professional sports we have the

ROGER MARIS COBWEB

The demand for Roger Maris' services for next year depends upon his performance this year. The cobweb has been inverted with demand reacting after a delay to supply; and the 1962 quasi-rent depended upon how ruthlessly Maris pursued the home-run mantle in 1961. Note that to introduce the concept of expectations does not alter the point, for the famous hog cycle—in which the sex urge of pigs responds to slaughtering prices in Chicago—is also one of expectations. Here one might note that an explosive cobweb is unlikely since the supply curve of talent in the quasi-rent range must be vertical and the height above the minimum price which Mr. Maris will accept and the depth below the maximum which

the Yankees will offer Mr. Maris depends upon bargaining technique. Below the minimum which Mr. Maris will take we have a horizontal supply curve and Mr. Maris leaves the market.

Whether marginal analysis of input pricing will work at all is doubtful. Whereas one can speak of the marginal steel worker without naming him it seems a little foolish to speak of the marginal quarterback of the Steelers. Marginalism seems to break upon the

BOBBY LAYNE RIGIDITY

There are possibilities of substitution of an indirect sort. Clearly one cannot field more than eleven laborers in a football game, "nor can one use two poor quarterbacks instead of one good one"; but one can use a better line to give a weaker passer more time or a faster fullback to make up for the absence of two first-class halfbacks. Such considerations obviously weigh with teams in their drafting and trading operations since Baltimore let Mr. Lipscombe go and the Giants put more effort into finding defensive personnel than into finding new offensive backs. But here one fails to see just how the Colts and the Giants compute the marginal returns of tackles, of pass receivers, and so forth. In baseball batting averages and earned-run ratings provide a better guide to marginal productivity computations; but in both sports the value of the marginal product is only indirectly and roughly related to these sporting measures since it is the effect upon the gate receipts which counts and gate receipts have no stable functional relationship with the sporting measures. In boxing the idea breaks down completely since the entire labor input is one and always tries to be its best. Thus the ultimate of the Bobby Layne Rigidity is the

ARCHIE MOORE INDIVISIBILITY

Having discussed the demand and cost structure of the professional sports industry certain parallels with other industries will be apparent. The firm of economic theory is the league, and the league is a natural monopoly with demand and cost and profit adjustments always tending toward unification of all league-firms into a single *firma-firmorum*.

The plant of economic theory is the game, which requires three factors of production: namely, land, labor, and labor. In different sports each of the factors has a critical minimum beyond which additions to output fall off rapidly; but the law of variable proportions is here invariable since two of the factors can be used simultaneously only in specified quantities and in some sports all three are subject to this limitation and the additional inputs logically come under the classification "repair and renewal." At this point one can also see the importance of institutionalism for the limits on the employment of labor trace back to ancient and irrational traditions of sportsmanlike behavior, and to break them by, say, fielding a fifth back armed with a switch blade would be impermissible to members of the tribal society despite the fact that any United Nations expert could point out the obvious technical advantages. To my knowledge only the Canadians have adopted the fifth back, and there is no evidence in published reports that even the Canadians have equipped this man

properly. On the other hand, economic sophistication of a high order is shown by the larger end zone and the elimination of the fourth down in a country with large unused areas of land and a small population.

We often think that if plant costs are constant (but here remember that the team or business firm does not constitute a plant) there can be no advantages of scale except as monopsonistic power is exerted; but we have already established those internal and external economies of scale called "league standing" and "fourth estate effect." Thus we justify horizontal integration in a natural monopoly.

Vertical integration takes different forms in different sports. We would have to stretch meanings to visualize vertical integration in boxing, but we are all familiar with the phenomenon in baseball. Here one familiar with the problems of underdeveloped countries and the earlier stages of industrialization will recognize the characteristic need to recruit and commit the labor force. It is also the arena of free contract negotiation; and is finally analogous to the tomato farms held by Heinz.

In American football there is still another organization often referred to as the university. The idea is to develop commitment before recruitment largely on the grounds that it is cheaper—or rather, on the grounds that the social costs of selection and training are shifted onto the community of academics, alumni, and taxpayers. But here we can go no further since this information is as well hidden as are the accounts of peasants.[10]

---

[10] The university farm team also appears to be the last stronghold of the third kind of

Variety of organization is found in the organization of recruitment more than in any other facet of the economy of professional sports. One can mention, in addition to the two forms already discussed, the feudal organization of village and county

integration problem. Most economists oppose integration of business firms either horizontally or vertically, but somehow manage at the same time to favor racial integration. This paradox is explained by the economic inefficiency of racial segregation, and the uneconomic character is perhaps sufficiently illustrated by an old lament of the Southwest which my daddy used to sing:

There was a blackguard from the South
For our sisters he was born too uncouth;
  He couldn't play Royal's
  Or even Frank Broyles',
So Syracuse hired the youth.

cricket, the climatic-linguistic character of ice-hockey recruitment, and less recently the religious qualifications for animal wrestling in the Roman arena. Here alone I feel economists should support the remaining elements of freedom, conflict, and competition in the business organization of professional sports.

Otherwise it is clear that professional sports are a natural monopoly, marked by definite peculiarities both in the structure and in the functioning of their markets. Consequently professional leagues have every economic ground to appeal to legislatures, to courts, and to the public on the ground that

We fall if you divide us;
We stand if Johnny Unitas.

THE BASEBALL PLAYERS' LABOR MARKET

Economist finds flaws in reserve clause. Free market rules seen as benefit to baseball industry.

By SIMON ROTTENBERG*

Since its inception in the 1870's, organized baseball has developed a market for baseball players and their

---

* Am indebted to my colleagues and the students of the Department of Economics at the University of Chicago for challenging discussions of this topic which I have had with them. I must lay claim, however, to any errors the paper still contains.

Although I have referred to a large number of different sources in the considerable literature on basball, I have found no document so valuable by far as the *Hearings before the Subcommittee on Study of Monopoly Power of the Committee on the Judiciary of the House of Representatives* (82nd Cong.,

1st sess.), Serial No. 1, Part 6: *Organized Baseball* (Washington, D.C.: Government Printing Office, 1952). The materials collected in this volume are massive and are indispensable for the understanding of the economics of this market. The volume will be cited henceforth, for brevity, as *Celler Hearings*, after Congressman Emanuel Celler, the committee chairman.

The companion piece to the hearings of the subcommittee is its report, *Organized Baseball: Report of the Subcommittee on Study of Monopoly Power of the Committee on the Judiciary, Pursuant to H. Res. 95, House of Representatives* (82nd Cong., 2d sess. [Washington, D.C.: Government Printing Office, 1952]). This document will be referred to henceforth as *Celler Report*.

services in which there is less than perfect freedom to buy and sell. In this paper I shall discuss analytically a number of market problems which are interesting because of some unusual characteristics of the baseball labor market and the organization of the baseball industry.

In the labor market, monopsony is more frank and explicit and less imperfect than in the more common case, in other industries, of covert antipirating agreements. The nature of the industry is such that competitors must be of approximately equal "size" if any are to be successful; this seems to be a unique attribute of professional competitive sports.

Before passing to the analytical questions, however, I must describe the structure of the industry and the rules of the market. The structure and the rules of the market for baseball players and their services are defined in seven documents which constitute the constitutional papers of the baseball industry. These documents are the Constitution of the National League of Professional Baseball Clubs, the Constitution of the American League of Professional Baseball Clubs, the Major League Agreement, the Major League Rules, the Major-Minor League Agreement, the Major-Minor League Rules, and the Agreement of the National Association of Professional Baseball Leagues (the minor leagues).[1]

The documents specify the procedures for their own amendment, and they are amended from time to time. They are enormously complex. This complexity arises, in part, from the ingenuity of club owners and business managers in doing violence to the purposes of the rules while obeying their letter. Let a rule be established proscribing a practice and inhibiting gainful action, and teams find some substitute for it, and an amended rule emerges. Complexity also arises from the effort to compromise inconsistent interests within baseball.

Taken all together, the documents constitute baseball as a collusive combination. The parties to this combination have agreed to be bound by rules that inhibit competition and to enforce these rules by extralegal sanctions.

The organized baseball industry[2] consists of two major leagues and a number of minor leagues. The number of minor leagues varies from time to time in response to changes in product-market conditions. In 1955 there were thirty-three minor leagues operating.[3]

Most leagues are composed of eight teams, but leagues of other sizes, for example, of six teams, are not uncommon. Sometimes a league begins a season with eight teams and

---

[1] The Baseball Blue Book, 1955 (Fort Wayne, Ind.: Bureau of the Blue Book, 1955).

[2] This paper is almost exclusively concerned with organized baseball. "Organized" baseball refers to the combination bound together by the constitutional documents I have enumerated. Baseball, outside of organized baseball, consists of amateur baseball, in which players receive no compensation for their play; semiprofessional baseball and the industrial leagues (composed of teams representing firms), in both of which a few players are paid for their playing services, but others are not; and a few fully professional leagues and clubs which are independent of organized baseball.

[3] For a record of the number of minor leagues from 1905 to 1951, see Celler Hearings, p. 992.

will lose a team or two that do not prosper and are abandoned in mid-season.

The major-league season provides for a schedule of 154 games played by each team; 77 games are played at its own home ball park and 77 in those of its opponents. Thus each team plays 22 games with each of the other seven teams in its league, 11 at home and 11 away.

The minor leagues are classified into categories defined by the sum of the populations of the cities of which is composed. These categories are called Open Classification, AAA, AA, A1, A, B, C, D, and E.[4]

The minor leagues are made up of teams that are either "independent" or are "farm" teams of a major-league team. Farm teams are either owned outright by a major-league team or controlled by "working agreements" which give the major-league club, in return for financial or other assistance, the right to acquire the services of a specified number of players of the minor-league teams. A farm system makes it possible for a major-league team to accumulate a pool of players from which it can make replacements on its own team, and it pro-

vides a place where promising players can be "seasoned" for major-league play.

Of approximately 260 minor-league teams operating in 1955, 155 were farms of the major-league teams, 40 owned outright and 115 controlled by working agreements. Farm teams are not equally distributed among the major-league teams. In 1955, for example, the St. Louis National League team controlled eighteen farm teams, while the Boston and the Chicago American League teams controlled only six farm teams each.[5]

Every team admitted to organized baseball has *territorial rights* in the city in which it is located. No team in organized baseball may play in the territory of any other team without the latter's consent.[6] Each team, therefore, monopolizes its own territory within organized baseball, and this monopoly right is a marketable commodity.

An elaborate system of rules has been devised to govern the contractual relationships between players and teams and among teams in the disposition of players' services. This system of rules structures the labor market and imposes restraints upon freedom in the market.

Until he signs his first contract with a team in organized baseball, a player is a *free agent* who may dispose of his services as he wishes, and teams may compete in bidding for him with relative freedom. In the market for free agents, competition is very intense. A star high-school player may have a large number of

----

[4] The number of leagues in each category in 1955 was as follows:

Classification		Aggregate Population Requirement	No. of Leagues
Open Classification		10,000,000	1
AAA		3,000,000	2
AA		1,750,000	3
A1		1,450,000	0
A		1,000,000	3
B		250,000	7
C		150,000	8
D	Up to	150,000	9
E	Up to	150,000	0

[5] *Baseball Official Guide, 1955* (St. Louis, Mo.: C. C. Spink & Sons, 1955), p. 162.

[6] *Baseball Blue Book, 1955*, p. 712.

representatives of different teams prepared to negotiate with him the day after his graduation from school.[7]

When bidding is heavy for the services of a particular free agent, the player is paid a *bonus* for signing a contract with one team rather than another. Bonuses of $100,000 or more to secure a player's signature are not unknown, although they have usually been much smaller.[8] The bonus can be thought of as part of the player's first year's salary or as an income supplement which is distributed over the length of his playing life. The size of the bonus is not the only dimension of bidders' offers. A free agent will also choose among alternative bidders on the basis of his estimates of his lifetime baseball earnings with each bidder, and these estimates are compounded of his estimates of his length of playing life (which may be longer with

one team than with another) and his estimates of his average annual earnings.[9]

When a player signs a contract, it must be a *uniform contract*, the terms of which are specified in detail by organized baseball. There is one uniform contract for the major leagues and another for the minors; the two are very similar. No deviation from the terms of the uniform contract is permitted without the approval of the appropriate executive officer of organized baseball, and deviation is rarely permitted.[10]

The uniform contract provides that, in consideration of the payment of the compensation provided for in the contract, the player "agrees to render skilled services as a baseball player." The team may terminate the player's contract if the player should "fail, in the opinion of the Club's management, to exhibit sufficient skill or competitive ability to . . . continue as a member of the Club's team."

Almost all contracts run for a one-year term. However, the uniform

---

[7] The rules do not permit negotiation with a high-school student until the day following his graduation.

[8] In an attempt to reduce the size of bonuses paid to free agents, baseball's rules have recently been changed to impose real costs upon teams contracting bonus players. A bonus player signed to a major-league team, for example, must be kept on the team roster for two years; normally a young player contracted by a major-league team would be sent to the minor leagues for several years of "seasoning." Bonus players, for this purpose, are defined as those who are paid in excess of a stipulated amount for their first year plus an extra sum in compensation for signing their first contracts. To skirt the rule, some teams are said to have paid the player less than this amount but to have employed his father in some nominal capacity at a high sarary, although the rules include in their definition of a bonus player payments made to other persons "for the use or benefit" of the player (*Baseball Blue Book, 1955*, pp. 513–14, 613–14, 729).

[9] Players under contract to Team A or its farm system are a non-competing group vis-a-vis players under contract to Team B or its farm system, because of the operation of the "reserve rule" to be discussed below. Average salaries may therefore vary among teams. On July 1, 1950, the mean salaries of the major-league teams ranged from $18,788 for the New York Yankees to $8,031 for the St. Louis Browns (*Celler Hearings*, p. 965). The range of salaries paid by different teams is also different, and a free agent, in computing his prospective earnings with different clubs, can be expected to consider the salary range of each of the bidders for his services and to estimate where, in the whole course of his playing career, he is likely to fall within it.

[10] *Baseball Blue Book, 1955*, pp. 509, 609.

player contract contains a renewal clause, conventionally called the *reserve clause*, which permits the the team to renew the contract for the following year at a price which the team may fix—subject, in the major leagues only, to the constraint that the salary in the following year shall not be less than 75 per cent of the salary in the current year. In the minor-league uniform contract there is no constraint at all on the price which the team may fix for the next season's services.

The team with which the player is contracted has exclusive right to the use of his playing services; he may not play baseball elsewhere without its consent. His contract may be assigned by this team to another team, and he is bound to report for play with the assignee team. No other team in organized baseball may employ him.

No team may negotiate with a player already under contract to another team. This is called *tampering* and is prohibited by the rules.[11] If any team wants to secure the services of a player contracted by another, it may negotiate with the team that owns the rights to his services for a purchase, but it may not bid the player away directly by contracting him.

Once a player has signed his first contract in organized baseball, therefore, he is no longer free to dispose of his services. He may withdraw from organized baseball and follow some other calling, but he may not choose freely among bidders for him within baseball.

The market for baseball players has really divided into three mar-

kets. One is the market for free agents, in which the player is the seller; another is the market for players who have already signed their first contracts, in which teams are both the sellers and the buyers; the third is the market for current services of contracted players, in which the player is the seller and the team that holds his contract is the buyer.

Some attempts have been made to enforce in the courts the exclusive right to contracted players' services which is conveyed by the uniform contract. On the principle that involuntary servitude is contrary to public policy, the courts have been reluctant to compel players to fulfil their contracts, to restrain them from performing for others, or to restrain others from employing them, and these attempts have met with little success.[12] Baseball has therefore resorted to extralegal sanctions to enforce exclusive rights. A player who refuses to play for a team by which he is contracted, or refuses to play for a team to which his contract has been assigned, is suspended; he may not be employed by another team in organized baseball.[13] If he finds employment in baseball outside of organized baseball, he is declared "ineligible" and may not play in organized baseball again until he

---

[11] *Ibid.*, pp. 511, 611.

[12] On the principle of a case decided in 1852 (*Lumley* v. *Wagner*) a contracted player may be restrained by a court of equity from making his services available to a third party if (1) the player is unique; (2) the contract is definite; (3) there is mutuality; and (4) the contract is not an unreasonable restraint of trade. There is some question whether players' contracts fulfil these conditions (Peter S. Craig, "Monopsony in Manpower," *Yale Law Journal*, March, 1953, p. 590).

[13] *Baseball Blue Book, 1955*, p. 538, 636.

is restored to eligibility; the length of time after his petition for reinstatement before he will be permitted to resume play will depend upon the evaluation of the gravity of his offense.[14] A team in organized baseball that employs a suspended or ineligible player will find that other teams will refuse to meet it on the field of play; a team outside of organized baseball that employs him will not be permitted to hire the ball park of a team in organized baseball; players who participate in contests in which an ineligible player takes part themselves become ineligible.[15]

The reserve rule is the heart of the limitation on freedom in the baseball labor market. A number of different defenses have been offered for it, some specious and others somewhat stronger.

The defense most commonly heard is that the reserve rule is necessary to assure an equal distribution of playing talent among opposing teams; that a more or less equal distribution of talent is necessary if there is to be uncertainty of outcome; and that uncertainty of outcome is necessary if the consumer is to be willing to pay admission to the game. This defense is founded on the premise that there are rich baseball clubs and poor ones and that, if the players' market were free, the rich clubs would outbid the poor for talent, taking all the competent players for themselves and leaving only the incompetent for the other teams. It will be seen later that the premise is false.

Most of the revenue of baseball clubs comes from admission receipts.[16] A rich club, therefore, is one located in an area where attendance at baseball games is high; a poor club is one whose attendance is low.

Attendance at baseball games, as a whole, is a function of the general level of income, the price of admission to baseball games relative to the prices of recreational substitutes, and the goodness of substitutes.[17]

[16] Combined major-league teams' revenue in 1950 was distributed by source as follows:

	Per cent
Home-game admissions	57.2
Road-game admissions	14.1
Exhibition games	2.8
Radio and television rights	10.5
Concessions (net)	9.2
Other	6.2

Approximately twenty-five cents of each admission price is paid to the visiting team; the remaining admission revenue is kept by the home team (*Celler Report*, p. 6).

[17] The following estimates show some trends related to baseball attendance:

	1929	1954
Expenditures for recreation as a percentage of total personal consumption expenditures	5.5	5.2
Admissions to specitied spectator amusements* as a percentage of expenditures for recreation	21.1	14.0
Spectator sports† as a percentage of admissions to specified spectator amusements	7.2	13.0
Professional baseball as a percentage of spectator sports	25.8	25.1‡

(Source: U.S. Department of Commerce, *National Income, 1954 Edition: Supplement to the Survey of Current Business* [Washington, D.C.: Government Printing Office, 1954], Table 30, pp. 206 ff.; *Survey of Current Business*, July, 1955, Table 30, p. 19; *Celler Report*, p. 12.)

[14] *Ibid.*, pp. 540, 637.
[15] *Ibid.*

Attendance at the games of any given team is a positive function of the size of the population of the territory in which the team has the monopoly right to play;[18] the size and convenience of location of the ball park;[19] and the average rank standing of the team during the season in the competition of its league. It is a negative function of the goodness of leisure-time substitutes for baseball in the area and of the dispersion of percentages of games won by the teams in the league.[20]

There is, in fact, a wide variation in attendance among teams. In the period 1931–50 the New York Yankees' aggregate paid attendance was 24,270,000, while that of the St. Louis Browns was 4,160,000.[21]

If, it is argued, other things being equal, a team in an area with a large population has larger revenues than

teams in less populous areas, then, in a free players' labor market, the former will get the most capable players, there will be wide variation among teams in the quality of play, contests will become certain, and attendance will decline.

The history of baseball seems, at least superficially, to support the position that the purpose of the reserve rule was to achieve balance of playing strength among teams. The first professional baseball league was the National Association of Professional Baseball Players, organized in 1870. It did not survive five seasons of play, and A. G. Mills, who first proposed the reserve rule, is reported to have said of its experience:

This condition was greatly aggravated by the general practice on the part of the richer clubs of stripping the weaker ones of their best playing talent. Then would follow the collapse of a number of these clubs in mid-season, leaving their players unpaid, while the winning clubs, owing to the disbandment of the weaker ones, would also frequently fall from inability to arrange a paying number of games.[22]

The National Association was succeeded by the National League, which was formed in 1876.

To bring the process of unequal distribution of talent to a halt, it was thought necessary to devise the reserve rule to permit the poorer teams to retain the services of players whom they would otherwise lose to teams prepared to pay higher salaries. If this was the purpose of the reserve rule, there seems to be some question whether it has been successful. A number of different measures suggest themselves for testing

---

* "Specified spectator amusements" are motion-picture theaters; legitimate theaters, opera, and entertainments of non-profit institutions (except athletics); and spectator sports.

† "Spectator sports" are professional baseball, football, and hockey; horse- and dog-race tracks; college football; and "others."

‡ 1950; information not available for 1954.

[18] Metropolitan area population per major-league team in 1950 ranged from 4,277,000 for each of the three teams in the New York area to 898,000 for Cincinnati and 857,000 for each of the two teams in St. Louis (*Celler Report*, p. 99).

[19] Major-league ball parks ranged in seating capacity in 1955 from 27,523 for Washington to 73,811 for Cleveland (*Baseball Blue Book, 1955*, pp. 18 ff.).

[20] That is to say, the "tighter" the competition, the larger the attendance. A pennant-winning team that wins 80 per cent of its games will attract fewer patrons than a pennant-winning team that wins 55 per cent of them.

[21] *Ibid.*, p. 100.

[22] *Celler Report*, p. 18, quoting *Spalding's Official Baseball Record, 1915*, p. 47.

the equality of distribution of player ability among teams. A simple test is one which counts the number of times each team has won its league pennant. In the period 1920–51 the New York Yankees led the American League in eighteen years, and the Chicago White Sox in none. In the National League, in the same period, the St. Louis Cardinals won in nine years, the New York Giants in eight, and the Philadelphia Phillies and Boston Braves in one year each.[23]

Clearly, there has been unequal distribution of talent. The Yankees have had better fortune than the others. By offering higher prices for the purchase of players' contracts from other teams, they have acquired players already under contract; by offering higher first-year salaries and prospects for higher professional lifetime earnings, they have induced the better free agents to sign with them; and by investing heavily in a farm system in the minor leagues, they have had access to a large pool of players from which the most capable could be drawn to the Yankees themselves.

By this simple empirical test, it can be seen that the reserve rule has not distributed players among teams perfectly equally; the teams that were prepared to outbid others for players have not been frustrated by the rule. The reason for this result will be shown later. It will also be shown that a market in which freedom is limited by the reserve rule cannot be expected to equalize the distribution of players among teams more than a market in which there is perfect freedom.

If the reserve rule does not, in fact, equalize the distribution of players, can it have some other result? By confronting each contracted player with an exclusive bidder, the rule can have the effect of depressing salaries, at least for some players. The relevance of salary levels to the rule was clearly seen in an official release of the National League on September 29, 1879, shortly after the adoption of the reserve rule for the first time.

The financial results of the past season prove that salaries must come down. We believe that players in insisting on exorbitant prices are injuring their own interests by forcing out of existence clubs which cannot be run and pay large salaries except at a large personal loss. . . . In view of these facts, measures have been taken by this league to remedy the evil to some extent in 1880.[24]

The "measures" taken were a secret agreement among the members of the league that each might reserve five players who could not be contracted by other teams. Over the years the number of players who might be reserved has been revised upward from time to time until now the major-league teams are permitted to reserve forty players and minor-league teams a smaller number, depending on their league classification.[25]

---

[23] *Celler Report*, p. 102. Operationally, perfect equality of distribution of players among teams may be made manifest in the following ways: every game ends in a tie; every team wins exactly half of the games it plays; every team, in an eight-team league, wins the pennant every eighth year.

[24] *Celler Hearings*, p. 139, quoting a release published in the *New York Clipper*, October 11, 1879.

[25] A class AAA team, for example, may reserve thirty-eight players, and a class D team, only twenty-one.

Two other rules affecting the disposition of players should be mentioned. The *draft* or *selection* rule prevents a player from being held indefinitely in a lower classification league if his services are wanted by a team of a higher classification. After a player in the minor leagues has served a stipulated number of years in the minor leagues,[26] he becomes eligible to be drafted (selected) by teams of higher classifications.[27] A player who is drafted has his contract taken up by the team that drafts him. The team that loses him is paid according to a schedule which appears in the constitutional documents; the price depends upon the league classification of the team from which the player is drafted and the classification of the team that drafts him.[28] Thus the draft is a forced sale at a previously stipulated price. A team of classification A or higher may lose only one player in each season by the draft, irrespective of the number of draft-eligible players it has under reserve; in leagues of lower classification than A any number of eligibles may be drafted from any team. Thus only as many players may be drafted from the higher minor-league teams as there are teams.[29]

An elaborate system of rules has been worked out for determining the priority of selecting teams in the draft process. First choice is given to teams of high league classification and last choice to low-classification teams; for teams of any given league classification, first choice is given to those that stood lowest at the end of the previous season, and last choice is given to those that stood highest. The system appears to give the advantage of first choice to the teams of any classification which need talented players most. The advantage, however, is largely illusory. A minor-league team that holds the contracts of, say, three players, each of whom, if sold, would be worth $40,000, will not be prepared to lose any of them for the substantially lower draft price. Since it does not know which of the three will be drafted, it will sell them all before the draft dates.[30] It sells, of course, to the highest bidder, without regard to the previous season's rank position of the bidding teams. In the end, therefore, it seems to be true that the players who are left to be drafted are those who are worth about the draft price. If there are bargains to be had, it is because someone miscalculated the

[26] For example, this number is five years in the Pacific Coast League (players in this league, and *only* in this league, may opt to sign a contract which exempts them from the draft; in November, 1955, there were only twenty-seven players in this league who had chosen to sign such a contract); four years in AAA leagues; and two years in D leagues (*Baseball Blue Book*, 1955, pp. 521–22).

[27] In November, 1953, 3,184 players were eligible to be drafted, of a total of about 6,900 players reserved by minor-league teams (*Sporting News*, November 23, 1955, p. 5).

[28] If a major-league team drafts a Pacific Coast League player, it must pay the team losing the player $15,000; if a major-league team drafts a class E player, it must pay the team that loses him $1,500; etc. (*Baseball Blue Book, 1955*, p. 521).

[29] *Ibid.*, pp. 768–69.

[30] Usually some days are set aside in November of each year for drafting; as soon as drafting by the major leagues is done, the minor leagues begin their own draft, in which teams in each league classification draft from teams in lower classifications.

market. As a result, few players are actually drafted.[31]

The *waiver*[32] rule limits the freedom of higher-classification teams to dispose of their players to lower-classification teams. A major-league team may freely sell a player's contract to another major-league team of its own league. However, it may not sell the contract to a team of the other major league or to a minor-league team without first asking the other teams of its own league in the first case, and the other teams of both major leagues in the second, to "waive" the player. If one or more of these teams refuses to waive, they say, in effect, that they are prepared to take over the player's contract at a waiver price specified in the rules (currently $10,000).[33]

A major-league player may not have his salary reduced during the season for which he is contracted and may not have it reduced for the following season, if he should stay in the major leagues, to less than 75 per cent of its current season level. A team that claims a player for whom waivers have been requested, therefore, says that the exclusive right to the use and disposition of the player's services is worth $10,000, given the salary costs which his contract attaches to him.

A team that has asked other major-league teams for waivers on a player so that it may assign his contract to a minor-league team may, if it wishes, withdraw its request for waivers if any of the major-league teams express an interest in having the player by filing a claim for him. Negotiations then often ensue, in which the team that owns the player tries to get from the team that wants him a price higher than the waiver price. If the negotiations are successfully consummated, the player's contract is assigned outright between the major-league teams; he does not

---

[31] In November, 1954, of the several thousand eligibles, thirteen players were drafted by major-league teams and forty-four by minor-league teams. Of the thirteen, only seven spent the full following season in the major leagues, none with distinction. The rule that only one player may be drafted in each year from the high-classification minor-league teams has permitted the major-league teams with farm systems to protect their reservoir of players by moving draft eligibles among their teams. For example, in November, 1955, the Montreal Royals, an AAA team which is the property of the Brooklyn Dodgers, had a roster of thirty-three players, of whom thirty-two were draft-eligible. By moving its promising draft-eligible players from its other farm teams to Montreal just before the draft dates, Brooklyn was assured that it would lose only one of them. The others, who were being protected so that Brooklyn would have a pool of talent from which to get replacements for its players in the future, were reshuffled among the Brooklyn farm teams when the period for drafting had expired. This process is repeated each year.

[32] *Baseball Blue Book, 1955,* pp. 529 ff., 749 ff.

[33] A major-league team may "optionally assign" a player whose contract it holds to a minor-league team within three years of the time it has contracted him without asking waivers. An optional assignment is one which gives the assignor team the right to recall the optioned player into its own service. It differs from an "outright" assignment, which transfers, for a consideration, the right to use or dispose of the player's services. The optional assignment is an exception to the waiver rule.

There is also a waiver rule affecting the assignment of minor-league players between minor-league teams of different classifications.

transfer on waivers. The rationale of the waiver rule is that it seeks to keep a player in the highest league classification for which his services are acceptable, if he is worth the waiver price, and despite the fact that he is worth more than this to a lower-classification team.[34] Only the bare bones of the market rules of the industry have been described in this paper. Their full texts and the exceptions which the rules permit can be found in the constitutional documents themselves. For our purposes the skeletal description given here suffices.

Very little information is available on player salaries. All contracts are registered with the relevant executive offices of major- and minor-league baseball, but salary information is not made public. The reports of player salaries which appear in the public press are said not to be reliable. Some salary data were divulged, however, by the congressional committee hearings of 1951.

The rules impose a minimum salary in the major leagues of $6,000 per year.[35] No other league has a minimum-salary rule. Neither does

any league have a maximum individual player salary rule. All leagues except the two major leagues and the only Open Classification league—the Pacific Coast League—have *team* maximum salary limits.[36]

On July 1, 1950, the range of major-league salaries was from $5,000[37] to $90,000 per year. The mean was $13,288, and the median $11,000.[38] In the minor leagues salaries were very much lower. Average salaries per player-month and monthly salary ranges in that year were reported to be as shown in Table 1.

TABLE 1
Average Salaries per Player-Month and Monthly Salary Ranges

League Classification	Mean	Median	Range
AAA	$876	$850	$200–$4,000
AA	639	600	300– 4,200
A	391	350	100– 1,555
D	192	165	80– 1,000

SOURCE: *Celler Hearings*, p. 965.

The large variation in players' salaries can be expected to attract many players who are hopeful that they will finally fall in the upper levels of the salary distribution. This will cause the average salary of baseball players to be below the level at which it would lie if the dispersion of salaries were smaller.

---

[34] That this is a "fact" may be demonstrated as follows: any major-league team can purchase a player of whom another major-league team wishes to dispose by offering a higher price for his contract than any minor-league bidder and by offering a price which is high enough so that it pays the team owning the player's contract to sell him to the bidding team rather than to employ him on one of its farm teams. The major-league team could do this if there were no waiver rule. If the waiver rule gives it a claim upon a player superior to that of a minor-league team, it is because the former can claim the player at a lower price than the latter is willing to pay for him.

[35] *Baseball Blue Book, 1955*, p. 543.

[36] For example, $7,000 per month per team in A1 leagues; $750 per month per team in E leagues. Each AAA and AA league may set its own team maximum; they were, for example, in 1951, American Asssociation (AAA), $13,800 per team-month; International League (AAA), 14,000 per team-month (*Celler Hearings*, p. 189; *Baseball Blue Book, 1955*, p. 739).

[37] $5,000 was the minimum established by the rules for major-league players at that time.

[38] *Celler Hearings*, p. 965.

Baseball-playing skills, at some level of proficiency, are, of course, widely distributed among the young male population of the United States and some other countries of the Western Hemisphere, and the supply of baseball-playing labor must be very elastic to price. In the lower minor leagues players make themselves available at prices which seem to be less than they could earn in some other employment. A congressional committee heard testimony from one former minor-league player that he accepted his first contract with a class D team in 1941 for a salary of $60 a month and that this was the common beginning wage in that classification at the time.[39] The worth of these earnings must surely have been reduced by some of the real costs which baseball players incurred. The same witness, for example, told the committee:

We used to finish a game in the evening, get on our bus, known as Stucker's Steamer. . . . The man who owned the club was named Rex Stucker. And this was an old, beat-up Ford, a bus, in which we had bunks in the back of the bus, and we used to pile all our suitcases, baseball bats and other things in this bus and then leave Sioux City about midnight and travel to Cheyenne, Wyoming. It is about 600 miles away. We were to get there at 4:30 the following afternoon and play a game in Cheyenne, Wyoming, that night. . . . That is a common practice in all minor leagues. . . . That is the common practice to save hotel bills.[40]

There are other disadvantages of life in the minor leagues. A player

under contract may have his salary reduced in midseason if he is assigned outright to another team of a lower classification, and he may have his contract terminated without notice.[41] Earnings in the lower minor leagues are so low that, at the end of each season, it is a common practice for class D teams to have a "players' night" to raise money that can be given to the players to permit them to pay the expenses of their transportation to their homes.

If players are willing to sell their services for such a wage and under such circumstances, it is perhaps because they derive very large psychic income from playing the game and because, on the average, the players in the lower leagues overestimate the probability that they will excel in play and be chosen to receive a higher salary with a team of a higher-classification league.

Experience diminishes uncertainty and increases knowledge, however, and players recalculate the probabilities which they assign to the occurrence of events. As they find that they have miscalculated, they withdraw from the market. The president of the association of minor leagues testified:

The turnover in B, C, and D (leagues) is terrific. . . . Boys may be in there a week or maybe 30 days. The turnover in the lower classifications is awfully heavy. . . . I suppose that a good many class D clubs have a turnover maybe five or six times during the season of almost their complete roster.[42]

---

[39] *Ibid.*, p. 349.
[40] *Ibid.*

[41] The president of the association of minor leagues told the Celler Committee of the no-notice rule: "That inspires the player to hustle a little all the time" (*ibid.*, p. 205).
[42] *Ibid.*, pp. 206, 213.

Especially in the major leagues players have opportunities for earning supplementary income which would not be available to them if they were not baseball players. They may be paid for speaking engagements or for product indorsements; between seasons, if they are employed as salesmen, say, of insurance or automobiles, they will be more successful because they are players; if they invest in retail or service establishments, they are more likely to prosper; if they play well, they may receive gifts from grateful fans; when they retire from baseball, they may teach at baseball schools; if they are engaged in business ventures, they will be rewarded in proportion to the favor in which they were held by the fans during their baseball careers.

The reserve rule, which binds a player to the team that contracts him, gives a prima facie appearance of monopsony to the market. Once having signed a first contract, a player is confronted by a single buyer who may unilaterally specify the price to be paid for his services. Each team and the players under contract to it appear in a labor market specific to them.[43] This market is distinct from those of other teams. No movement among markets, either of buyers or sellers, is permitted. In each market the team operates as buyer; the players, as sellers. While there is no competition on the buying side, there is intense competition on the sellers' side.

In such a market rational maxi-

mizing teams[44] might be expected to behave like discriminating monopsonists. Each player will have his supply price; if he is offered less than this, he will prefer to work at some other occupation. The supply price will vary among individuals. For each of them it ought to be related to how much he can earn in the next best employment outside of baseball, with the appropriate adjustments made for the plaudits of the crowd, for the supplementary income opportunities baseball provides, for the convenience of seasonal employment and the inconvenience of constant

---

[43] In the case of farm systems, the system defines the limits of the market; all the teams in the system coalesce into a single buyer for market purposes.

[44] The question may be asked whether it is sensible to assume that baseball-team owners are rational maximizers of money quantities. Representatives of organized baseball often say that the owners are interested more in providing opportunities for wholesome sport than they are in turning a profit. It was said in 1951 that ten of the sixteen major-league primary owners had their main business interests outside of baseball, and the Celler Committee heard testimony that, as of July, 1951, of 2,287 officers and directors of minor-league teams, only 291 made their living primarily from baseball. If baseball entrepreneurs get large psychic income from their association with the game, they will be willing to pay a price for engaging in the baseball business. This does not mean necessarily that they will be prepared to take a loss on their baseball operations but only that they are prepared to take a smaller return from baseball investment than their capital would earn in some other use. Still, one major-league property is reported to have sold in recent years for three and a half million dollars and another is said to be up for sale, at this writing, for four million dollars. The most expensive major-league property has been estimated to be worth fifteen million dollars and the average six million dollars. It seems unlikely that people will subject capital of this magnitude to large risk of loss for the pure joy of association with the game.

travel, and so on. A maximizing team would be expected to pay different salaries to different players, even though they are of the same quality, but only just about the salaries that are necessary to prevent them from withdrawing their services.

Actually, however, teams seem to pay, in the major leagues, much more than this. Here a paradox emerges. If baseball players have, on the average, no skills other than those necessary to play baseball proficiently, then their next best wage would be relatively low. Why are they paid so much more?

To begin with, it is undoubtedly correct that the player will not be paid more than he is worth to the team, his worth being determined by that part of the team's revenue which is attributable to his capacity to attract patrons to the ball park, net of the price paid for his contract to another team or the cost of his development. Nor will he receive less than his reservation price. The salary he receives, therefore, must fall somewhere between these limits; the question is: Why does it not fall at the bottom of the range?

The answer must be that the player is not without his defenses, even if he is in a monopsonistic market. He may withhold his services, and, in fact, each year there are a few holdouts who refuse to sign contracts providing for salaries that are unacceptable to them. In the end they usually sign, either because they become convinced, after a time, that the team will not offer more or because the team raises its offer. But sometimes players hold out for the full season. These may simply be cases of irrational behavior on the part of the player; though he is able

to earn only $5,000 in another employment, he may sometimes refuse to accept $15,000 for playing baseball if he believes he is worth $20,000. But, if, in truth, he is worth $20,000, then it pays the team to offer $16,000. Thus the process by which the salary is fixed assumes the characteristics of bargaining, and the level at which it falls is a function of the shrewdness and guile of the parties in devising their bargaining strategies. Moreover, the teams cannot push the salary "too low" even for those who do sign, because it does not pay to have discontented players. Player performance is determined in part by natural abilities like sharpness of eye, perception of space, and muscular co-ordination but also in part by the effort the player exerts. A player who is unhappy about his salary will perhaps not play as well as one who is not.

The solution to the problem of individual salary levels is not, however, completely indeterminate within the limits of the range which has been specified, as it would be in a classic duopoly case. This is so because, while each player has a monopoly of his own services, he is not truly unique, and there are more or less good substitutes for him. His salary is therefore partially determined by the difference between the value productivities and costs of other players by whom he may be replaced.

A rational team will seek to maximize the rent it derives from each player. It will be indifferent between two shortstops, one of whom is worth $30,000 and costs $20,000, and the other of whom is worth $20,000 and costs $10,000. It will prefer the first if it can have him for $19,000;

but it will prefer the second if it must pay the first $21,000 to induce him to play. It will be prepared to pay a Babe Ruth a fabulous salary, simply because there are no very good substitutes for him, and he is worth so much more to the team than any other player. But if a Ruth insisted upon receiving his full worth, it would pay to employ in his stead some other person of less skill on whom some positive rent would be earned. The team would keep a Ruth even if he insisted upon receiving his full value only if all other players also insisted upon receiving theirs and if rents were therefore zero for all of them. Since it is incredible that all players should, in fact, exact their full worth, it follows from this analysis that at least some players are exploited.[45]

It has been suggested,[46] however, that, while major-league players, and especially the star players of the major leagues, may be exploited, it does not follow that all players taken together are. The process by which players are brought to the major leagues can be likened to that by which paying oil wells are brought in or patentable inventions discovered. In all these cases there is heavy investment in the discovery of knowl-

edge. When it is discovered, the returns on it are high, but these returns must compensate for the losses incurred on the attempts which failed. In this schematic conception minor-league players who do not qualify for major-league play are like dry wells and research which does not yield a patent. They are paid more than they are worth because they may turn out to be of major-league caliber. To their cost must be added the cost of scouts and try-out camps and other costs of finding players and assessing their capacities. The monopsony gains in the major leagues are merely compensation for investment losses in scouting and in the operation of farm teams, and returns to investment in baseball, like returns to investment in oil and in research, should be no higher than returns to capital used in other ventures. If they were higher, capital would flow from other uses to investment in baseball.

This suggestion has a great deal of analytical merit. Its power is reduced somewhat, however, by the restraints on freedom of entry in the baseball industry. If the returns on oil investments or on investment in research are very much larger than returns on other investment, new entrants are free to search for oil and knowledge. But the rule of "territorial rights," which gives monopoly rights to desirable locations in the product market to teams currently in organized baseball, and the system of private sanctions for the enforcement of the rule put serious disabilities upon prospective new entrants into the baseball industry. If, therefore, there are monopoly gains arising from the characteristics of the baseball labor market, they are reinforced by re-

---

[45] Representatives of organized baseball testified before the Celler Committee that players receive their full value. "If the players are dissatisfied, they are traded to other teams which will pay them more." This belief is, of course, not consistent with the other, also held by baseball representatives, that the reserve rule has the effect of balancing team strength by permitting poorer clubs, which pay less than the richer clubs, to retain players to whom the latter are prepared to pay a higher wage.

[46] I am indebted for the immediately following idea to Professor Gary S. Becker.

straints on competition in the product market.

Is it clear that the reserve rule is necessary to achieve more or less equality of play among teams? Assume that teams are distributed among locations, as they are in fact, so that the revenues of some are very much larger than those of others. Assume a free players' labor market, in which players may accept the offer of the highest bidder and teams may make offers without restraint.

At first sight, it may appear that the high-revenue teams will contract all the stars, leaving the others only the dregs of the supply; that the distribution of players among teams will become very unequal; that contests will become less uncertain; and that consumer interest will flag and attendance fall off. On closer examination, however, it can be seen that this process will be checked by the law of diminishing returns, operating concurrently with each team's strategic avoidance of diseconomies of scale.

Professional team competitions are different from other kinds of business ventures. If a seller of shoes is able to capture the market and to cause other sellers of shoes to suffer losses and withdraw, the surviving competitor is a clear gainer. But in baseball no team can be successful unless its competitors also survive and prosper sufficiently so that the differences in the quality of play among teams are not "too great."

If the size of a baseball team is thought of as the number of players under contract to it, each player being weighted by some index of his quality, then diseconomies of scale set in at some point when a team too far outstrips its competitors, and they

become larger in proportion to the size of the differences.

Two teams opposed to each other in play are like two firms producing a single product. The product is the game, weighted by the revenues derived from its play. With game admission prices given, the product is the game, weighted by the number of paying customers who attend. When 30,000 attend, the output is twice as large as when 15,000 attend. In one sense, the teams compete; in another, they combine in a single firm in which the success of each branch requires that it be not "too much" more efficient than the other. If it is, output falls.

A baseball team, like any other firm, produces its product by combining factors of production. Consider the two teams engaged in a contest to be collapsed into a single firm, producing as output games, weighted by the revenue derived from admission fees. Let the players *of one team* be one factor and all others (management, transportation, ball parks, *and the players of the other team*), another. The quantity of the factor —players—is measured by making the appropriate adjustment for differential qualities among players, so that a man who hits safely in 35 per cent of his times at bat counts as more than one who hits safely only 20 per cent of the time. Given the quantity of the other factors, the total product curve of the factor— players of one team—will have the conventional shape; it will slope upward as the "quantity" of this factor is increased, reach a peak, and then fall. It will not pay to increase this factor without limit. Beyond some point—say, when a team already has three .350 hitters—it will not pay to employ another .350 hitter. If a team goes on increasing the quantity of the factor, players, by hiring additional stars, it will find that the total output—that is, admission receipts— of the combined firms (and, therefore, of its own) will rise at a less rapid rate and finally will fall absolutely. At some point, therefore, a first star player is worth more to poor Team B than, say, a third star to rich Team A. At this point, B is in a position to bid players away from A in the market. A's behavior is not a function of its bank balance. It does what it calculates it is worthwhile to do; and the time comes when, in pursuing the strategy of its *own* gains, it is worthwhile, whatever the size of its cash balance, to forego the services of an expert player and see him employed by another team.

The wealthy teams will usually prefer winning to losing.[47] If they do, they will prefer winning by close margins to winning by wide ones. If their market behavior is consistent with this objective—that is, if they behave like rational maximizers— playing talent will be more or less equally distributed among teams.

It does not require collusion to bring about this result. It is not senseless to expect it to be produced by a free labor market in which each team is separately engaged in gainful behavior. The position of organized baseball that a free market, given the unequal distribution of revenue, will result in the engrossment of the most competent players by the wealthy teams is open to some question. It seems, indeed, to be true that a market in which freedom is limited by a reserve rule such as that which now governs the baseball labor market distributes players among teams about as a free market would.

Players under contract to a team may be used by that team itself, or they may be sold to another team. Each team determines whether to use a player's services itself or to sell him, according to the relative returns on him in the two uses. If the return will be higher from sale, he will be sold, and vice versa. Now, if he can be sold to another team for a price higher than his worth to his present team, it is because he is worth more to the team that buys him than to the team that sells him. It follows that players will be distributed among teams so that they are put to their most "productive" use; each will play for the team that is able to get the highest return from his services.[48] But this is exactly the result which

---

[47] It should not be thought that wealthy teams will invariably want to assemble winning combination of players, either in a free market or in a market governed by the reserve rule. A team will seek to maximize the difference between its revenue and its costs. If this quantity is maximized, for any given club, by assembling a team of players who are of lower quality than those of another club in its league, it will pay the former to run behind.

[48] The sale of a player's contract occurs in a market in which the seller is a monopolist and the buyer an oligopsonist. The selling price will be not less than the player's capitalized value to the team that owns his contract (the difference between his average yearly product to it and his average yearly salary, multiplied by the estimated number of remaining years of his playing life and appropriately discounted). It will not be more than his capitalized value to the team for which his product would be higher than for any other team. The price will fall between these limits, at a point determined by bargaining strategies and the player's capitalized value to other would-be buyers.

would be yielded by a free market. The difference is only that in a market subject to the reserve rule part of the price for the player's services is paid to the team that sells his contract, and part of his value is kept by the team that holds his contract; in the free market the player gets his full value.

If players were not indentured to teams but were free to accept the offers of the highest bidders, would the amount of investment in the training of players and the quality of play fall? In such a market, players will bear a larger proportion of the cost of training, and the wages they receive will have to compensate for this cost. If it pays now, in a monopsonistic market, to invest in training and development, it will also pay to do so in a free market. There will be cases in which players will reject a higher salary in the major leagues in order to remain longer in the minors and acquire skills that will assure even larger earnings in the future, just as medical students, receiving a negative income, now reject factory work at some positive wage.

Are there other alternatives to the reserve rule? Are there some other rules which would tend to produce a more or less equal distribution of playing talent among teams and which would not be defective on some other criterion?

Let there be a free players' market and let the total revenues of all teams in the major leagues be pooled and shared equally by all teams, perhaps after adjusting for differences in operating costs associated with differences in the size of franchise cities. All teams will then be equal in capacity to bid for talent. There will be no incentive, however, for any

single team to win or to assemble a winning combination. Win or lose, play badly or well, it will receive its equal slice of pie. It will pay for all teams, taken together, to play well enough, on the average, so that revenue will not fall off faster than costs. But any individual team, by employing only men whose supply prices are low, whatever their quality, can then take advantage of the gains yielded by the expenditures of the others. No team will be willing to spend if it cannot be assured that others will also do so. Each team will therefore tend to buy the cheapest playing services in the market. A rule of equal sharing of revenue leads to the equal distribution of mediocre players among teams and to consumer preference for recreational substitutes.

As another possibility, let teams bid for players and players accept offers, subject only to the constraint that a ceiling is imposed on the salaries that may be paid to individual players. The allocational effects of this rule would appear to depend upon the level of the ceiling. If the maximum salary permitted by the rule is higher than the highest wage paid to any player in a free market, the effect can be nothing but zero. It may appear that if the ceiling is sufficiently lower than this, so that more than one team is prepared to pay the specified maximum price to the highest-salaried player, the rule will begin to have some positive effects, and that, the lower the maximum salary, the larger will be the effects. On closer view, this is seen to be not true. Suppose the maximum is placed at some level, x. Players who would be worth more than x in a free market will then distribute themselves among teams on other criteria than the yearly salary, and teams will bid for players by offering other quantities than price; for example, perquisites or the security of long-term contracts.[49] Teams which, in the absence of a maximum salary rule, would have outbid other would-be buyers of a player's services with cash will outbid them with non-money offers, and the distribution of players among teams will be left unaffected. If complementary roles are devised and successfully enforced (such as rules forbidding the payment of perquisites, contracts for longer than one year, secret understandings, and employment of players' relatives), so that the cash price is the whole price received by the player, those who receive the maxi-

mum will tend to accept, among competing bids, those from the teams which paid the highest average salary, for they will then be combined with higher-priced (and better) players, and the probability that they will share in World Series bonus earnings will be higher.[50] Even if players worth the maximum wage or more are distributed randomly (thus, in the long run, equally) among teams, they will be exploited; the market will not be free for them.

As still another possibility, let there be a free players' labor market and let franchises be distributed so that the size of the product market is equal for all teams. Suppose, for example, that all teams are located in markets whose population is two million. Thus, in the New York area there will be six teams rather than three; in the Chicago area, three rather than two; and so on. If attendance is a unique function of the size of the market, such a distribution of teams may equalize revenues among teams. But, as has already been shown,[51] attendance is a function of several variables. If psychic income is not zero for all team owners, or if it is larger for some than others, and if consumer income levels, the convenience of reaching the ball park, the taste for recreation relative to other objects of expenditure, or the taste for baseball (within recreational expenditures) is not equal among cities, differences in revenues will occur. When they do, a self-generating process begins to

---

[49] An interesting subsidiary question is: What effect will long-term contracts, rather than one-year contracts, have on player salaries if the market is free and the contracts are enforceable? Players will accept a lower annual salary if they have the security of a long contract, but they will demand a higher annual salary because it will then be impossible for them to accept a higher offer from another team during the life of the contract. Assuming that players estimate their future prospects correctly, those who expect to do well will take only a one-year contract. Teams will be prepared to pay a higher annual salary because they have the security of having a player's services for a long period; but they will pay a lower annual salary because they run the risk that the quality of his play will decline during the life of the contract. If they estimate a player's future correctly, they will sign a long-term contract with those who will do well in the future and a one-year contract with those who will not. On the assumption of correct estimation of the future on both sides of the market, the outcome seems to be that there will be no difference in the annual salary whatever the length of the contract.

[50] Part of the revenues of each annual World Series is distributed to players of the teams which are in the upper half of the major leagues' rank standings at the season's end.

[51] Above, pp. 62–63.

operate to increase the magnitude of the differences. If the revenues of Team A are larger than those of Team B for any of the foregoing reasons, despite the equality of market size, Team A is in a position to contract the better players by offering a higher price;[52] Team A then wins more games than B, and its relative attendance and revenues increase. Now it is in a still better position to outbid B for players. Equal division of markets may, however, tend to result in a somewhat more equal distribution of players among teams than unequal division of markets.

Finally, let teams bid for players and let players accept offers, subject to the constraints that a low ceiling is imposed on the number of players that may be under contract to any team and that the control of players in the minor leagues is prohibited. Suppose no team is permitted to contract, directly or indirectly, more than, say, fifteen players.[53] The

smaller the number of players each team is permitted to contract, the more equally will talent be distributed among teams. But it must be kept in mind that player limits are inhibitions on freedom to contract and, therefore, inconsistent with market freedom. Like other rules which have been discussed, they lead to exploitation by preventing some players from contracting with a team prepared to pay a higher price for their services; they receive less than they would be worth in a free market uninhibited by rules.

Markets in which the freedom to buy and sell is constrained by the reserve rule or by the suggested alternatives to it do not promise better results than do markets constructed on the postulate of freedom. It appears that free markets would give as good aggregate results as any other kind of market for industries, like the baseball industry, in which all firms must be nearly equal if each is to prosper. On welfare criteria, of course, the free market is superior to the others, for in such a market each worker receives the full value of his services, and exploitation does not occur.

---

[52] It may, of course, not do so (see p. 73, n. 47).

[53] The reader is reminded that major-league teams are now permitted by the rules to have an active roster of twenty-five players during the playing season (and, for one year from the date of their discharge from military service, up to five more who have returned from the service); that they may have an additional fifteen players under contract who are out on option to play

wih minor-league teams, subject to recall; and that they may hold several hundred players indirectly by contracting them to minor-league teams which they own or with which they have working agreements.

THE ECONOMICS OF RECREATION: PROGRESS AND PROBLEMS

Recreation resource decisions not subject to evaluation solely by market test. Recreation has social benefits as well as private.

By OMER L. CAREY*

The problem of evaluating the economic benefits of recreation has been receiving increased attention in recent years but progress has been slow. Why is the economic evaluation of recreation benefits a problem and what are the roadblocks to the solution of this problem?

The evaluation of the benefits derived from recreation is a problem to the extent that recreational facilities are provided through the public budget and not subject to evaluation by a market test. The market place services several sectors of the demand for recreation and economists have largely ignored these private sectors of recreation in their research.

Private firms in recreation are not concerned with the problem of evaluating recreation benefits to the individual except as it is reflected in that individual's "willingness to pay" for the service provided. The price mechanism, moreover, provides the measure for expected future returns utilized by the firm in its capital budgeting decision. Any benefits not

captured by the price mechanism are not included in the calculation. Likewise, any costs incurred by society as a whole, rather than the firm, are not included in the investment decision.

In the public sector, however, recreation is provided free or at nominal cost. Under these conditions, the price mechanism does not provide a meaningful guide to consumer preference or consumer willingness to pay. Furthermore, in the federal sector, social benefits and social costs are relevant to the investment decision due to the span of decision-making. For public decision groups that are less than nationwide, i.e., a state or local unit, social costs and benefits realized outside the unit need not be considered.

The effort to evaluate the benefits of recreation has not gone unopposed. Some writers have stated flatly that it cannot be done because the benefits of recreation are intangible and do not lend themselves to economic evaluation.[1] This argument has been examined and answered in

* The author wishes to thank Idaho State University for the research grant for typing expenses of the original drafts of this paper and Arthur Hillabold and Cornelius Hofman for helpful criticism and suggestions on an earlier draft of this paper. However, the opinions and errors are solely the responsibility of the author.

[1] Roy A. Prewitt, *The Economics of Public Recreation—An Economic Study of the Monetary Evaluation of Recreation in the National Parks* (U.S. Department of the Interior, National Park Service, 1949), p. 27; C. Frank Brockman, *Recreational Use of Wild Lands* (New York: McGraw-Hill, 1959), p. 185.

detail by others;[2] therefore, it will not be answered here except to note that this is the problem facing all consumers—the problem of comparing an item with a monetary cost and a nonmonetary benefit. Intangibles (for example, symphony music) are sold in the market place. The presence of intangibles is not the primary obstacle to the evaluation of recreation benefits; rather, it is the fact that recreation is institutionally a public good (and frequently a free good) and thus not subject to market evaluation.

Much of the current interest in evaluating recreation benefits is centered on the federal sector. Multiple-purpose river-basin proponents desire an allocation of project costs to recreation, so that the benefits derived by these users can be recognized. Costs allocated to recreation are non-reimbursable from power revenues and benefits attributed to recreation would improve the benefit-cost ratio of the project.

A series of controversies involving the National Park Service has emphasized the need for evaluating the benefits of recreation. The National Park Service does not accept the multiple-use philosophy of the U.S. Forest Service. The Park Service views the purpose of the national parks and monuments as education and each unit as an "outdoor museum." Any use of resources within the system not conforming to this

purpose is opposed—a policy which has produced interagency conflicts as well as conflicts with private interests. Dams have been proposed by federal agencies—supported by elaborate benefit-cost analysis—for Yellowstone National Park, Big Bend National Park, Glacier National Park, and various national monuments. The Park Service has opposed these dams as nonconforming uses. These conflicts were settled in the political sphere; however, sound economic analysis might have reduced the heat and increased the light.

Recreation activities are now being proposed by various federal agencies as a cure for non-urban depressed areas. These proposals are based on the assumption that, if the area is not suited for other economic activities, it will at least be suitable for recreation.

The techniques utilized to date have largely been the result of attempts to find answers for the resource decisions mentioned above. For this reason, the techniques are specific and problem oriented rather than general approaches to an economic theory of recreation. This problem-oriented approach to evaluating the economic benefits of recreation has produced diverse definitions of recreation "benefits," creating problems of comparison with alternative values of resource use.

The following section examines the various techniques developed for evaluating recreation benefits from public facilities. Most of the progress reported in this section has been achieved in the last 10 years. While this progress may be commendable, there are many unsolved problems.

---

[2] For example, Robert K. Davis, "The Value of Outdoor Recreation: An Economic Study of the Maine Woods" (unpublished doctoral dissertation, Harvard University, Cambridge, 1963), p. 15.

TECHNIQUES OF EVALUATING RECREATION BENEFITS

Recreation facilities are provided free or at nominal cost by government at all levels; and therein lies the reason for the difficulty in evaluating recreation benefits. Recreation, at the point of supply, is frequently a free good; hence, at the margin, its monetary value is zero. Many approaches have been devised by economists, however, in an effort to approximate a market solution.

Consumer Surplus as a Measure of the Recreation Benefit

One of the earlier attempts at evaluating recreation benefits involved an effort to determine the "value in exchange." Hotelling, in a study for the Park Service, suggested a method of evaluating consumer surplus in recreation.[3] From Hotelling's presentation, Andrew H. Trice and Samuel E. Wood developed a method for the Feather River Project.[4] The Trice-Wood model is regarded in this paper as representative of the "consumer-surplus" approach in evaluating recreation benefits.

The first step in the Trice-Wood method was to survey park visitors and to determine their points of origin. A "cost-of-travel" index was then computed, based upon distance traveled, days on the trip, days in the recreation area, and the number of persons sharing expenses. An array was made of "per-visitor-day" costs of travel, and the costs of the

more distant visitors were used to establish the "market value" of a day of recreation. This market value was assumed to be the value of the benefit received by each visitor. The difference between the actual travel costs incurred by the visitor and this derived benefit was regarded as consumer surplus. The authors contend that the aggregate consumer surplus was an approximation of the total value of the resource to consumers.

There are several criticisms of this method of evaluation:

1. It does not measure the value of recreation; rather it is a value derived from the value of the services and goods received. Advocates of this approach of using the value of goods and services as a proxy for the value of the recreation benefit contend that the expenditures for goods and services reflect consumer willingness to pay for the recreational experience.

The simplification of assuming that the "on-site" experience is *the* recreation benefit involved in the trip poses a major problem. The food consumed may not be a "means to an end" but rather an "end" in itself. The tourist may have saved vacation money to dine in nice restaurants; he orders steak not merely to live but because he enjoys it. His food expenditures are not measuring the value of a visit to a recreation site; rather, they are measuring his subjective valuation of the eating experience. Marion Clawson recognizes this problem in his current writings.[5]

[3] Prewitt, *op. cit.*

[4] Andrew H. Trice and Samuel E. Wood, "Measurement of Recreation Benefits," *Land Economics*, August 1958, 195–207.

[5] Marion Clawson, "Private and Public Provision of Outdoor Recreation Opportunity," *Economic Studies of Outdoor Recreation*, ORRRC Study Report 24 (Washington, D.C., 1962), 75–76.

Using expenditure data to derive a value for the recreation benefit includes expenditures that would have been incurred even if the visitor had stayed home. If expenditure data were otherwise acceptable for deriving the value of the recreation benefit, the data could be adjusted to correct this deficiency; however, Trice and Wood make no attempt to do this.

2. The consumer-surplus approach has other shortcomings in addition to its use of expenditure data. It charges the entire cost of the trip to the recreational opportunity, even though there might have been visits to other recreation areas on the same trip. While this assumption may be satisfactory for some recreational attractions, its validity in studies of most recreation sites or vacation trips is doubtful.

3. Lawrence Hines criticizes the consumer-surplus approach on more theoretical grounds.[6] Hines points out that this method requires, at the least, the qualification that the marginal utility of money be constant, and that the individual preference scales be identical. Few would contend that these qualifications are even approached in the situations posited by Trice and Wood.

These criticisms appear to make the consumer-surplus approach of questionable value. The continued use of this approach by the California Department of Water Resources probably is due more to the lack of a clearly superior method of valuation than the merits of the present

method. The problem is: Does the consumer-surplus method lead to better allocation decisions than the use of pure judgment?

Willingness to Pay as a Measure of the Recreation Benefit

Currently the most popular approaches to the problem of determining recreation benefits involve attempts to determine the users' willingness to pay for the use of recreational facilities. These two methods are Clawson demand curves and consumer surveys.

CLAWSON DEMAND CURVES. Marion Clawson of Resources for the Future recommends the construction of demand curves for recreation rather than attempting to derive a value for the recreation benefit.[7] He would do this by estimating the demand curve for the *total recreational experience,* and then by estimating the demand curves for the recreational opportunity itself from the first curve. The resulting demand curve could be used by government to experiment with fees either as a rationing device or as an income device, and to provide an insight into the value of the facility if fees were imposed.

Clawson contends that a visit to an outdoor recreation area is more than just the experience at the recreation site. He states that the recreational experience consists of five phases, all of which affect the ultimate evaluation of the benefits, and identifies these as: (1) the planning

[6] Lawrence C. Hines, "Measurement of Recreation Benefits: A Reply," *Land Economics,* November 1958, p. 367.

[7] Clawson, *Methods of Measuring the Demand for and Value of Outdoor Recreation,* RFF Reprint No. 10, Resources for the Future, Inc. (Washington, D.C., 1959).

or anticipation phase; (2) the travel to the recreation site; (3) the on-site experience; (4) the return home; and (5) the recollection of the experience.[8] For some recreational experiences, such as camping, the largest expenditures may occur during the planning or anticipation phase. If the user is on a vacation trip, the expenditures incurred on the trip to and from the site may involve far greater sums than those incurred at the site itself.

Point-of origin information is needed for constructing the curve for the total recreational experience. Points of origin are grouped into areas according to distance from the recreation site, and the number of visitors per 100,000 population in each area is computed. A total monetary cost per visit is estimated for each distance zone and then the information is plotted on a graph. Clawson contends that the resulting curve is an *approximation* to a demand curve for the total recreational experience.

The demand schedule for the total recreational experience is then used to estimate the curve for the recreation site itself. Two assumptions are required for this estimate. First, it is assumed that visitors view an increase in fees as no more serious than a proportional increase in the total cost of visiting the area; second, it is assumed that the experience of visitors from one zone provides an indication of what people in other zones would do, if costs in *money and time* were the same.

The demand curve for the recreation site itself is obtained by computing the attendance by zone per 100,000 population, for various levels of entrance fees. These fees would increase the average cost per visit; and, as the average cost per visit of one zone approaches that of another zone, it is assumed that the attendance per 100,000 population of the two zones would be similar. If we use the data of attendance by zone per 100,000 population for each level of entrance fees, the total visits to the recreation site are computed for each level of fees and then plotted on graph paper. It is Clawson's contention that the resulting curve *approximates* the true demand curve for the recreational opportunity itself. From cost information and data from the demand schedule, it is possible to compute the value of the resource, as a recreation site, by capitalizing the net profit resulting from the imposition of the most profitable fees.

Three practical difficulties of this method are immediately apparent:

1. It is assumed that the experience of visitors from one zone provides an indication of what people in other zones would do if costs in *money and time* were the same. The demand curve analysis deals only with the monetary costs—time is not considered. As distance from the recreation site increases, time costs may become a greater obstacle to visits than the money costs.

2. The demand curve analysis assumes that the recreational experience involves only one major recreation site. This assumption may be appropriate for visitors living near the site; but many visitors may travel great distances and may visit several sites. In addition, the principal purpose of the trip may have been for

[8] Clawson, "Private and Public Provision of Outdoor Recreation Opportunity," *op. cit.*

reasons not related to recreation; therefore, the visit to the site would have been only incidental to the trip.

3. The demand curve may vary considerably among visitors; not only because of differing preference scales, but also because of differing reasons for the visit. For example, Dinosaur National Monument is located in western Colorado and eastern Utah near U.S. Highway 40. The museum and quarry unit attracts many visitors, most of whom stay only a few hours. For many of these visitors, the visit to Dinosaur is only incidental to the main purpose of the trip; the relevant cost would be the cost of the detour from U.S. 40.

The canyonlands of Dinosaur attract a much smaller number of visitors than do the museum and quarry. As this is less accessible, these visitors invest greater time and money in the visit and, very probably, would have a significantly different demand curve than would the museum and quarry visitors. A still smaller group of visitors, numbering only a few thousand, visit Dinosaur to travel down either the Green or Yampa river canyons in boats. For these users, the visit is the primary purpose of the trip, and monetary costs are considerably higher than for the previous two groups; consequently, their demand curve would probably vary a great deal from either of the other two groups.

Most national parks and national forests have varied recreational uses and are used more intensively by some visitors than by others. An "average" demand curve for many recreation sites would appear to have little value.

Since Clawson's original formulation in 1959, his approach has received considerable attention.[9] In a recent paper, Jack L. Knetsch recognizes some of the criticisms and limitations of the original Clawson approach, and suggests areas for additional research and refinements in the technique.[10] Clawson's approach is probably the most popular current approach; however, the problems involved appear to limit its practical application to a narrow range of recreational problems.

CONSUMER SURVEYS TO DETERMINE WILLINGNESS TO PAY EOR RECREATIONAL OPPORTUNITIES. Probably the most recent study of this type was performed by Robert Davis.[11] Davis attempted to compute the value of recreation for three areas in the Maine woods by the use of a questionnaire and a bidding game to determine the willingness to pay of the users. He notes that there have been at least two other interview studies of willingness to pay although neither produced definitive results.[12]

[9] For an interesting recent application of the Clawson technique, see William C. Brown, Ajmer Singh, and Emery Castle, "An Economic Evaluation of the Oregon Salmon and Steelhead Sport Fishery" (mimeographed report to the Oregon State Game Commission, 1963).

[10] Jack L. Knetsch, "Outdoor Recreation Demands and Benefits," review draft, January 1963, Resources for the Future (Washington, D.C., 1963).

[11] Davis, op. cit.

[12] Ibid., pp. 25 ff. Audience Research, Inc. ("Outdoor Recreational Activities and Preferences of the Population Living in the Region of the Delaware River Basin" for the National Park Service, 1958), asked for a daily use fee. Bruce E. Stewart, "Recrea-

The procedure used by Davis to determine willingness to pay consisted of an interview which included five types of questions. These were: (1) details of the trip, including expenditures, times, budgets, activities, visits, and the like; (2) the respondent's outdoor recreation habits aside from the trip; (3) open-end questions dealing with reasons for choosing the area, the degree of satisfaction, areas that are substitutes, and a few others; (4) personal information including leisure time, type of residence, education, income, and occupation; and (5) preferences in outdoor recreation, including willingness to pay. The interview and bidding game were constructed so that they would minimize adverse reaction by the respondent.[13]

This method would be rather expensive in terms of time and money for most recreational decisions. On the other hand, it has certain advantages over Clawson's method for determining users' willingness to pay. If we use Davis' method the different classes of recreation users can be separated so that a willingness to pay can be determined for each group. Neither travel time nor the purpose of the trip would affect the validity of the results obtained by Davis' method. Further studies of this type would appear to be very beneficial, particularly if the results could be validated by controlled experiments with user fees.

Impact upon a Predetermined Area as a Measure of the Recreation Benefit

This approach does not attempt to value the recreation benefit itself; rather it attempts to determine the economic impact of the recreation site as a guide to the investment decision. At least two methods have been suggested for determining the economic impact.

GROSS VOLUME OF BUSINESS GENERATED BY REASON OF THE OUTDOOR RECREATIONAL OPPORTUNITY. This method has been very popular with the National Park Service and state and local chambers of commerce,[14] and it is frequently used by the U.S. Fish and Wildlife Service as one method of assessing the benefits from their projects.[15] This method has some serious shortcomings and is receiving little attention in current economic literature. Among its shortcomings are: (1) the expenditures may not really be new or increased expenditures, but merely transferred from one area to another; (2) much of the expenditures may occur outside the area in which the

---

tional Use of Private Land in a Portion of Eastern Maine" (unpublished Master's thesis, University of Maine, 1961), inquired about willingness to pay for improvements that respondents thought desirable.
[13] *Ibid.*, 34–35.

[14] To list only a few: "Economic Effects of Establishing National Parks" and "Economic Effects of the Blue Ridge Parkway" (unpublished papers by the National Park Service, Department of the Interior); Robert Wallace, *An Evaluation of Wildlife Resources in the State of Washington*, Washington State University, Bureau of Economic and Business Research (Pullman, 1956); Donald Greenway and Robert Lanzillotti, *The Washington Tourist Survey*, Washington State University, Bureau of Economic and Business Research (Pullman, 1950).
[15] *Water Project Planning Policy*, Hearings of the 88th Congress, Interior and Insular Affairs Committee, U.S. Congress and House of Representatives.

outdoor recreation site is located; and (3) "gross-volume" data between any two industries are not comparable, therefore, the gross-volume data for outdoor recreation cannot be meaningfully compared with the gross volume of business generated by alternative investments.

Gross-volume data were converted to personal income by Robert Edminster, University of Utah, in a study for the Park Service.[16] In this study gross-volume data were obtained and input-output analysis was then utilized to determine the relationship between gross tourist expenditures and personal income generated in the five county area studied. This "personal income generated" is a better measure of the economic impact upon an area than the gross-volume data and it may be satisfactory for some decisions. However, it certainly does not measure the benefits from recreation sites except under a very narrow definition of benefits, and it would not be appropriate for problems such as the Dinosaur National Monument controversy.

VALUE ADDED BY OUTDOOR RECREATION EXPENDITURES. This method is a refinement of the gross-expenditure method in that the data are adjusted for funds leaving the area, and the value added by the recreation expenditures is computed. The value-added approach was used in a recent study by the University of New Mexico to compare the value

added by alternative uses of the water resources of New Mexico.[17] This technique, as used in the New Mexico study, seems appropriate; however, it does not measure the value of the recreation benefit. It is a measure of the value of other services consumed in connection with the use of the recreational opportunity, and is thus inappropriate for many comparisons among alternative investments.

Cost of Alternative Facilities as a Measure of Benefit from the Public Facilities

Two different alternative-cost methods have been utilized; namely, the cost of comparable private alternatives and the cost of comparable public alternatives.

1. The National Park Service estimates a value for recreation days spent at Bureau of Reclamation reservoirs based upon a 1950 study of comparable private opportunities.[18] Using the 1950 study and incorporating changes in the consumer cost-of-living index, the Park Service computed a benefit of $1.60 per user day.

This practice had been criticized by Warren C. Robinson on both theoretical and practical grounds.[19] Two of the readily apparent objections to this method are: (1) national averages for the value of the user

[16] Robert Edminster, *An Economic Study of the Proposed Canyonlands National Park and Related Recreation Resources* (University of Utah, Bureau of Economic and Business Research, Salt Lake City, 1962).

[17] Nathaniel Wollman, *The Value of Water in Alternative Uses* (University of New Mexico, Albuquerque, 1963).

[18] Warren C. Robinson, "Economic Evaluation of Outdoor Recreation Benefits," *Economic Studies of Outdoor Recreation*, ORRRC Study Report 24 (Washington, D.C., 1962), p. 64.

[19] *Ibid.*

day would have little significance for any specific reservoir or recreational opportunity, and (2) the passage of time renders this price less meaningful even if it is adjusted for changes in the cost of living.

While this method has been criticized, it does enable the Park Service to place at least some value on the recreation benefits inherent in a multiple-purpose river-basin project, it is practical from an administrative point of view, and it is easily understood. The problem, then, becomes: Is a poor estimate of benefits better than no estimate of benefits? Which practice produces the least distortion of actual benefits?

2. Edward Ullman and Donald Volk computed the benefits of a proposed new reservoir by studying the attendance at alternative reservoirs, and then computing the savings for these users who would use the new reservoir if it were available.[20] This annual savings could then be capitalized to compute a value for the reservoir's recreation benefit. This method shows promise for recreation studies of proposed new sites.

Opportunity Cost of the Recreation Site

If an acceptable value of the recreation benefit is lacking, it would be helpful in the decision to know at least the value of benefits foregone.

William Atkinson, utilizing the "marginal method" developed by Henry J. Vaux,[21] computed the ratio of the value of "timber per man days of recreation use" for a number of forests and parks and arrayed these values in descending order. Atkinson defined the "marginal area" by the highest ratio found among parks and the lowest ratio in timberland. If a proposed area has a ratio of "timber values per man day of recreation use" higher than this marginal ratio it should be utilized for timber production. If, on the other hand, it has a ratio lower than the marginal ratio, it would be better used for recreational purposes.

The marginal method, as a decision tool, has several obvious weaknesses, and these are recognized by its proponents. (a) No provision can be made for historical and scientific values that may be present on the proposed site. (b) All user days are weighted equally, whether they represent a picnic or mountain climbing. Yet, the willingness to pay by the users may be considerably different. (c) The problem of forecasting future attendance, particularly for undeveloped areas, presents some difficulties. Other weaknesses could also be enumerated which limit its application; nevertheless, when a better measure of recreation benefits is lacking, a knowledge of the opportunity costs is relevant to the decision.[22]

[20] Edward L. Ullman and Donald J. Volk, "An Operational Model for Predicting Reservoir Attendance and Benefits: Implications of a Location Approach to Water Recreation" (preliminary), Washington University (St. Louis, April 1961).

[21] William Allen Atkinson, "A Method for the Recreational Evaluation of Forest Land" (unpublished Master's thesis, University of California, Berkeley, 1956).

[22] For an additional application of the opportunity cost concept to recreation, see Omer L. Carey, "The Application of the Economic Criteria for Government Investment in National Parks—The Dinosaur National Monument Controversy" (unpublished doctoral dissertation, Indiana University, Bloomington, 1962).

SUMMARY AND CONCLUSIONS

The Prewitt study in 1949 marked the first serious attempt to apply economic theory to an evaluation of recreation benefits. Interest by economists in regional planning, urban redevelopment, multiple-purpose river-basin planning, and agriculture and forestry spurred the development of the economics of recreation. Though progress has been rapid, the problems are impressive.

Unfortunately, the research to date has emphasized problem solving rather than a broad approach to the economics of recreation. Clawson and Knetsch have been moving in the direction of a broad approach but at the present time there is no agreement on definitions. For example, as shown in this paper, the meaning of the word "benefits" varies greatly, depending upon the author. Much needs to be done in expanding the horizons of research into the more general area of recreation; however, the research to date can provide meaningful information for certain types of decisions.

If the decision involves an already-established attraction, the Clawson approach appears to show promise and is currently the most popular. The interview method used by Davis, however, allows a better analysis of the demand for recreation at a given site than the Clawson approach. The different recreational uses can be distinguished and the users can be separated by desired characteristics. The interview method allows a separate demand schedule for each type of user to be computed rather than the "average" demand schedule resulting from Clawson's study. On the other hand, Davis' method has the same weakness of the Clawson approach —it cannot deal with a newly developed or planned recreation site.

The approach used by Ullman and Volk in their Missouri studies seems to be the most promising for undeveloped or planned recreation sites. It would appear that a need exists for an Ullman-Volk-type study of a planned recreation development followed by comparable studies of the same site after a suitable period of use.

For those areas interested in the economic impact of a proposed recreation development upon the area, the personal-income-generated approach used by Edminster should give satisfactory results. The gross-volume approach, favored by the National Park Service, chambers of commerce, and others, probably has no value other than impressively large totals. The Edminster approach, however, is not relevant for national decisions unless the aim is the economic development of the area in question.

The value-added approach used by Wollman in the New Mexico study is a useful tool in evaluating the alternative uses of a resource. Its great shortcoming is the fact that it can only recognize previous market transactions; nonmonetary benefits of a resource are ignored and consumer willingness to pay is not evaluated. However, a knowledge of the economic effects of various decisions regarding resource use would be helpful to the decision-makers. In this sense, the value-added approach is an opportunity-cost approach.

Existing techniques can yield information useful to most recreation resource decisions; however, they cannot provide the answer to these dilemmas. These approaches cannot incorporate nonmarket values into the solution and are limited in their use of market value. For some resource decisions, market values may be the relevant criteria but for the other decisions, such as those involving national parks, where the investment involved is not marginal and where the results of the action may be irreversible, nonmarket values cannot be ignored. Current approaches to evaluating recreation benefits can make explicit the market value opportunity costs but can give no guidance to the nonmarket costs and benefits of the decision.

POLITICS

AN ECONOMIC THEORY OF POLITICAL ACTION IN A DEMOCRACY

Goal of government said to be attainment of income, power, and prestige. Only if perfect altruists hold power is goal to maximize social welfare.

By ANTHONY DOWNS*

I

In spite of the tremendous importance of government decisions in every phase of economic life, economic theorists have never successfully integrated government with private decision-makers in a single general equilibrium theory. Instead they have treated government action as an exogenous variable, determined by political considerations that lie outside the purview of economics. This view is really a carry-over from the classical premise that the private sector is a self-regulating mechanism and that any government action beyond maintenance of law and order is "interference" with it rather than an intrinsic part of it.[1]

However, in at least two fields of economic theory, the centrality of government action has forced economists to formulate rules that indi-

cate how government "should" make decisions. Thus in the field of public finance, Hugh Dalton states:

As a result of [the] operations of public finance, changes take place in the amount and in the nature of the wealth which is produced, and in the distribution of that wealth among individuals and classes. Are these changes in their aggregate effects socially advantageous? If so the operations are justified; if not, not. The best system of public finance is that which secures the maximum social advantages from the operations which it conducts.[2]

A similar attempt to differentiate the operations "proper" to government from those "proper" to private agents has been made by Harvey W. Peck, who writes: "If public operation of an enterprise will produce a greater net social utility, the services rendered by this enterprise should belong in the category of public goods."[3] In addition, several welfare

---

* The argument presented in this article will be developed further in my forthcoming book, *An Economic Theory of Democracy*, to be published by Harper & Row.
[1] See Gerhard Colm, *Essays in Public Finance and Fiscal Policy* (New York: Oxford University Press, 1955), pp. 6–8.

[2] *The Principles of Public Finance* (London: George Routledge & Sons, Ltd., 1932), pp. 9–10.

[3] *Taxation and Welfare* (New York: Macmillan Co., 1925), pp. 30–36, as quoted in

economists have posited general principles to guide government action in the economy. For example, Abba P. Lerner indirectly states such a rule when he says: "If it is desired to maximize the total satisfaction in a society, the rational procedure is to divide income on an equalitarian basis."[4]

Admittedly, this list of examples is not very long, primarily because overt statements of a decision rule to guide government action are extremely rare in economic theory. However, it does not unduly distort reality to state that most welfare economists and many public finance theorists implicitly assume that the "proper" function of government is to maximize social welfare. Insofar as they face the problem of government decision-making at all, they nearly all subscribe to some approximation of this normative rule.

The use of this rule has led to two major difficulties. First, it is not clear what is meant by "social welfare," nor is there any agreement about how to "maximize" it. In fact, a long controversy about the nature of social welfare in the "new welfare economics" led to Kenneth Arrow's conclusion that no rational method of maximizing social welfare can possibly be found unless strong restrictions are placed on the preference orderings of the individuals in society.[5]

The complexities of this problem have diverted attention from the second difficulty raised by the view that government's function is to maximize social welfare. Even if social welfare could be defined, and methods of maximizing it could be agreed upon, what reason is there to believe that the men who run the government would be motivated to maximize it? To state that they "should" do so does not mean that they will. As Schumpeter, one of the few economists who have faced this problem, has pointed out:

It does not follow that the social meaning of a type of activity will necessarily provide the motive power, hence the explanation of the latter. If it does not, a theory that contents itself with an analysis of the social end or need to be served cannot be accepted as an adequate account of the activities that serve it.[6]

Schumpeter here illuminates a crucial objection to most attempts to deal with government in economic theory: they do not really treat the government as part of the division of labor. Every agent in the division of labor has both a private motive and a social function. For example, the social function of a coal-miner is removing coal from the ground, since this activity provides utility for others. But he is motivated to carry out this function by his desire to earn income, not by any desire to benefit others. Similarly, every other agent in the division of labor carries out his social function primarily as a means of attaining his own private ends: the enjoyment of income, prestige, or power. Much of economic theory consists in essence of proving

_____

Harold M. Groves (ed.), *Viewpoints in Public Finance* (New York: Henry & Co., 1948), p. 551.

[4] *The Economics of Control* (New York: Macmillan Co., 1944), p. 32.

[5] *Social Choice and Individual Values* (New York: John Wiley & Sons, 1951).

_____

[6] Joseph A. Schumpeter, *Capitalism, Socialism, and Democracy* (New York: Harper & Row, Publishers, 1950), p. 282.

that men thus pursuing their own ends may nevertheless carry out their social functions with great efficiency, at least under certain conditions.

In light of this reasoning, any attempt to construct a theory of government action without discussing the motives of those who run the government must be regarded as inconsistent with the main body of economic analysis. Every such attempt fails to face the fact that governments are concrete institutions run by men, because it deals with them on a purely normative level. As a result, these attempts can never lead to an integration of government with other decision-makers in a general equilibrium theory. Such integration demands a positive approach that explains how the governors are led to act by their own selfish motives. In the following sections, I present a model of government decision-making based on this approach.

II

In building this model, I shall use the following definitions:

1. Government is that agency in the division of labor which has the power to coerce all other agents in society; it is the locus of "ultimate" power in a given area.[7]

2. A *democracy* is a political system that exhibits the following characteristics:

a. Two or more parties compete in periodic elections for control of the governing apparatus.

b. The party (or coalition of parties) winning a majority of votes gains control of the governing apparatus until the next election.

c. Losing parties never attempt to prevent the winners from taking office, nor do winners use the powers of office to vitiate the ability of losers to compete in the next election.

d. All sane, law-abiding adults who are governed are citizens, and every citizen has one and only one vote in each election.

Though these definitions are both somewhat ambiguous, they will suffice for present purposes.

Next I set forth the following axioms:

1. Each political party is a team of men who seek office solely in order to enjoy the income, prestige, and power that go with running the governing apparatus.[8]

2. The winning party (or coalition) has complete control over the government's actions until the next

[7] This definition is taken from Robert A. Dahl and Charles E. Lindblom, *Politics, Economics, and Welfare* (New York: Harper & Row, 1953), p. 42. However, throughout most of my analysis the word "government" refers to the governing party rather than the institution as here defined.

[8] A "team" is a coalition whose members have identical goals. A "coalition" is a group of men who co-operate to achieve some common end. These definitions are taken from Jacob Marschak, "Towards an Economic Theory of Organizationn and Information," in *Decision Processes*, ed. R. M. Thrall, C. H. Coombs, and R. L. Davis (New York: John Wiley & Sons, 1954), pp. 188–89. I use "team" instead of "coalition" in my definition to eliminate intraparty power struggles from consideration, though in Marschak's terms parties are really coalitions, not teams.

election. There are no votes of confidence between elections either by a legislature or by the electorate, so the governing party cannot be ousted before the next election. Nor are any of its orders resisted or sabotaged by an intransigent bureaucracy.

3. Government's economic powers are unlimited. It can nationalize everything, hand everything over to private interests, or strike any balance between these extremes.

4. The only limit on government's powers is that the incumbent party cannot in any way restrict the political freedom of opposition parties or of individual citizens, unless they seek to overthrow it by force.

5. Every agent in the model—whether an individual, a party, or a private coalition—behaves rationally at all times; that is, it proceeds toward its goals with a minimal use of scarce resources and undertakes only those actions for which marginal return exceeds marginal cost.[9]

From these definitions and axioms springs my central hypothesis: political parties in a democracy formulate policy strictly as a means of gaining votes. They do not seek to gain office in order to carry out certain preconceived policies or to serve any particular interest groups; rather they formulate policies and serve interest groups in order to gain office. Thus their social function—which is to formulate and carry out policies when in power as the government—

is accomplished as a by-product of their private motive—which is to attain the income, power, and prestige of being in office.

This hypothesis implies that, in a democracy, the government always acts so as to maximize the number of votes it will receive. In effect, it is an entrepreneur selling policies for votes instead of products for money. Furthermore, it must compete for votes with other parties, just as two or more oligopolists compete for sales in a market. Whether or not such a government maximizes social welfare (assuming this process can be defined) depends upon how the competitive struggle for power influences its behavior. We cannot assume a priori that this behavior is socially optimal any more than we can assume a priori that a given firm produces the socially optimal output.

I shall examine the nature of government decision-making in two contexts: (1) in a world in which there is perfect knowledge and information is costless and (2) in a world in which knowledge is imperfect and information is costly.

III

The analysis of government decision-making in a perfectly-informed world is intended only to highlight the basic relationship between a democratic government and its citizens. This relationship can be stated in the following set of propositions:

1. The actions of the government are a function of the way it expects voters to vote and of the strategies of its opposition.

2. The government expects voters

---

[9] The term "rational" in this article is synonymous with "efficient." This economic definition must not be confused with the logical definition (i.e., pertaining to logical propositions) or the psychological definition (i.e., calculating or unemotional).

to vote according to (a) changes in their utility incomes from government activity and (b) the strategies of opposition parties.

3. Voters actually vote according to (a) changes in their utility incomes from government activity and (b) the alternatives offered by the opposition.[10]

4. Voters' utility incomes from government activity depend on the actions taken by government during the election period.

5. The strategies of opposition parties depend on their views of the voters' utility incomes from government activity and on the actions taken by the government in power.

These propositions actually form a set of five equations containing five unknowns: expected votes, actual votes, opposition strategies, government actions, and individual utility incomes from government activity. Thus the political structure of a democracy can be viewed in terms of a set of simultaneous equations similar to those often used to analyze an economic structure.

Because the citizens of our model democracy are rational, each of them views elections strictly as means of selecting the government most beneficial to him. Each citizen estimates the utility income from government action he expects each party would provide him if it were in power in the forthcoming election period; that is, he first estimates the utility in-

come Party A would provide him, then the income Party B would provide, and so on. He votes for whatever party he believes would provide him with the highest utility income from government action. The primary factor influencing his estimate of each party's future performance is not its campaign promises about the future but its performance during the period just ending. Thus his voting decision is based on a comparison of the utility income he actually received during this period from the actions of the incumbent party and those he believes he would have received had each of the opposition parties been in power (I assume that each opposition party has taken a verbal stand on every issue dealt with concretely by the incumbents). This procedure allows him to found his decision on facts rather than on conjectures. Of course, since he is helping to choose a future government, he modifies his analysis of each party's past performance according to his estimate of probable changes in its behavior. Nevertheless, the current record of the incumbents remains the central item in his evaluation.

The government also makes decisions rationally, but its behavior is not so easy to analyze, because it is engaged in political warfare with its opponets. Each party resembles a player in an N-person game or an oligopolist engaged in cut-throat competition. However, the conjectural variation problem is somewhat simplified, because the incumbent party must always commit itself on each issue before the opposition parties do. Since it is in power, it must act whenever the occasion for a decision arises, if failure to respond is counted

---

[10] In a perfectly informed world, voters always vote exactly the way government expects them to, so the relationships expressed in Nos. 2 and 3 are identical. But in an imperfectly informed world, the government does not always know what voters will do; hence Nos. 2 and 3 may differ.

as a form of action. But the opposition, which is not responsible for the government, can wait until the pressure of events has forced the governing party to commit itself. Thus opposition parties have a strategic advantage—which incidentally makes the analysis of interparty warfare simpler than it would be if all parties revealed their strategies simultaneously.

However, I shall not explore party strategies in a perfectly informed world, because nearly all the conclusions that could be drawn are inapplicable to the imperfectly informed world in which we are primarily interested. Only one point should be stressed: in a world where perfect knowledge prevails, the government gives the preferences of each citizen exactly the same weight as those of every other citizen. This does not mean that its policies favor all citizens equally, since strategic considerations may lead it to ignore some citizens and to woo others ardently or to favor some with one policy and others with another. But it never deliberately eschews the vote of Citizen A to gain that of Citizen B. Since each citizen has one and only one vote, it cannot gain by trading A's vote for B's, *ceteris paribus*. In short, the equality of franchise is successful as a device for distributing political power equally among citizens.

IV

Lack of complete information on which to base decisions is a condition so basic to human life that it influences the structure of almost every social institution. In politics especially, its effects are profound. For this reason, I devote the rest of my analysis to the impact of imperfect knowledge upon political action in a democracy.

In this model, imperfect knowledge means (1) that parties do not always know exactly what citizens want: (2) that citizens do not always know what the government or its opposition has done, is doing, or should be doing to serve their interests; and (3) that the information needed to overcome both types of ignorance is costly—in other words, that scarce resources must be used to procure and assimilate it. Although these conditions have many effects upon the operation of government in the model, I concentrate on only three: persuasion, ideologies, and rational ignorance.

V

As long as we retain the assumption of perfect knowledge, no citizen can possibly influence another's vote. Each knows what would benefit him most, what the government is doing, and what other parties would do if they were in power. Therefore, the citizen's political taste structure, which I assume to be fixed, leads him directly to an unambiguous decision about how he should vote. If he remains rational, no persuasion can change his mind.

But, as soon as ignorance appears, the clear path from taste structure to voting decision becomes obscured by lack of knowledge. Though some voters want a specific party to win because its policies are clearly the most beneficial to them, others are highly uncertain about which party they prefer. They are not sure just what is happening to them or what would happen to them if another

94 THE DAILY ECONOMIST

party were in power. They need more facts to establish a clear preference. By providing these facts, persuaders can become effective.

Persuaders are not interested per se in helping people who are uncertain become less so; they want to produce a decision that aids their cause. Therefore, they provide only those facts which are favorable to whatever group they are supporting. Thus, even if we assume that no erroneous or false data exist, some men are able to influence others by presenting them with a biased selection of facts.

This possibility has several extraordinarily important consequences for the operation of government. First, it means that some men are more important than others politically, because they can influence more votes than they themselves cast. Since it takes scarce resources to provide information to hesitant citizens, men who command such resources are able to wield more than proportional political influence, *ceteris paribus*. The government, being rational, cannot overlook this fact in designing policy. As a result, equality of franchise no longer assures net equality of influence over government action. In fact, it is irrational for a democratic government to treat its citizens with equal deference in a world in which knowledge is imperfect.

Second, the government is itself ignorant of what its citizens want it to do. Therefore it must send out representatives (1) to sound out the electorate and discover their desires and (2) to persuade them it should be re-elected. In other words, lack of information converts democratic government into representative govern-

ment, because it forces the central planning board of the governing party to rely upon agents scattered throughout the electorate. Such reliance amounts to a decentralization of government power from the planning board to the agents.[11] The central board continues to decentralize its power until the marginal vote-gain from greater conformity to popular desires is equal to the marginal vote-loss caused by reduced ability to co-ordinate its actions.

This reasoning implies that a democratic government in a rational world will always be run on a quasi-representative, quasi-decentralized basis, no matter what its formal constitutional structure, as long as communication between the voters and the governors is less than perfect. Another powerful force working in the same direction is the division of labor. To be efficient, a nation must develop specialists in discovering, transmitting, and analyzing popular opinion, just as it develops specialists in everything else. These specialists are the representatives. They exercise more power, and the central planning board exercises less, the less efficient are communication facilities in society.

The third consequence of imperfect knowledge and the resulting need for persuasion is really a combination of the first two. Because some voters can be influenced, specialists in influencing them appear. And, because government needs intermediaries between it and the people, some of these influencers pose as

---

[11] Decentralization may be geographical or by social groups, depending upon the way society is divided into homogeneous parts.

"representatives" of the citizenry. On one hand, they attempt to convince the government that the policies they stand for—which are of direct benefit to themselves—are both good for and desired by a large portion of the electorate. On the other hand, they try to convince the electorate that these policies are in fact desirable. Thus one of their methods of getting government to believe that public opinion supports them is to create favorable opinion through persuasion. Though a rational government will discount their claims, it cannot ignore them altogether. It must give the influencers more than proportional weight in forming policy, because they may have succeeded in creating favorable opinions in the silent mass of voters and because their vociferousness indicates a high intensity of desire. Clearly, people with an intense interest in some policy are more likely to base their votes upon it alone than are those who count it as just another issue; hence government must pay more attention to the former than the latter. To do otherwise would be irrational.

Finally, imperfect knowledge makes the governing party susceptible to bribery. In order to persuade voters that its policies are good for them, it needs scarce resources, such as television time, money for propaganda, and pay for precinct captains. One way to get such resources is to sell policy favors to those who can pay for them, either by campaign contributions, favorable editorial policies, or direct influence over others. Such favor buyers need not even pose as representatives of the people. They merely exchange their political help for policy favors—a transaction eminently rational for both themselves and the government.

Essentially, inequality of political influence is a necessary result of imperfect information, given an unequal distribution of wealth and income in society. When knowledge is imperfect, effective political action requires the use of economic resources to meet the cost of information. Therefore, those who command such resources are able to swing more than their proportional weight politically. This outcome is not the result of irrationality or dishonesty. On the contrary, lobbying in a democracy is a highly rational response to the lack of perfect information, as is government's submission to the demands of lobbyists. To suppose otherwise is to ignore the existence of information costs—that is, to theorize about a mythical world instead of the real one. Imperfect knowledge allows the unequal distributions of income, position, and influence—which are all inevitable in any economy marked by an extensive division of labor—to share sovereignty in a realm where only the equal distribution of votes is supposed to reign.

VI

Since the parties in this model have no interest per se in creating any particular type of society, the universal prevalence of ideologies in democratic politics appears to contradict my hypothesis. But this appearance is false. In fact, not only the existence of ideologies, but also many of their particular characteristics, may be deduced from the premise that parties seek office solely for the income, power, and prestige that accompany it.[12] Again, imperfect knowledge is the key factor. In a complex society the cost in time alone of comparing all the ways in which the policies of competing parties differ is staggering. Furthermore, citizens do not always have enough information to appraise the differences of which they are aware. Nor do they know in advance what problems the government is likely to face in the coming election period.

Under these conditions many a voter finds party ideologies useful because they remove the necessity for relating every issue to his own conception of "the good society." Ideologies help him focus attention on the differences between parties; therefore, they can be used as samples of all the differentiating stands. Furthermore, if the voter discovers a correlation between each party's ideology and its policies, he can rationally vote by comparing ideologies rather than policies. In both cases he can drastically reduce his outlay on political information by informing himself only about ideologies instead of about a wide range of issues.

Thus lack of information creates a demand for ideologies in the electorate. Since political parties are eager to seize any method of gaining votes available to them, they respond by creating a supply. Each party invents an ideology in order to attract the votes of those citizens who wish to cut costs by voting ideologically.[13]

This reasoning does not mean that parties can change ideologies as though they were disguises, putting on whatever costume suits the situation. Once a party has placed its ideology "on the market," it cannot suddenly abandon or radically alter that ideology without convincing the voters that it is unreliable. Since voters are rational, they refuse to support unreliable parties; hence no party can afford to acquire a reputation for dishonesty. Furthermore, there must be some persistent correlation between each party's ideology and its subsequent actions; otherwise voters will eventually eschew ideological voting as irrational. Finally, parties cannot adopt identical ideologies, because they must create enough product differentiation to make their output distinguishable from that of their rivals, so as to entice voters to the polls. However, just as in the product market, any markedly successful ideology is soon imitated, and differentiation takes place on more subtle levels.

Analysis of political ideologies can be carried even further by means of a spatial analogy for political action. To construct this analogy, I borrow and elaborate upon an apparatus first used by Harold Hotelling in his famous article "Stability in Competition."[14] My version of Hotelling's spatial market consists of a linear scale running from zero to one hundred in the usual left-to-right fashion. To render it politically meaningful, I make the following assumptions:

---

[12] I define "ideologies" as verbal images of "the good society" and of the chief policies to be used in creating it.

[13] In reality, party ideologies probably stem originally from the interests of those persons who found each party. But, once a political party is created, it takes on an existence of its own and eventually becomes

relatively independent of any particular interest group. When such autonomy prevails, my analysis of ideologies is fully applicable.

[14] *Economic Journal*, XXXIX (1929), 41–57.

1. The political parties in any society can be ordered from left to right in a manner agreed upon by all voters.

2. Each voter's preferences are single-peaked at some point on the scale and slope monotonically downward on either side of the peak (unless it lies at one extreme of the scale).

3. The frequency distribution of voters along the scale is variable from society to society but fixed in any one society.[15]

4. Once placed on the political scale, a party can move ideologically either to the left or to the right up to but not beyond the nearest party toward which it is moving.[16]

5. In a two-party system, if either party moves away from the extreme nearest it toward the other party, extremist voters at its end of the scale may abstain because they see no significant difference between the choices offered them.[17]

Under these conditions Hotelling's conclusion that the parties in a two-party system inevitably converge on the center does not necessarily hold true. If voters are distributed along the scale as shown in Figure 1, then Hotelling is right. Assuming that Party A starts at position 25 and Party B at 75, both move toward 50, since each can gain more votes in the center than it loses at the extremes because of abstention. But, if the distribution is like that shown in Figure 2, the two parties diverge toward the extremes rather than converge on the center. Each gains more votes by moving toward a radical position than it loses in the center.

This reasoning implies that stable government in a two-party democracy requires a distribution of voters roughly approximating a normal curve. When such a distribution exists, the two parties come to resemble each other closely. Thus, when one replaces the other in office, no drastic policy changes occur, and most voters are located relatively close to the incumbent's position no matter which party is in power. But when the electorate is polarized, as in Figure 2, a change in parties causes a radical alteration in policy. And, regardless of which party is in office, half the electorate always feels that the other half is imposing policies upon it that are strongly repugnant to it. In this situation, if one party keeps getting re-elected, the disgruntled supporters of the other party will probably revolt; whereas if the two parties alternate in office, social chaos occurs, because government policy keeps changing from one extreme to the other. Thus democracy does not lead to effective, stable government when the electorate is polarized. Either the distribution must change or democracy will be replaced by tyranny in which one extreme imposes its will upon the other.

---

[15] Actually, this distribution may vary in any one society even in the short run, but I assume it to be fixed in order to avoid discussing the complex of historical, sociological, psychological, and other factors which cause it to change.

[16] It cannot go beyond the adjacent parties, because such "leaping" would indicate ideological unreliability and would cause its rejection by the electorate.

[17] This is equivalent to assuming elastic demand along the scale, as Smithies did in his elaboration of the Hotelling model (see Arthur Smithies, "Optimum Location in Spatial Competition," *Journal of Political Economy,* XLIX [1941], 423–39).

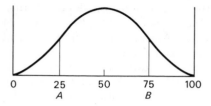

0   25   50   75   100
         A   B

FIGURE 1

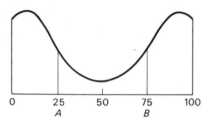

0   25   50   75   100
         A   B

FIGURE 2

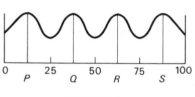

0   P   25   Q   50   R   75   S   100

FIGURE 3

Hotelling's original model was limited to the two-firm (or two-party) case, because, when three firms existed, the two outside ones converged on the middle one, which then leaped to the outside to avoid strangulation. Since this process repeated itself endlessly, no stable equilibrium emerged. But, in my model, such leaping is impossible, because each party has to maintain continuity in its ideology. Hence this model can be applied to multiparty systems without resulting in disequilibrium.

Multiparty systems are most likely to exist when the distribution of voters is multimodal, as shown in Figure 3. A separate party forms at

each mode, and each party is motivated to stay at its mode and to differentiate itself as completely as possible from its neighbors. If it moves to the left so as to gain votes, it loses just as many votes to the party on its right (or loses them because of abstention if it is an extremist party at the right end of the scale), and vice versa. Thus its optimal course is to stay where it is and keep other parties from approaching it. In a multiparty system, therefore, we find conditions exactly opposite to those in a viable two-party system. Whereas in the former each party links itself to a definite ideological position and stresses its differences from other parties, in the latter both parties move toward the political center so as to resemble each other as closely as possible.

This conclusion implies that voters in multiparty systems have a wider range of choice than voters in two-party systems and that each choice in this range is more definitely linked to some ideological position. Thus it appears that the electorate exercises a more significant function in a multiparty system than in a two-party system, because only in the former does it make much difference which party gets elected.

However, appearances are deceiving in politics, because in fact the government in a multiparty system is likely to have a less definite, less coherent, and less integrated program than the government in a two-party system. This paradoxical outcome arises from the necessity in most multiparty systems of forming coalition governments. Since voters are scattered among several modes, only rarely does one party obtain the support of a majority of those voting. Yet, in most democracies, the government cannot function without at least the indirect support of a majority of voters. Even in systems in which the legislature selects the government, a majority of its members must support the coalition chosen to govern before the coalition can take office. If we assume that representation in the legislature is "fair"—that each member represents the same number of citizens—then even a coalition government must receive the indirect support of a majority in order to govern.

Such support can be maintained only if the government implements at least some policies that appeal to —are ideologically near—each cluster of voters whose support it needs. If a majority of voters are massed in one relatively narrow band on the left-right scale, then the government can chose all its policies from within this band. Hence its policies will form a fairly cohesive set embodying the ideological viewpoint associated with that area of the scale. This outcome is typical of a two-party system.

But in a multiparty system there are many modes scattered across the whole scale. Therefore, in order to appeal to a majority of voters, the government must be a coalition of parties and must include in its policy-set some policies espoused by each party in the coalition. In this manner it "pays off" voters at each cluster in return for their support. However, the result is that its program contains policies reflecting a wide variety of ideological viewpoints, so that no real cohesion or integration about any one Weltanschauung is possible. This outcome necessarily occurs whenever the distribution of voters along the scale is so scattered that only a very wide band can encompass a majority.

Consequently, a multiparty system offers voters an ostensible choice between definite, well-integrated policy-sets in each election, but only rarely does one of these sets actually govern. Usually a coalition governs, and its policies are likely to be less definite and less well integrated than those of the government in a two-party system. This is true even though voters in the latter are offered only two relatively unintegrated alternatives which closely resemble each other. No wonder politics often seems confusing.

Whether a political system has two or more parties depends on the distribution of voters along the scale and on the electoral rules governing the system. To demonstrate this dual dependence, I use the concept of "political equilibrium." A state of political equilibrium exists when no new parties can successfully be formed and when no existing party is motivated to move away from its present position.

The limit to the number of new parties that can be formed successfully springs from my definition of success as ability to gain the income, power, and prestige that go with office; that is, as ability to get elected. If the constitution calls for the election of a legislature by proportional representation and the subsequent formation of a government by the legislature, then many parties can be formed, because any given party can get at least some of its members elected by winning the support of only a small proportion of the citizens. Once elected, these members have a chance to share in the fruits of office by joining a coalition government. Hence it follows from my hypothesis about party motivation that many parties are likely to exist in a proportional representation system. Their number is limited only by the number of seats in the legislature and by the necessity of formulating ideologies sufficiently different from those of existing parties to attract votes away from them.[18] New parties continue to form until the distribution of voters is "saturated" —until there is not enough ideological "room" between existing parties to support others significantly different from them.

In an electoral system in which a plurality is necessary for victory, the limit on successful party formation is much more stringent. Since the only way to insure a plurality against all opponents is to win a majority of votes, small parties tend to combine until two giants are left, each of which has a reasonable chance of capturing a majority in any given election. Where these two parties are located on the ideological scale depends upon the distribution of voters, as explained before.

Actually, the policy position and stability of the government in a democracy are relatively independent of the number of parties; they follow primarily from the nature of the distribution of voters along the left-right scale.[19] If a majority of voters are massed within a narrow range of

that scale, democratic government is likely to be stable and effective, no matter how many parties exist. As noted earlier, the government can formulate a policy-set which appeals to a majority of voters and yet does not contain policies embodying widely disparate points of view. But, if the government can win the support of a majority only by adopting a scattering of policies chosen from a broad range of viewpoints, these policies tend to cancel each other out, and the government's net ability to solve social problems is low. Thus the distribution of voters—which is itself a variable in the long run— determines whether or not democracy leads to effective government.

VII

When information is costly, no decision-maker can afford to know everything that might possibly bear on his decision before he makes it. He must select only a few data from the vast supply in existence and base his decision solely upon them. This is true even if he can procure data without paying for them, since merely assimilating them requires time and is therefore costly.

The amount of information it is rational for a decision-maker to acquire is determined by the following economic axiom: It is always rational to perform any act if its marginal return is larger than its marginal cost. The marginal cost of a "bit" of information is the return foregone by devoting scarce resources —particularly time—to getting and using it. The marginal return from a "bit" is the increase in utility income received because the information enabled the decision-maker to

---

[18] The number of sufficiently different parties a system can support depends upon the shape of the distribution of voters along the scale.

[19] However, because the preferences of rising generations are influenced by the alternatives offered them, the number of parties is one of the factors that determine the shape of the distribution of voters.

improve his decision. In an imperfectly informed world, neither the precise cost nor the precise return is usually known in advance; but decision-makers can nevertheless employ the rule just stated by looking at expected costs and expected returns. This reasoning is as applicable to politics as it is to economics. Insofar as the average citizen is concerned, there are two political decisions that require information. The first is deciding which party to vote for; the second is deciding on what policies to exercise direct influence on government policy formation (that is, how to lobby). Let us examine the voting decision first.

Before we do so, it is necessary to recognize that in every society a stream of "free" information is continuously disseminated to all citizens. Though such "free" data take time to assimilate, this time is not directly chargeable to any particular type of decision-making, since it is a necessary cost of living in society. For example, conversation with business associates, small talk with friends, reading the newspaper in a barber shop, and listening to the radio while driving to work are all sources of information which the average man encounters without any particular effort to do so. Therefore, we may consider them part of the "free" information stream and exclude them from the problem of how much information a decision-maker should obtain specifically to improve his decisions.

The marginal return on information acquired for voting purposes is measured by the expected gain from voting "correctly" instead of "incorrectly." In other words, it is the gain in utility a voter believes he will re-

ceive if he supports the party which would really provide him with the highest utility income instead of supporting some other party. However, unless his vote actually decides the election, it does not cause the "right" party to be elected instead of a "wrong" party; whether or not the "right" party wins does not depend on how he votes. Therefore, voting "correctly" produces no gain in utility whatsoever; he might as well have voted "incorrectly."

This situation results from the insignificance of any one voter in a large electorate. Since the cost of voting is very low, hundreds, thousands, or even millions of citizens can afford to vote. Therefore, the probability that any one citizen's vote will be decisive is very small indeed. It is not zero, and it can even be significant if he thinks the election will be very close; but, under most circumstances, it is so negligible that it renders the return from voting "correctly" infinitesimal. This is true no matter how tremendous a loss in utility income the voter would experience if the "wrong" party were elected. And if that loss is itself small—as it may be when parties resemble each other closely or in local elections—then the incentive to become well informed is practically nonexistent.

Therefore, we reach the startling conclusion that it is irrational for most citizens to acquire political information for purposes of voting. As long as each person considers the behavior of others as given, it is simply not worthwhile for him to acquire information so as to vote "correctly" himself. The probability that his vote will determine which party governs is so low that even a trivial cost of procuring information outweighs its return. Hence ignorance of politics is not a result of unpatriotic apathy; rather it is a highly rational response to the facts of political life in a large democracy.

This conclusion does not mean that every citizen who is well informed about politics is irrational. A rational man can become well informed for four reasons: (1) he may enjoy being well informed for its own sake, so that information as such provides him with utility; (2) he may believe the election is going to be so close that the probability of his casting the decisive vote is relatively high; (3) he may need information to influence the votes of others so that he can alter the outcome of the election or persuade government to assign his preferences more weight than those of others; or (4) he may need information to influence the formation of government policy as a lobbyist. Nevertheless, since the odds are that no election will be close enough to render decisive the vote of any one person, or the votes of all those he can persuade to agree with him, the rational course of action for most citizens is to remain politically uninformed. Insofar as voting is concerned, any attempt to acquire information beyond that furnished by the stream of "free" data is for them a sheer waste of resources.

The disparity between this conclusion and the traditional conception of good citizenship in a democracy is indeed striking. How can we explain it? The answer is that the benefits which a majority of citizens would derive from living in a society with a well-informed electorate are indivisible in nature. When most members of the electorate know what policies best serve their interests, the government is forced to follow those policies in order to avoid defeat (assuming that there is a consensus among the informed). This explains why the proponents of democracy think citizens should be well informed. But the benefits of these policies accrue to each member of the majority they serve, regardless of whether he has helped bring them about. In other words, the individual receives these benefits whether or not he is well informed, so long as most people are well informed and his interests are similar to those of the majority. On the other hand, when no one else is well informed, he cannot produce these benefits by becoming well informed himself, since a collective effort is necessary to achieve them.

Thus, when benefits are indivisible, each individual is always motivated to evade his share of the cost of producing them. If he assumes that the behavior of others is given, whether or not he receives any benefits does not depend on his own efforts. But the cost he pays does depend on his efforts; hence the most rational course for him is to minimize that cost—in this case, to remain politically ignorant. Since every individual reasons in the same way, no one bears any costs, and no benefits are produced.

The usual way of escaping this dilemma is for all individuals to agree to be coerced by a central agency. Then each is forced to pay his share of the costs, but he knows all others are likewise forced to pay. Thus everyone is better off than he would be if no costs were borne, because everyone receives benfits which

(I here assume) more than offset his share of the costs. This is a basic rationale for using coercion to collect revenues for national defense and for many other government operations that yield indivisible benefits.[20] But this solution is not feasible in the case of political information. The government cannot coerce everyone to be well informed, because "well-informedness" is hard to measure, because there is no agreed-upon rule for deciding how much information of what kinds each citizen "should" have, and because the resulting interference in personal affairs would cause a loss of utility that would probably outweigh the gains to be had from a well-informed electorate. The most any democratic government has done to remedy this situation is to compel young people in schools to take courses in civics, government, and history.

Consequently, it is rational for every individual to minimize his investment in political information, in spite of the fact that most citizens might benefit substantially if the whole electorate were well informed. As a result, democratic political systems are bound to operate at less than maximum efficiency. Government does not serve the interests of the majority as well as it would if they were well informed, but they never become well informed. It is collectively rational, but individually irrational, for them to do so; and, in the absence of any mechanism to insure collective action, individual rationality prevails.

---

[20] See Paul A. Samuelson, "The Pure Theory of Public Expenditures," *Review of Economics and Statistics*, XXXVI (November, 1954), 387–89.

VIII

When we apply the economic concept of rationality to the second political use of information, lobbying, the results are similarly incompatible with the traditional view of democracy. In order to be an effective lobbyist, a citizen must persuade the governing party that the policies he wants either are already desired by a large number of other citizens or are sufficiently beneficial to the rest of the electorate so that it will, at worst, not resent the enactment of these policies. To be persuasive, the would-be lobbyist must be extremely well informed about each policy area in which he wishes to exert influence. He must be able to design a policy that benefits him more than any other would, to counter any arguments advanced by opposing lobbyists, and to formulate or recognize compromises acceptable to him. Therefore, being a lobbyist requires much more information than voting, since even well-informed voters need only compare alternatives formulated by others.

For this reason, the cost of acquiring enough information to lobby effectively is relatively high. A lobbyist must be an expert in the policy areas in which he tries to exert influence. Since few men can afford the time or money necessary to become expert in more than one or two policy areas (or to hire those already expert), most citizens must specialize in a very few areas. Such behavior is rational even though policies in many areas affect them to some extent. Conversely, only a few specialists will actively exert pressure on the government in any one policy area. As a result, each need not heavily discount his own impact because of the large number of other persons influencing the decision, as he does in regard to voting. On the contrary, for those few lobbyists who specialize in any given area, the potential return from political information may be very high—precisely because they are so few.

The men who can best afford to become lobbyists in any policy area are those whose incomes stem from that area. This is true because nearly every citizen derives all his income from one or two sources; hence any government policy affecting those sources is of vital interest to him. In contrast, each man spends his income in a great many policy areas, so that a change in any one of them is not too significant to him. Therefore, men are much more likely to exert direct influence on government policy formation in their roles as producers than in their roles as consumers. In consequence, a democratic government is usually biased in favor of producer interests and against consumer interests, even though the consumers of any given product usually outnumber its producers. Tariff legislation provides a notorious example of this bias.

It should be stressed that such systematic exploitation of consumers by producers acting through government policy is not a result of foolish apathy on the part of consumers. In fact, just the opposite is true. Government's anticonsumer bias occurs because consumers rationally seek to acquire only that information which provides a return larger than its cost. The saving a consumer could make by becoming informed about how government policy affects any one product he purchases simply does not recompense him for the cost of informing himself—particularly since his personal influence on government policy would probably be slight. Since this is true of almost every product he buys, he adopts a course of rational ignorance, thereby exposing himself to extensive exploitation. Yet it would be irrational for him to act otherwise. In other words, lobbying is effective in a democracy *because* all the agents concerned—the exploiters, the exploited, and the government—behave rationally.

IX

Clearly, rational behavior in a democracy is not what most normative theorists assume it to be. Political theorists in particular have often created models of how the citizens of a democracy ought to behave without taking into account the economics of political action. Consequently, much of the evidence frequently cited to prove that democratic politics are dominated by irrational (non-logical) forces in fact demonstrates that citizens respond rationally (efficiently) to the exigencies of life in an imperfectly informed world.[21] Apathy among citizens toward elections, ignorance of the issues, the tendency of parties in a two-party system to resemble each other, and the anti-consumer bias of government action can all be explained logically as effi-

[21] In this sentence the word "irrational" is not the opposite of the word "rational," as the synonyms in parentheses show. Admittedly, such dual usage may cause confusion. However, I have employed the word "rational" instead of its synonyms "efficient" throughout this article because I want to emphasize the fact that an intelligent citizen always carries out any act whose marginal

cient reactions to imperfect information in a large democracy. Any normative theory that regards them as signs of unintelligent behavior in politics has failed to face the fact that information is costly in the real world. Thus political theory has suffered because it has not taken into account certain economic realities.

On the other hand, economic theory has suffered because it has not taken into account the political realities of government decision-making. Economists have been content to discuss government action as though governments were run by perfect altruists whose only motive was to maximize social welfare. As a result, economists have been unable to incorporate government into the rest of economic theory, which is based on the premise that all men act primarily out of self-interest. Furthermore, they have falsely concluded that government decision-making in

all societies should follow identical principles, because its goal is always the maximization of social welfare. If my hypothesis is true, the goal of government is attaining the income, power, and prestige that go with office. Since methods of reaching this goal are vastly different in democratic, totalitarian, and aristocratic states, no single theory can be advanced to explain government decision-making in all societies. Nor can any theory of government decision-making be divorced from politics. The way every government actually makes decisions depends upon the nature of the fundamental power relation between the governors and the governed in its society; that is, upon the society's political constitution. Therefore, a different theory of political action must be formulated for each different type of constitution.

I conclude that a truly useful theory of government action in a democracy—or in any other type of society—must be both economic and political in nature. In this article I have attempted to outline such a theory. If nothing else, the attempt demonstrates how much economists and political scientists must depend on each other to analyze government decision-making, which is the most important economic and political force in the world today.

---

return exceeds its marginal cost. In contrast, he does not always make use of logical thinking, because, under some conditions, the marginal return from thinking logically is smaller than its marginal cost. In other words, it is sometimes rational (efficient) to act irrationally (non-logically), in which case an intelligent man eschews rationality in the traditional sense so as to achieve it in the economic sense. This is really what is meant by the sentence in the text to which this footnote is attached.

THE ECONOMY OF PATRONAGE

Patronage maintains political organizations. Desire to maximize votes not necessarily prime objective of political bosses.

By JAMES Q. WILSON

There is a growing interest in the development of descriptive models of political competition and decision-making. This interest often reflects a dissatisfaction on the part of economists and political scientists with theories of government and public finance which view the state as a selfless, disembodied agent which maximizes a "social welfare function" or simply buys and sells essential public services. In many of these recent models, the key assumption is that government is run by coalitions (political parties) whose leaders act so as to maximize their vote.

Anthony Downs, in his theoretical treatment of democracy in terms of an economic model, postulates that the party and the party leaders are motivated by the desire for the power, income, and prestige that accrue to those who gain and hold political office.[1] Thus, winning and retaining political office is the pri-

mary task, and for this maximizing the vote is usually essential. It is "usually" essential because in those cases where there is little popular interest in the outcome, it is often to the advantage of the party to turn out a small vote which is known to be favorable rather than a large vote which may be unpredictable. Strictly speaking, Downs' model calls for the maximization of the probability of winning office rather than votes. But in all important contested elections, maximizing the vote is essential, and it is with such elections that this paper is concerned.

Downs' model accounts for a great deal of political activity, but not all. In some cases, particularly at the city or county level, a party will organize, not to defeat its opponents, but to create a "nuisance" value that can be exchanged for pay-offs. Republican politicians in Democratic cities often seek, not to maximize their vote (or even win any vote at all), but to obtain patronage jobs and favors from the Democratic politicians in exchange for *not* competing vigorously in the general elections. Similarly, certain political organizations have been known to accept electoral defeat rather than win with a slate of candidates that is unacceptable to the party leaders. The party may have had such candidates forced upon it by a demand for "reform" or by a split in the party itself. To win

[1] *An Economic Theory of Democracy* (New York: Harper & Row, 1957). See also his later treatment, "Why the Government Budget Is Too Small in a Democracy," *World Politics*, XII (July, 1960), 541–63.

I would like to express my appreciation to Anthony Downs for his helpful comments on various drafts of this paper, as well as to Edward C. Banfield, on whose ideas I have drawn freely. I am indebted to the Social Science Research Council for financial support of the research on part of which this paper drew. Responsibility for the views herein is, of course, mine.

the election with undesirable candidates (for example, candidates who are likely to engage in large-scale political reforms, attempt to create their own machine, or upset established party arrangements) is to jeopardize the party leadership. (To lose with Taft would have been more acceptable, to certain Republican leaders in 1944 and 1948, than to win with Dewey.) Control of the party leadership may be valued over Pyrrhic victories at the polls. V. O. Key, Jr., notes the extent to which the Republican party in southern states seeks principally to take advantage of federal patronage (when the Republicans are in power nationally) and to wield influence in national conventions.[2] Sayre and Kaufman observe the tendency of the Republican party in New York City to play the "minority game" by placing "the survival of the organization as well as the personal interests of their followers and supporters" ahead of electoral victory, and to seek this organizational goal by extracting considerations from their adversaries through bargaining.[3]

This essay will analyze a special case of the political party, the big-city "machine." The leader of a machine, like the leader of any other large organization, has many goals, and his problem typically is not how to maximize the attainment of one but how to balance the demands of all. To make this clearer, I will consider the machine in terms of the manner in which it allocates its re-

sources. Those resources, it is assumed, consist primarily of patronage. The thesis of this paper is that machines specifically and political parties generally allocate patronage so as to maintain their organizations and that this goal may or may not be compatible with the desire to maximize votes, depending on the position of the leader and the character of the situation.

I

Assume the existence of a city political organization which has a large but not infinite stock of patronage at its disposal.[4] For purposes of

<hr/>

[2] *Southern Politics in State and Nation* (New York: Alfred A. Knopf, Inc., 1951).

[3] Wallace S. Sayre and Herbert Kaufman, *Governing New York City* (New York: Russell Sage Foundation, 1960), p. 179.

[4] A "machine" is defined as that kind of political party which sustains its members through the distribution of material incentives (patronage) rather than non-material incentives (appeals to principle, the fun of the game, sociability, etc.). "Patronage" is customarily used to refer to all forms of material benefits which politicians may distribute to party workers and supporters. Here it will be used to refer (generally) to the fund out of which the patronage jobs and favors are provided and (specifically) to the jobs and favors themselves. "Patronage jobs" are all those posts, distributed at the discretion of political leaders, the pay for which is greater than the value of the public services performed. This "unearned increment" permits the machine to require that the holder perform party services as well. Useful studies of machines and patronage include Frank Kent, *The Great Game of Politics* (Garden City, N.Y.: Doubleday & Co., 1923); David H. Kurtzman, *Methods of Controlling Votes in Philadelphia* (Philadelphia: University of Pennsylvania Press, 1935); Sonya Forthal, *Cogwheels of Democracy* (New York: William-Frederick Press, 1946); and Harold Gosnell, *Machine Politics, Chicago Model* (Chicago: University of Chicago Press, 1937). Recent studies include Martin Meyerson and Edward C. Banfield, *Politics, Planning, and the Public Interest* (Glencoe, Ill.: Free Press,

simplicity, assume further that these jobs and favors are the only form of patronage (although, in fact, other forms—such as graft—are common) and that their monetary values are suitable for attracting, holding, and promoting voters and political workers. Thus, most of the jobs would be similar in character and carry moderate salaries (say, $4,000 to $6,000 a year), but jobs would be available at higher pay levels as well. The city is divided into wards or districts of approximately equal size, each of which is headed by a ward leader.

The leader of the machine is the "boss." He is selected by the ward leaders from among their number and he is ultimately accountable to them. He requires their support for his elevation. However, once he is selected he acquires considerable power over them because of his control of patronage and his ability to decide (or greatly influence) who will be slated for elective office. It is much easier to create a boss than to destroy one. It is difficult for the ward leaders to expel him, for it requires concerting the action of all against one, a willingness to accept short-term penalties in the hope of long-term advantage, and acceptance of the cost of disrupting the machine by internecine warfare and thus reducing its ability to defeat the opposition party. But *in extremis*, the ward leaders will attempt to expel him. Even though the boss acquires great power over his lieutenants, it

is not unlimited power. If he makes gross errors or asks his followers to commit political suicide, they, like the subjects of Hobbes' Leviathan, will feel entitled to assert their right of self-defense.

The conditions of life in the city are assumed to be much as they are in any city, with the population distinguished by significant differences in income, prestige, political opinions, loyalties, and values. Assume that many, but not all, voters can be induced to vote for the machine's slate of candidates by having paid political workers who can perform favors canvass them. The value of these favors to the voter will vary somewhat with the skill of the worker offering them.

Patronage, thus, has at least four functions: (1) It is a means available to the boss to induce his ward leaders to support him as boss. The boss's control over patronage is a principal source of his authority, at least in all cases short of outright rebellion by a majority of the ward leaders. The boss, to state it bluntly, uses patronage to pay his colleagues for obeying his orders. (2) Patronage is a means whereby the boss induces elective office-holders to surrender to him all or part of their legally vested discretionary powers. A condition of their nomination for elective office is that they permit the machine (that is, the boss) to dispense the jobs and favors they will acquire upon election. The boss then uses this stock of patronage to "bribe" these officials when necessary to follow his lead in matters of public policy. Each elective official has some legal powers. These powers can be seen as a collection of potential "vetoes" over the policies of others. The boss pays the officials

1955); Sayre and Kaufman, *op cit.*; and Frank J. Sorauf, "Patronage and Party," *Midwest Journal of Political Science*, III (May, 1959), 115–26, and "State Patronage in a Rural County," *American Political Science Review*, L (December, 1956), 1046–56.

with favors for not exercising those vetoes. (3) Patronage is used to induce precinct captains to work for the machine by getting out the vote and dispensing favors to voters. This function is, of course, only analytically distinct from the others, since almost *all* jobs are ultimately given to persons who do some work for the organization. The crucial factors are the reason for which the jobs are given, the intermediaries through which they must pass, and the nature of the benefits accruing to the boss from their expenditure. (4) Patronage, finally, is used to induce at least some voters to support the machine. Often these favors are not directly exchanged for votes. Rather, many voters support the party of their precinct captains in hope of future reward, or to deter possible reprisals, or simply to maintain good relations with a potentially useful and certainly powerful organization.

The boss must balance his expenditures of patronage among these four functions. Patronage spent for any of these ends involves an opportunity cost in terms of other ends. All the goals are, of course, related, and none may be ignored entirely. The important question concerns the conditions under which the boss may or must spend excessively for one purpose at the expense of others. Equally important, the tactics and administrative methods called for by seeking one goal (say, spending to attract voters) are sometimes dysfunctional to the tactics and methods appropriate to other goals. Thus, emphasizing vote maximization over other ends is not only costly in terms of resources (patronage) but also tends to the creation of structural rigidities and the development of patterns of expectations which reduce the effectiveness of the resources that are spent on the other ends.

II

This can best be seen by considering the conditions favorable to heavy expenditures for each purpose and the organizational consequences of such outlays.

1. *Maintaining leadership.* The boss is likely to emphasize this goal when a serious challenge to his own authority arises. Such challenges are more common when the total stock of incentives (patronage) has been sharply reduced, thus intensifying conflict over its distribution. Tammany Hall in the Borough of Manhattan in New York City has been gripped by a prolonged internecine war. The Democratic party of Chicago, on the other hand, has a stable and unchallenged leadership. One factor (although by no means the only one) contributing to the situation in Manhattan is the shortage of patronage by which loyalty could be maintained and rivals bought off.

Although no over-all totals are known and none could probably be discovered by any feasible research strategies, some ward and district comparisons can be made.[5] In each of two typical Manhattan congressional districts (which in turn are made up of smaller party districts), there may be as many as 115 or 120

---

[5] So much secrecy is maintained in city politics that no exact data on patronage may ever be obtained in cities of any size. For a patronage count in a rural county, see Douglas St. Angelo, "Political Patronage in a Rural County" (unpublished Master's thesis, Department of Political Science, University of Chicago, 1957).

jobs available but probably the number is no higher than 80 or 90. In congressional districts of similar size in Chicago, on the other hand, the number of jobs may be in excess of 450 and is undoubtedly more than 350. In smaller units, the comparisons are equally striking. In a Manhattan assembly district, there may be as many as 50 jobs available; in a ward of comparable size in Chicago, there are 165 or more. This comparative shortage of material rewards in Manhattan, combined with the recent weakness in party leadership, has meant that the machine is much more unstable than its counterpart in Chicago. Its ability to punish or defeat dissidents is decidedly less and its power to co-opt ambitious leaders has been diminished.

There is some evidence that, as a result of this state of affairs, Carmine G. De Sapio, the threatened leader of Tammany Hall, allocates such resources as he does possess so as to improve his own immediate position in the organization rather than maximize the party's vote. Thus, dissident factions (for example, the so-called "reform" clubs) are deprived of patronage and their pro-De Sapio rivals are awarded it instead—even though the dissident group is often the more effective at winning votes for the party ticket in general elections.[6] [Editors' note: The threat to De Sapio was real. He subsequently lost his congressional seat to a reform candidate, Edward Koch, the first event in a long downhill course that ended with De Sapio's conviction on

charges of conspiracy to bribe a public official.] In those districts where dissident clubs could use patronage to good advantage in campaigns, they are denied it because of intra-organizational conflict. This may well reduce the vote of the party.

Even when the boss himself is reasonably secure, his ward leaders must maintain their positions. Control of patronage is customarily a means whereby they defend themselves against challenges and exercise discipline. Although the boss uses his ultimate control over patronage to command the loyalty of the ward leaders, he relinquishes, within that framework, power to make specific recommendations to the ward leaders. The power of a ward leader over the jobs assigned to him is called, in Chicago, the power to "vice them downtown"—that is, the power to replace one worker on the payroll with another. When one ward leader is replaced by another, his power to "vice" workers is transferred by the boss to the new leader. Struggles for power within ward organizations are not infrequent, and vicing occurs in many cases without regard for the ability of the workers as vote-getters. Thus, just as the boss's use of patronage may be costly in terms of a vote-maximization goal (because he must hold the allegiance of ward leaders whose wards do not produce votes in proportion to the patronage invested in them), so also the ward leader's use of patronage may be similarly costly (because he may be compelled to vice able precinct workers whom he regards as potential rivals).

Were vote-maximization the single goal, and were the boss secure in his position, patronage would be allocated to the wards in accord with its

[6] See James Q. Wilson, "Egghead Politics in Manhattan," in E. C. Banfield (ed.), *Urban Government: A Reader in Politics and Administration* (Glencoe, Ill.: Free Press, 1961).

marginal product (see below). But no boss is perfectly secure, and few are even comfortably secure. Thus, the marginal-product principle of patronage distribution does not apply. Instead, a machine such as that in Chicago (and to some extent in Manhattan) adopts, as a rule of thumb, the principle of distributing jobs on a roughly equal basis to all ward leaders. Although this will be modified by local conditions, the principle of equal distribution regardless of the marginal product of patronage persists for several reasons. First, most wards or districts are usually about equal in size, and thus each can make a plausible case for equality. Second, equal distribution is usually insisted upon (at least tacitly) by ward leaders as a condition of the boss's selection. Third, since the wards most responsive to patronage are usually in a minority (and, with continued prosperity and social mobility, will become more so), any attempt to change the equality principle could be defeated by the more numerous wards which would lose patronage as a consequence of any change in the rules in the direction of a greater "rationality." In any case, equal distribution means the boss does not have to distinguish between "good" and "bad" wards. In contesting for jobs, ward leaders often present the argument that "ward n has more jobs than we and therefore we are entitled to an increase." The boss, within limits, must try to meet these claims, for the support of the ward leaders would be jeopardized by any great and obvious discrepancies in the allocation of jobs, even though such discrepancies could be justified by the high marginal product of the jobs if spent in the relatively few most responsive wards.

This principle of equal disrtibution is, of course, modified over time to take account of special circumstances. In some cases, that modification reflects an attempt to increase the party vote. Recently in Chicago, at least two ward leaders were able to appeal to the boss for more jobs, in effect on the grounds that the marginal product of such favors should be at least as high in their wards as elsewhere. But just as often, modifications of the principle of equal distribution have little to do with vote maximization. Some ward leaders are simply more powerful than others. This may be because they hold elective office and, by the formal powers attaching to that office, are in a position to bargain with the boss about issues in city politics. A city official, for example, who is legally endowed with the power to approve a proposed course of action can use the leverage gained thereby to bargain for more jobs. To be sure, as long as the boss is in command, he can check a rebellious ward leader by refusing to reslate him for his elective office, thereby ending his legal power to affect decisions. The ward leaders know this, and therefore use their bargaining resources cautiously (unless the boss, as in Manhattan, shows signs of weakness; then they will act with great vigor to improve their positions). But they are nonetheless able to influence the allocation of jobs at the margin, and since only a few ward leaders hold elective office, inequalities in the ability to earn patronage are created which have no necessary relation to the utility of patronage in producing votes.

Further, some ward leaders may be more powerful than others because they are important sources of party funds; they may have seniority and the confidence of other ward leaders who see in these more powerful men possible successors to the boss when the latter retires or is ousted; or they may be particularly skilful and thus able to control with some precision the votes of their citizens, thereby giving them more deliberate influence over those members of the party leadership who are running for office. Such ward leaders in Chicago are called the "Big Boys," and often their precedence is recognized by placing them on the select executive committee of the county political organization. Sometimes, as in New York, the formal rules of the party create inequalities. There, district leaders have different voting strengths in the councils of the party, ranging from one-sixth of a vote (in cases where the district has been subdivided and votes must be shared with other leaders as well as with one's female co-leader) to one full vote (in cases where the district has not been subdivided and where the female co-leader is completely under the control of the male leader).[7]

2. *Bargaining with elective officials.* In most American cities, the mayor lacks sufficient formal political power to accomplish his ends. The boss, even if he is also the mayor, must therefore overcome potential vetoes by assembling power informally. It is necessary that he do this in part because no city is composed exclusively of wards filled with

voters responsive to organization politics and the dispensation of favors. In addition to the "river wards" there are others, called in Chicago "newspaper wards" and in New York "silk-stocking" districts, which will respond much less, if at all, to the infusion of patronage.

Indeed, in some, citizens will be annoyed by the appearance of paid political workers at their door to solicit their vote, and outraged by any suggestion that they "sell" their votes. In such areas, patronage will have a negative marginal product. It will be costly in terms of votes.

If the boss were acting so as to maximize votes, he would take steps to insure that an alternative set of appeals were developed for wards which responded negatively to patronage. Not only would patronage be denied to the ward leaders in those areas, but the boss would dispense with the ward leader and his staff altogether. Their presence would be a conspicuous symbol of presumably evil machine politics. Instead, the boss might choose to work through existing neighborhood and civic organizations. Speakers with high prestige would be sent into the area to address meetings of these clubs. Elaborate statements of policy would be prepared and distributed. Debates would be arranged between candidates. Public issues in which articulate citizens in these wards were interested would be taken up and sponsored by the boss. Presumably, the wards which respond positively to patronage will be uninterested in substantive policies and issues, and thus advocating these programs will cost nothing in the river wards. In fact, of course, some such projects—for example, urban

[7] See Sayre and Kaufman, *op. cit.*, 136–37, on the practice of splitting leadership votes in Tammany Hall.

renewal or slum clearance—do affect the river wards considerably. When they do, some voters will complain and the programs may have to be modified.

If the boss feels it necessary to appeal strongly to the newspaper wards, he will have to spend his patronage resources heavily in bargaining with elected officials in order that desirable civic projects will be approved. This will divert resources from voter appeals in the river wards. Further, by weakening or destroying the organization in the newspaper wards, it will cause dissatisfaction in the machine. As a result, more resources will have to be diverted to mollifying this discontent and preventing rebellion. As a matter of fact, the extensive civic program undertaken by Mayor Daley in Chicago has had just this effect. River ward leaders have felt, quite rightly, that they were slighted.[8] Although spending patronage to overcome legal vetoes is, logically, compatible with vote maximization in some areas, among its consequences often are conditions which make the boss more concerned about maintaining his position. This is a result of the fact that he has two constituencies: the party constituency, which is most powerful in the river wards and on whom he is dependent for his position; and the electoral constituency, which is becoming larger outside the river wards and to which he must appeal for votes. Indeed, it is this latent incompatibility between constituencies which is the central problem for most party leaders, including those who are not machine bosses. There are few, if any, cases in which the appeals useful in holding the loyalty of party workers are the same as, or even compatible with, the appeals necessary to attract voters. In a machine, this is because newspaper wards usually outnumber river wards. In a party which relies on intangible appeals rather than patronage, it is because party activists often require more extreme commitments to principles or programs than will be tolerated by the more moderate and diverse electorate.[9]

3. *Maximizing the vote.* The boss will be in a position to act to maximize the vote of his party when his own position in the organization is relatively secure and when the formal centralization of power in the city government is such that little need be spent on paying officials not to veto the policies of the boss. Given the opportunity to make vote maximization his primary goal, the boss might wish to do so for a variety of motives. One of these often is a desire to improve his standing with his party nationally. By delivering a large vote to the ticket, the boss can become a man of power and prestige in the councils of his party and perhaps create an opportunity for elevation to higher office.

Under these conditions, the allocation of patronage to maximize the vote would logically be a straightforward problem. It would only be necessary for the boss to discover what the marginal return from patronage

---

[8] See James Q. Wilson, *Negro Politics: The Search for Leadership* (Glencoe, Ill.: Free Press, 1960), chap. iv.

[9] See Edward C. Banfield, *Political Influence* (Glencoe, Ill.: Free Press, 1961), for a discussion of the conflict between party and electoral constituencies in the Chicago machine.

is in each of the city's wards. Patronage would be spent in order to equalize its marginal product. Ideally, the last increment of patronage would produce the same number of additional votes no matter in which ward it was spent.[10]

Such a procedure would require that the boss have centralized control of patronage in his hands and that he be able to redistribute it at will. Both these conditions are in conflict with the use of patronage to maintain the boss's position in the organization. As indicated above, ward leaders resist marked inequities in patronage distribution. They would particularly oppose the pursuit of a goal that implies the possibility that some would receive very little patronage or even none at all.

It is often observed that "local party conditions" or "internecine warfare" prevents a city organization from giving full support to the national ticket. Such comments imply that the absence of full support is the exception. In fact, it is more nearly the rule. Giving all-out support to the national ticket is a luxury which only secure bosses with no other pressing demands on their resources can afford. Maintaining the organization locally comes first in every case. In addition, national

offices are either poor in patronage (as is the case with a congressman) or the ratio between effort required and probability of gain is excessively large (as is the case with the presidency). Local offices (such as state's attorney, sheriff, mayor, county clerk, or governor) are either richer in patronage than national offices or, if they are not richer, at least the likelihood of capturing them is more directly related to the machine's local efforts. An all-out campaign for the presidency by a city machine is often risky; defeat may easily be the result of factors over which the organization has no control (party organization elsewhere, national mood, unexpected dramatic events, etc.). Thus, even when it is legitimate to assume that the overriding goal of the party is to maximize the vote, one must carefully specify for which offices this hold true.

4. *Attracting workers.* Of all the functions of patronage, the one most likely to be compatible with vote maximization would presumably be its use to pay party workers. Incentives cannot be given to voters if there are no workers to distribute them. Even here, however, there are important limitations on the freedom of the boss to pursue the logically best course of action. Ideally, patronage would be used as an *incentive* to extract more work, rather than as a *reward* to compensate for past attainments. A worker who does well (who produces a high party vote) can be treated in one of two ways: he can be given a better-paying job and allowed to remain in the area where he did so well; or he can be given a better-paying job and then transferred to an area where the marginal product of additional

[10] Patronage may be spent in various ways: money can be given directly to the voter (either as a gift, a favor, or to hire him as an election-day worker), or the money can be used to place additional full-time, paid precinct workers in the area to canvass for votes, or both. For purposes of this analysis, it is not important which way the patronage is spent. In most city machines, money is spent in most wards to hire workers. It is of interest, but not crucial, to know how much work can be extracted from those hired before they cease to value the job.

increments of paid workers is higher and where his skills can therefore be put to better use. Ideally, in short, a system of transferals would be employed by the boss to test whether vote increases are the result simply of spending patronage or whether they are the result of spending patronage through particularly skilful workers. This transfer system would be modified to the extent that a worker's familiarity with his precinct is a condition of his success. Too frequent transfer would inhibit efficient political work. The boss must thus be constantly alert to vote losses that result from lack of familiarity with the neighborhood which cannot be offset by worker skill.

It is obvious that this "ideal" personnel system is not employed. The most valuable jobs are given to political workers in most cases as "rewards" and not as "incentives." The best workers are often given the best precincts—that is, precincts where maintaining a high vote level is not arduous—as well as the best jobs. New men or less skilful or energetic men are often assigned to the "tough" precincts, where the party's vote is low and where increasing it is laborious. Getting a "soft" precinct is frequently held to be one of the rewards of good work for the machine.[11] This means that if votes

in wards which are responsive to canvassing by paid workers are a function of the number of such workers modified by the skill of the workers (a variable of unknown magnitude), then the machine in reality does not test the productivity of its resources. Those resources are probably underutilized in any city organization because the task of maintaining the position of the boss and the ward leaders overrides the presumed goal of obtaining an optimal vote.

Other factors are also at work inhibiting the most efficient use of patronage. Some groups and individuals within the machine develop vested claims in their jobs. These claims may develop for a variety of reasons, but once they have been acknowledged, the machine must honor them to maintain confidence that machine commitments are reliable. Rules, promises, and agreements are essential to order; they must be maintained for their own value, even though the distribution of patronage which results is valueless in terms of producing votes. For the boss to concert activity toward common goals, individuals must have stable expectations as to the

---

[11] Relatively few precinct workers canvass their areas vigorously or frequently. Once they acquire a patronage job and become a member in good standing of the local political club or ward-headquarters, they often concern themselves more with the social and fraternal advantages of membership (getting away from the wife a few nights a week, playing cards with "the boys," and swapping political yarns). The club system in Manhattan seems to be more conducive to this kind of sociability than the ward-headquarters system in Chicago. But in both cases, precinct workers canvass principally their friends and a small group of voters who are well known and who can be relied upon. This renders most city machines very vulnerable to demographic changes which break up established contacts and introduce new elements into the neighborhood. The personnel management policies of a city machine would strike a corporate sales manager as notoriously lax and archaic. See Robert Heilbroner, "Carmine de Sapio: The Smile on the Face of the Tiger," *Harper's Magazine* (July, 1954), p. 30, for an account of the vulnerability of the Manhattan organization to "reform" challenges.

consequences of alternative courses of action. The "rule of law" is essential to the maintenance of the organization, and although the maintenance of the organization is in itself essential to maximizing the vote, the necessary means (in this case, the rule of law) may be antithetical to vote maximization because it compels the boss to recognize unproductive patronage commitments. These commitments may arise in various ways: (*a*) Ethnic groups may lay claim to particular jobs—that is, may assert that the job, once granted a member of that group, be always offered to a member of that group. (*b*) Individuals who have been rewarded by the party may seek to pass their position on to a person of their, rather than the party's, choice. Father-to-son bequests, in which a property right in the job is simply assumed to exist, are not unheard of. (*c*) Individuals to whom political debts are due require that those debts be honored. The party realizes it must honor them in order that future creditors will have confidence in the reliability of the party as a debtor. Often these debts are related to vote maximization—for example, a popular candidate of the opposition party (or of an opposition faction within the machine) may be induced to abandon elective politics in exchange for a valuable job. Just as frequently, such debts have little to do with vote maximization but arise instead from personnel problems or special services rendered within the organization. (*d*) Labor unions lay claim to certain categories of jobs as a condition of their support (in time, energy, and money). For example, plumbing inspectors are recruited from the plumbers' union, electrical inspectors from the electricians'

union, and so forth. No one can be certain what would be the consequences of withdrawing such jobs from the union or, what amounts to the same thing, of treating the holders of these jobs as if their only superiors were the machine leaders. It is unlikely, however, that the gain in votes from allotting jobs to labor leaders exceeds the opportunity costs of failing to spend those jobs in responsive wards.

The boss, even under the best of circumstances and disregarding the rigidities built into the patronage system by the factors mentioned above, can only redistribute patronage at the margin. A boss, on ascending to power, cannot call in all the chips and redistribute them. That he will not upset existing arrangements is typically a condition of his election as a leader. For example, when Richard J. Daley was chosen Democratic county leader in Chicago in 1955, he was not given carte blanche to reorganize the party to facilitate its recovery from the administration of Mayor Martin Kennelly, which had sharply reduced patronage and created factions within the organization. Rather, jobs are vacated and become available for redistribution at a certain rate. A vigorous boss will try to increase that rate by various expedients. In the first place, he will try to create new jobs. This requires new sources of revenue. In large American cities today, newspapers and civic associations place constraints on the boss in this respect. If no "newspaper" wards existed, he could ignore demands for economy, but newspaper wards invariably exist. Organized guardians of the civic purse will permit him to increase city expenditures through certain kinds of projects (for example, urban renewal, street-lighting, street-cleaning, building inspection, fire and police protection) but not through others (increasing the staffs of aldermen, multiplying executive secretariats, and hiring men to do jobs which machines can do better —such as operating elevators, sweeping streets, etc.). The problem is that the creation of new jobs is very expensive. Since new expenditures will be costly in votes in newspaper wards unless civically approved "end products" emerge, the goals of these expenditures must be accomplished. Further, many projects (such as urban renewal) which interest civic groups require a rather high level of technical expertise. Thus, the number of patronage jobs created by new expenditures is always far less than the total number of new jobs created. In the second place, the boss may try to form coalitions with the leaders of other political units (for example, the county or the state) whereby the boss contributes to electoral victory in return for additional jobs allotted him by his allies in the other jurisdictions. Diverting resources to accomplish the election of officials outside the city means, of course, that resources for electing officials within the city are reduced.[12] Whether the expected utility of the additional jobs will offset the diversion of city election resources is something which the boss can only estimate very imprecisely.

Finally, some patronage jobs are scarcely used for party purposes at all because the jobs are so unattractive (for example, unskilled highway laborers in a rural county) that the party must offer them to anyone who will take them. Thus, Professor Sorauf, in interviewing 123 of the 138 Republican highway workers in a rural Pennsylvania county, discovered that fewer than one-half the laborers had ever performed any party services either before or after their appointment with the exception of making a contribution to the party coffers, while almost all the supervisors ("caretakers") had campaigned. Indeed, fewer than half the laborers stated they had even voted a straight Republican ticket.[13]

III

It may be objected to this analysis that any act which is intended to maintain the organization is an act which will increase the capability of the organization to maximize its vote. In the long run, this is probably true for most political machines. The machine must replenish its stocks of incentives, and winning public offices which control these stocks is therefore essential (except in those cases where, in effect, the local organization is "subsidized" by gifts of patronage from higher levels of the party). The only response to this objection is that taking the long view collapses all the interesting questions and obscures the nature of the month-to-month, year-to-year problems which confront the party leader. At the most general level of analysis, to assume that the party

---

[12] This reduction in resources for city elections is usually less than that diverted to the county or state campaign because of the prevalence of straight-ticket voting. Usually, working for a slate is as easy as working for one candidate. This may not be true if the ticket is weak or if the party is particularly interested in one office which is notably rich in patronage.

---

[13] Sorauf, "State Patronage in a Rural County," *op. cit.*, 1048–50.

acts solely to maximize its vote to win office is satisfactory. But at the most general level, relatively few interesting or important hypotheses can be deduced from a model relying on such a motivational assumption. For the party to act as if vote maximization were its goal, it would have to be relieved of the necessity of hiring the contributions of essential actors—ward leaders, elective officials, and precinct workers. The prospect of winning an election would have to be a sufficient inducement for these contributors. Such a prospect would be sufficient only if one assumed that the party, as Downs states, is a "coalition"—a body of men who have certain ends in common and co-operate to attain them.[14] The point of this paper is that there are only certain conditions under which a party can act as a coalition; these conditions are usually only partially present, and sometimes they are not present at all.

I have, in effect, substituted an alternative model of the party machine. In this model, the machine, like most utilitarian organizations, exists primarily to satisfy the individual motives of the participants. All these participants have in common is the belief that, so long as it continues to be a source of valued rewards, the organization ought to be maintained.[15] In this sense, my

model is simlar to that proposed by Downs. In both cases, the operating principle is the same: reward the members. We differ in that in my model, the boss realizes that, to satisfy his followers and thereby maintain his own position as boss, he will have to seek several subsidiary ends, of which vote maximization is only one. The variety of goals arises from the fact that the boss needs to reward not only voters but ward leaders, precinct workers, and elective officials as well. The demands of each group are not always compatible with the demands of other groups, and thus resources (patronage) must be allocated among competing ends.

Since the general goal of organizational maintenance must be translated into at least four (and possibly more) operational goals, and since these ends are at least partially incompatible, it becomes difficult or impossible to predict how the boss will act *knowing only the assumptions of the model.* The extent to which he will act to maximize the party's vote (or, more generally, the party's probability of winning elections) will depend on his assessment of certain environmental factors (particularly his judgment as to the probability of obtaining a certain net income of resources) and of the "balance of power" obtaining within the machine itself.

---

[14] Downs, *op. cit.*, p. 24.

[15] The theory of organizations which underlies much of the foregoing analysis is derived from Peter B. Clark and James Q. Wilson, "Incentive Systems: A Theory of Organizations," *Administrative Science Quarterly*, Vol. V (September, 1961). The major premises of that theory are found in Chester I. Barnard, *The Functions of the Executive* (Cambridge, Mass.: Harvard University Press, 1938). Banfield's *Political Influence* is a recent study of politics in Chicago employing a theory of incentives and analyzing in particular the changes in incentive systems dictated by ecological and social changes. A more or less explicit application of this model is James Q. Wilson, "Two Negro Politicians: An Interpretation," *Midwest Journal of Political Science*, IV (November, 1960), 346–69.

The Daily Economist

EDUCATION

ECONOMICS OF THE UNIVERSITY

Expert says university long overdue for economic analysis. Creates model for others to apply to their own institutions.

By ALLAN M. CARTTER

There are few other commodities more eagerly sought, more haphazardly selected, more irrationally priced, more undervalued in the act of consuming it, more misleadingly represented by some producers, and more enjoyed by the labor force engaged in its production, than higher education. In this economic Wonderland it is not surprising that a theory of the university has not yet emerged, for things are only rarely what they seem and even the most selective colleges or universities bewail their limitations in detecting skim milk masquerading as cream. It is also not surprising that a paper should have been invited on this theme for this particular meeting, for few other economists since Veblen's delightful polemic on *The Higher Learning in America* have been more outspoken critics of educational folklore than the distinguished President-elect of the Association. Having had the signal fortune of being his colleague for a decade (but the more dubious fortune of being on the receiving end as one of his deans for the last four of those years), I am perhaps more acutely aware of the pitfalls of supposing to be a rational man in an intentionally irrational universe.

Some of our academic colleagues would deny the relevance of economic rationality to such a serious matter as education—economics is for the world of wheat, automation, and stock markets, they would argue, while higher education is the world of humane learning, scholarly inquiry, and freedom of the spirit. The "economics of the university," they would feel, is in the same category as positing the economics of the Church. As one of my theological friends once noted: "After all, Judas was the economist among the disciples, and look how that turned out!"

Somewhat surprisingly, until very recently economists have also treated the university as sacrosanct and have spent their energies looking out through its windows at the rest of the world instead of viewing their own natural habitat.[1] Perhaps fear-

---

[1] By contrast the sociologists have been less reticent, beginning with Logan Wilson's *The Academic Man* in 1942. Among the more interesting studies of the intellectual and social environment of academia are Paul Lazarsfeld's *The Academic Mind* (1958), T. Caplow and J. McGee, *Academic Marketplace* (1958), and David Riesman, *Constraint and Variety in American Education* (1958).

ing that a closer look would reveal an Augean Stable, they have spent thousands of man-years analyzing the behavior of business firms, financial entities, governments, households, trade-unions, entrepreneurs, and most any other variety of institution and have scarcely given a thought to that one with which they are most closely and dependently connected. In the light of developments of the last several years, one qualification should be added: we are at last developing a macroeconomic view of education,[2] but we have not even begun to develop a counterpart view of education analogous to the theory of the firm.

Before examining what it is that an economist might say about his own institution, let me suggest why so little has been done in the past. First, as academicians I think we have always felt that the university was misunderstood and undervalued by the world at large, and consequently that an uninformed public was safer than an informed one. We have carried this distrust of knowledge and distaste for public debate so far that we are content to be uninformed about our own institutions. Some professors even today believe that A.A.U.P. Committee Z has been too zealous (a few presidents think that is what the "Z" stands for) and has somehow committed a breach of good manners by discussing mundane salary matters in public.

Second, I believe many of us—perhaps less so economists than phi-losophers or classicists—fear that to study the university as an economic institution may ultimately result in the wholesale application of business procedures and principles to education. In an age of mass education and the burgeoning "multi-versity" there is a real danger of developing inflexible bureaucratic rules and formulae; and the scholar has some justification in holding to "a little rationality is a dangerous thing" philosophy.

Third, most university administrators in the seventy-five years ending with the recent war—and many even today—feel that matters of university finance, salaries, and even teaching loads are none of the faculty's business. This play-your-cards-close-to-your-chest attitude may arise for one of two reasons: because the president views himself in the role of employer and the faculty as employees, or because the president sees himself in the role of mediator, and to reveal too much to the faculty will commit him to a similar clean breast with the board of control. The latter view is certainly preferable to the former, although neither fosters informative research on the institution. It should be added, however, that the president may in effect be right (even if for the wrong reason), for too much information can fan the rivalries and petty jealousies which seem to breed particularly on college and small university campuses.

Finally, for a variety of reasons, existing data on educational institutions, even were it all to be freely available, is extremely poor. University accounting procedures are devised, not to show the health of an institution, but to satisfy trustees

---

[2] I refer here to the seminal work of Schultz, Harris, and Machlup among the more senior members of the profession, and of Becker, Bowen, and Weisbrod among the younger members.

and government auditors. Because universities rely on the largesse of philanthropy or state legislatures for capital needs, not only accounting provisions for replacement needs but the whole concept of depreciation and obsolescence tend to be absent. One ironic result is that despite fifteen years of persuasive argument the universities have never been able to convince the Congress that 20 percent overhead on grants and contracts is not pure profit, while an identical project with a business firm would safely allow 30 percent to 50 percent. The Office of Education has collected educational statistics for a century but cannot even provide information on the number of full-time-student equivalents in higher education today, much less the kind of cost data which would be of primary use to economists. Despite the rapid and continuing expansion of college enrollments, no one has done a real study of incremental costs, comparing, say, expansion of existing institutions versus the founding of new ones. One other example suggests the shocking state of the arts in analyzing the market for academic personnel. Most everyone has been making dire predictions about the shortage of faculty trained at the doctorate level. The N.E.A. studies since 1953 have indicated a sharp reduction in the percentage of new faculty with the Ph.D., and the Office of Education, the Fund for the Advancement of Education, the graduate deans, and some of the President's most important advisory groups have estimated the large cumulative deficits in the production of Ph.D.'s. Recent studies now suggest that over the last decade the percentage of teaching faculty holding

the doctorate has actually risen in the four-year colleges and universities from approximately 44 percent to 51 percent. There is much in our own house to put in order, and we may be in the embarassing position of having cried wolf when it was only a tabby cat, and thus being friendless if a real wolf appears.

Turning to the individual institution, the closest analogy one can draw between a university and a business firm is to picture the former as a firm producing multiple products. This "firm" operates under conditions of variable proportions, with cost interdependencies producing a strong incentive for vertical integration, particularly in a backward direction. That is to say, once one is committed to the production of Ph.D.'s, cost factors necessarily impose the adoption of undergraduate programs producing baccalaureates. The reverse has not been true in the past, for liberal arts colleges have not been driven by economic factors to integrate forward into university status. Prestige factors have occasionally brought this about, and judging from the postwar success of major universities in raising private endowments and attracting massive federal support, there may be emerging long-run economic factors which will entice more frequent attempts at forward integration. The movement of such colleges as Wesleyan, Dartmouth, Lawrence, and Reed towards full university status may indicate a new trend.

The evidence of the pressure for vertical integration is that no major graduate school today is without an undergraduate base with the single exception of the Rockefeller Institute (which is removed from financial constraints with an endowment equal to approximately $1 million per student). Clark, Johns Hopkins, and Chicago at one time or another attempted to be purely graduate institutions, but without success. It is self-evident that the additional investment and incremental costs of adding undergraduates to a graduate establishment are relatively low. Only minor additions are needed to library and laboratory facilities, dormitories are largely self-financing and not even necessary in an urban setting, and courses can be predominantly taught by advanced graduate students and junior nontenure faculty. To use an example on the last point, in 1962–63 instruction in the Faculty of Arts and Sciences at Harvard was provided by 1,103 individuals, 27 percent of whom were tenured faculty members, 21 percent were instructors and assistant professors, and 52 percent were part-time instructors. (These are numbers of persons, not full-time equivalents.)

The incremental cost of adding graduate programs to an existing undergraduate college are extremely high—or stated more correctly, are extremely high if quality programs are to be offered. Judging from the rash of institutions now beginning doctoral work, this is not self-evident, and forward integration is proceeding on some campuses despite the economics of the case. It is one thing for Michigan State, Duke, or Brandeis to become full-fledged universities overnight with fully adequate resources at hand; it is quite another for Melrose College and Omaha Normal (I hope these are fictitious names) to initiate doctoral programs willynilly. To cite one example which should give pause for thought,

there are today at least fifteen or twenty universities offering the Ph.D. in a variety of fields whose library holdings are less than 150,000 volumes—barely a creditable collection for a good small liberal arts college.

I once attempted a rough cost estimate for a private university which indicated yearly costs of approximately $900 for the first two undergraduate years, $1,300 for the upperclass years, and $2,700 for the graduate school. This report is probably still gathering dust in the files of some academic vice-president, for his reaction was: "Most interesting, but for Heaven's sake don't show it to the President or the Board!" Cost figures for a major state system a year or two ago were, if I remember correctly, $32 per credit hour for freshmen and sophomores, $45 for juniors and seniors, and $162 for graduate education. These are at least suggestive of differential cost levels and should raise two other warning flags. If we did, indeed, have accurate cost studies, I doubt we should any longer be able to tell the private university undergraduate that he pays only 35–40 percent of his educational costs. Tuition may be that proportion of total university expenditure, but I suspect the undergraduate comes close to paying the entire educational and general expense attributable to undergraduate education. And second, if the university costed out the graduate school of arts and sciences as it frequently does its schools of medicine and law, the deficit might be a source of extreme delight to our medical and legal brethren. If my suspicions are correct, the president who jealously protects the innocence of both his faculty and his board of control by permitting only fuzzy consolidated financial reports to see the light of day begins to take on the characteristics of wisdom and sanctity.

The economist is unlikely to make much headway in cost studies of individual institutions without the full support of the administration. Can he nevertheless make a contribution in studying such problems as optimum size, the relationship between cost and quality, the market for academic personnel, etc.? There are many fascinating questions in this realm, and issues of public policy demand answers even if imprecise ones. There are currently a number of centers where economists are engaged in research into various aspects of the economics of education: Schultz and Bowman at Chicago; Weisbrod and Hansen at Wisconsin; Bowen and Machlup at Princeton; Fein and Rivlin at Brookings; Hirsch and others at U.C.L.A.; Becker at Columbia; Harris at San Diego; and others too numerous to name. In the four short years since Schultz's presidential address to the A.E.A. meeting in St. Louis, the economics of education has become a popular enough subject to run the danger now of becoming fashionable.

To add one more center, such an interest has developed even in the citadel of college and university presidents—the American Council on Education. Our work to date has focused chiefly on the university sector, with particular attention to graduate education. Some preliminary research results may be of interest, since they bear closely on some of the above questions.

Members of the audience may have participated in a major survey conducted last spring evaluating quality in graduate education. Professors in thirty separate disciplines in the 106 largest universities were asked to rate the quality of graduate faculty in their respective fields in each institution, and also to judge the effectiveness of doctoral programs. We were fortunate in receiving nearly an 80 percent response to the 5,400 questionnaires. Although detailed results will be published next summer, a summary of findings for the most prestigious economics departments is given in Table 1.

One hundred seventy-three out of 219 economists receiving the questionnaire returned usable replies. Table 1 lists the first twenty departments in order by quality of faculty. Columns 3, 4, and 5 indicate the rank resulting from the judgments of department chairmen, distinguished senior scholars (who have never served as chairmen except in a temporary acting capacity), and knowledgeable junior scholars not more than ten years beyond the receipt of the Ph.D. Columns 6 through 9 show rankings as seen by respondents currently employed in four regions. Column 10 indicates the judgment of a small select panel of experts, including some past and present officers of this Association, editors of major economic journals, and others recognized for their scholarly attainments.

I am aware of the limitations of such subjective evaluations—that they are based only partly on firsthand knowledge, are influenced by hearsay, incorporate halo effects, are subject to time lags, etc. As one of our respondents quoted Dr. Johnson, "A compendium of gossip is still gossip." Despite some very real limitations, however, I believe such evaluations more clearly reflect repu-

TABLE 1
Ranking of Quality of Faculty for Leading Economics Departments, Spring 1964

Rank	Institution	Department Chairmen	Junior Scholars	Senior Scholars	East	Midwest	South	West	Expert Panel
(1)	(2)	(3)	(4)	(5)	(6)	(7)	(8)	(9)	(10)
1	Harvard	1	1	1	1	1	2	1	3
2	M.I.T.	1	1	2	3	2	1	2	1
3	Chicago	5	3	3	4	5	3	4	5
4	Yale	3	3	5	2	4	5	5	1
5	California (Berkeley)	7	5	4	5	3	4	3	6
6	Stanford	4	6	6	6	6	7	6	4
7	Princeton	6	7	7	7	7	6	7	7
8	Michigan	9	8	9	9	9	9	8	8
9	Columbia	9	9	8	8	12	8	11	11
10	Wisconsin	8	9	10	10	8	13	9	13
11	Minnesota	13	11	11	13	11	11	12	9
12	Northwestern	11	13	12	11	13	12	10	11
13	Carnegie Tech	12	12	14	11	10	10	19	9
14	Pennsylvania	14	15	13	14	15	16	13	13
15	Johns Hopkins	15	14	15	15	14	14	14	15
16	U.C.L.A.	19	16	16	18	16	15	15	15
17	Cornell	16	18	17	16	21	17	16	17
18	Duke	17	20	18	17	20	18	17	18
19	Purdue	17	19	19	18	17	26	17	20
20	Michigan State	21	23	22	24	19	25	20	24
173	Number of respondents in each category	41	59	73	65	49	35	24	13

tation and accomplishment than do such "objective" measures as number of books in the library, Nobel laureates on the faculty, Woodrow Wilson fellows enrolled, or dollars of research grants from government or foundations. The present study was designed to answer some of the criticisms of Keniston's study in 1957 and Hughes's studies in 1924 and 1934. Keniston used only chairmen, and Hughes used small select panels; the reader of the A.C.E. study will be able to give any weighting he wishes to the eight various subsamples.

Among the more interesting conclusions is the close correlation of ratings among the three ranks (particularly of the junior and senior raters), and the variance with the fifteen-member experts' panel. More detailed analysis of absolute scores than shown here would characterize the easterners as being uncharitable to everyone, including many of their own institutions. The westerners and southerners are most charitable to everyone, although most noticeably to themselves. The midwesterners play out their role of middlemen, showing the least regional bias. Most respondents also leaned over back-

TABLE 2
Top Ranking Economics Departments

Institution	Rank According to "Effectiveness of Doctoral Program"	Rank According to "Quality of Graduate Faculty"
M.I.T.	1	2
Harvard	2	1
Yale	3	4
Stanford	4	6
California (Berkeley)	5	5
Princeton	6	7
Chicago	7	3
Wisconsin	8	10
Michigan	9	8
Northwestern	10	12
Carnegie Tech.	11	13
Minnesota	12	11
Johns Hopkins	13	15
Columbia	14	9
Pennsylvania	15	14
Duke	16	18
Cornell	17	17
Purdue	18	19
U.C.L.A.	19	16
North Carolina (Chapel Hill)	20	21

ward in rating their present university attachment and their doctoral institution, rating their current department on the average 17 percent higher than outsiders did, and rating their doctoral alma mater 9 percent above the evaluation of non-alumni. If one were to assume that these differences reflected bias, not better informed judgments, and corrected for them, the top of the list would read M.I.T., Harvard, Yale, Chicago, etc.

Table 2 summarizes the results of a second question on the effectiveness of the doctoral program, where the respondent was asked to take into consideration the accessibility of the faculty, library and research facilities, quality of other students, the intellectual climate, curriculum, etc. In effect this asked where the informed respondent, knowing what he now knows, would go to study economics if he were starting over gain. The good small departments in private universities generally moved up the scale and the larger departments slipped. Chicago and Columbia show the most marked differences, for reasons which I shall let others interpret.

Table 3 compares the 1964 findings on faculty quality (combined scores) with the earlier Keniston and Hughes rankings. Whether or not one agrees with the precise rankings, the noticeable movements appear to be in keeping with what one knows of changes over time. Hopkins has declined relatively, particularly since 1957. M.I.T. has soared to the top. Columbia has gradually lost its commanding position of the 1920's, and Wisconsin is completing a cycle by

TABLE 3
Leading Economics Departments in 1924, 1957, and 1964

1924[a]	1957[b]	1964[c]
1. Harvard	Harvard	Harvard
2. Columbia	Chicago	M.I.T.
3. Chicago	Yale	Chicago
4. Wisconsin	Columbia	Yale
5. Yale	California	California
6. Johns Hopkins	Stanford	Stanford
7. Michigan	Princeton	Princeton
8. Pennsylvania	Johns Hopkins	Michigan
9. Illinois	Michigan	Columbia
10. Cornell	Minnesota	Wisconsin
11. Princeton	Northwestern	Minnesota
12. California	Duke	Northwestern
13. Minnesota	Wisconsin	Carnegie Tech.
14. Northwestern	Pennsylvania	Pennsylvania
15. Stanford	Cornell	Johns Hopkins
16.		U.C.L.A.
17.		Cornell
18.		Duke
19.		Purdue
20.		Michigan State

(Lines indicate a shift of more than two positions in rank order.)

[a] From Raymond M. Hughes Report to the Association of American Colleges, Jan., 1925. The results are summarized in *American Universities and Colleges*, 1st ed. (American Council on Education, 1928), and in the Keniston report.

[b] From Hayward Keniston, *Graduate Study and Research in the Arts and Sciences at the University of Pennsylvania* (University of Pennsylvania Press, 1959), Appendix.

[c] From Table 1 above.

climbing again after a sharp drop in the postwar period. (Yale can be thankful that no rating was done in the 1940's.) Most interesting is the relative stability of the top departments—a phenomenon peculiar to economics alone of the major disciplines studied. Between 1924 and 1957, Illinois dropped out of the first fifteen and Duke was added. In 1964, two institutions not included in previous studies, M.I.T. and Carnegie Tech, placed high on the list, but the same fourteen survivors of the "Class of '24" are still among the first seventeen (U.C.L.A. has bumped Duke for inclusion). By contrast, in a field such as botany, only seven of the original fifteen are still among the leaders today.

How can we make such quality ratings more than an interesting compendium of gossip? An economist might ask: What is the cost of quality? What are the economic constraints on improving quality? What degree of concentration exists in output, research support, fellowship funds, etc.? What is the relationship between quality and size? Is the concept of optimum size relevant to higher education? One brief paper cannot answer adequately these and the many other interesting related

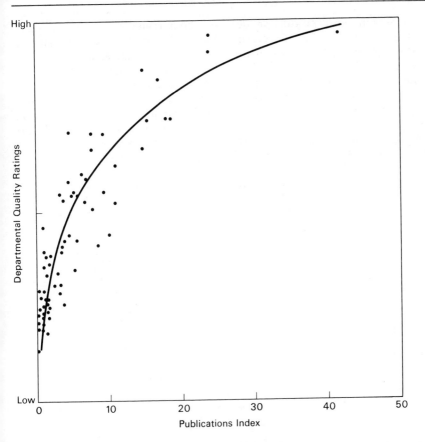

FIGURE 1 Publications Index and Quality of Graduate Faculty for 72 Leading Economics Departments, 1964

questions, but a few tentative conclusions will be suggested, and others will be included in the later publication of the study results.

First, the subjective ratings indicated above are closely correlated with the quantity of scholarly publications originating in the various departments. Figure 1 compares for economics the index of quality with a publications index. The latter is based on a count of all articles, communications, and book reviews appearing in six major nonspecialized economics journals and all books reviewed or noted in the *American Economic Review* during the period January, 1961, through June, 1964. Weights were assigned to various types of publications, counting a substantive book as 10, 3.3 for a textbook, 2.5 for an edited volume, 2.5 for substantive articles, 1 for notes and communications, and .5 for book reviews. In the case of joint authorship these scores were divided evenly among authors. Scholarly output, as measured by "article equivalents" per year in this index, is highly concentrated in a few institutions; the ten most productive departments accounted for 56 percent and the top twenty-five departments for nearly 90 percent of all publications reviewed. At the other extreme, about twenty-five of the seventy-two Ph.D. granting departments placed no more than a single article in these journals, and nearly a dozen departments accounted for not more than

one book review in nearly four years. Even allowing for the fact that it is easier to place an article in a reputable journal if one's address is Cambridge or Berkeley, the poorer departments were so unproductive that the President-elect of the Association, were he to be treated as a department all by himself, would have ranked thirty-seventh.

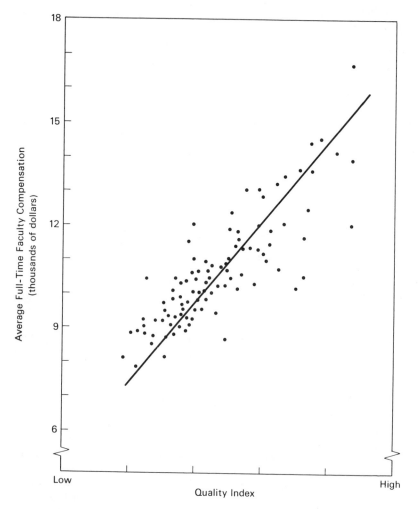

FIGURE 2   Average Faculty Compensation (A.A.U.P.) and Quality of Graduate Faculty of 97 Leading Universities, Spring, 1964

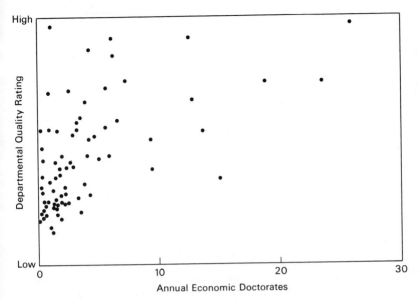

FIGURE 3 Average Annual Doctorates Awarded in Economics (1953–62) and Subjective Quality Ratings (1963–64) of 70 Leading Graduate Economics Departments

This evidence may lend support to Stigler's Law, which maintains that there are not more than fourteen really first-class scholars in any field of study.[3] The market being what it is, no single department can afford to hire them all, just as no single museum can afford to purchase all the Rembrandts. A department building around scholar number fifteen cannot hope to achieve distinction, says George Stigler, and the first fourteen men distribute themselves so that there are normally only a half dozen or so really outstanding departments. Fortunately, in our study Chicago emerged third in faculty quality, thus lending comfort to Stigler's plea for "selective eminence," and credence to the ob-jectivity of economists (most particularly since only 7 percent of those participating in the ratings are present faculty or former Ph.D.'s from that eminent institution).

A second conclusion I would offer is that quality is expensive, and that it is most closely correlated with the level of faculty salaries. Figure 2 illustrates this relationship by comparing average quality ratings for ninety-seven universities reporting A.A.U.P. faculty salary data. The coefficient of correlation is .872, and if we were to measure the elasticity of quality in response to salary level, the scatter would suggest a moderately high elasticity at low salary levels, diminishing as both salaries and quality rise.

Third, although there are obvious quality advantages associated with size, the actual correlation between

[3] George J. Stigler, *The Intellectual and the Marketplace* (Free Press of Glencoe, 1963).

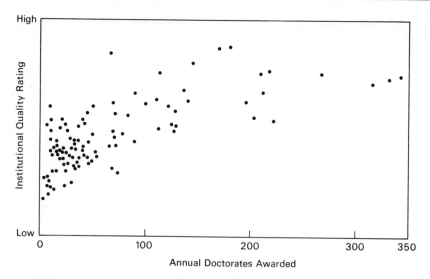

FIGURE 4   Average Annual Doctorates Awarded (1953–62) and Subjective Quality Ratings (1964) of 103 Leading Graduate Institutions

the two is rather poor. Two scatter diagrams indicate this, Figure 3 plotting annual doctorates awarded in economics during 1953–62 against quality rating, and Figure 4 plotting overall quality with total doctorates awarded. Economics is a particularly interesting case, since six institutions among the top half of the quality list produced less than ten Ph.D.'s in the last decade, while nine departments with twenty-five or more doctorates awarded in the decade were on the bottom half of the list.

Fourth, and perhaps most interesting, Figure 5 relates educational and general income per full-time student "unit" to overall size of institution.[4] For the top twenty-five universities in terms of quality there appear to be marked economies of scale; the scatter for all other universities in the study exhibits an almost precisely horizontal line of best fit. The latter supports the hypothesis that higher education, for the typical institution, tends to exhibit constancy of costs over a wide range of scale. The interesting study made by Russell and Reeves thirty years ago[5] —one of the few early educational studies which asked the kinds of questions an economist would like to pose—is probably still valid today, indicating that liberal arts colleges experience significant economies of scale up to an enrollment of about 1,000 to 1,500 and thereafter costs remain almost exactly constant per unit for any particular level of educational quality.

The theory of the firm is tradi-

[4] Full-time undergraduate students are the unit of measure. Graduate and professional students were counted as three units, and part-time students were converted to full-time equivalents by multiplying by .4.

[5] John Dale Russell and Floyd W. Reeves, *The Evaluation of Higher Institutions*, Vol. VII, *Finance* (University of Chicago Press, 1935).

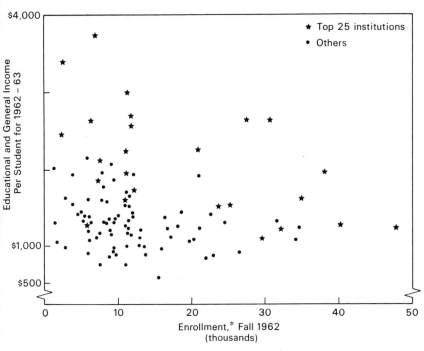

FIGURE 5   Educational and General Income per Student by Size of Enrollment

tionally two dimensional, dealing with quantity and cost (or price) assuming either a standardized product or a clearly differentiated one with a separate identifiable demand. Higher education pretends to produce certain standardized commodities (e.g., B.A.'s M.A.'s Ph.D.'s) but in fact qualitatively exhibits wide range and variety. Qualitative measures are becoming more common today in higher education, as studies of student test scores, fellowship data, institutional finance, and subjective ratings proliferate. These open new and interesting avenues for the economist in the study of higher education and may indeed help us to develop a more sophisticated economics of educational institutions. Howard Bowen's Committee of this Association looked at cost and size a few years ago.[6] I have concentrated on the relationship of quality to some cost factors (i.e., salaries) and to size as represented by degree production. Perhaps the study I have reported on above will be a useful tool in developing a more relevant three-dimensional model.

The present paper has hardly more than scratched the surface, but

[6] Report of the A.E.A. Committee on Graduate Education in Economics, *American Economic Review*, Sept., Pt. 2, 1953.

I hope it will encourage others to undertake research on that over-looked but fascinating institution—their own university.

THE DISTRIBUTION OF COSTS
AND DIRECT BENEFITS
OF PUBLIC HIGHER EDUCATION:
THE CASE OF CALIFORNIA

Subsidies for higher education on rise, but upper income families benefit most. Is California model for trend in U.S.?

By W. LEE HANSEN
and BURTON A. WEISBROD*

ABSTRACT

This paper explores the general nature of income redistribution effects of the financing of public higher education in California. The amount of available subsidy (full cost less student charges) varies dramatically among the three higher education systems—University, State College, and Junior College. Since eligibility for the higher-subsidy institutions is positively related to family income level, and since actual attendance among those eligible increases as family income rises, the result is that the distribution of subsidies actually favors upper income families.

These subsidies are then compared with total state and local taxes paid. The results show that families with children enrolled in public higher education receive positive net transfers (subsidy less taxes paid) and that these net transfers are an increasing fraction of average family money income.

The public higher education system in the United States provides—or, at least, offers—a public subsidy to young people of college age. The extent to which the young people actually receive the subsidy depends on (1) whether they can qualify for admission, (2) whether they avail themselves of the opportunity to attend, and (3), if they do, what quantity and quality of education they receive. As a result, the amount of subsidy received through the public financing of higher education varies greatly from one person to another. Our objective in this paper is to estimate (1) the amount of subsidies received through higher education, (2) the variation in subsidies received by students depending upon the amount of schooling and the kind of

---

* This paper is an extension of material contained in Chapter IV of our forthcoming book, *Benefits, Cost, and Finance of Public Higher Education* (Chicago: Markham Publishing Co., 1969). Hereinafter this volume is referred to as *Higher Education*.

schooling they obtain, and (3) the extent to which these subsidies are received in different amounts by students whose families are at different socioeconomic levels.[1] Attention is restricted to undergraduate education, and the data used are for public education in California. While higher educational systems differ among states, it would appear that the results for California are broadly characteristic of those for a number of other states.

A knowledge of the magnitude and distribution of subsidies or direct benefits provided through public higher education, or, indeed, through any public program, is important for what it suggests as to appropriate pricing, tax, and expenditure policy. By "appropriate" we mean policies that will be efficient, in the sense of doing the most to raise output, and at the same time equitable, in the sense of doing the most to achieve society's distribution goals, such as providing greater equality of opportunity for young people. We can illustrate some of the possibilities. For those "eligible" for higher education, uniform subsidies may provide a "windfall" to the more financially able while doing little to facilitate college attendance by the less well-off. This might argue for some kind of flexible pricing system in higher education, though much the same effect might be achieved less directly through the tax system. For those "not eligible" for public higher education, the provision of other kinds of subsidies or

direct-benefit programs may not only yield substantial societal benefits but also help to achieve greater equality, not only of educational opportunity but of opportunity in general.

SUBSIDIES STUDENTS CAN RECEIVE

The amounts of public higher education subsidies that can be received by college students are determined largely by the costs—instructional and capital—of providing instruction to them.[2] But, in addition, the number of years of instruction received is also relevant. Table 1 indicates how the amount of subsidies received will differ, given various assumed patterns of progression through the educational system in California—a state which, like many others, has three different higher education subsystems. First, the annual as well as the cumulative subsidy in each of the systems is shown (lines 1–6). Second, we have also attempted to show how these subsidies will vary, based on several assumed patterns of transfer from one type of institution to another (lines 7–12). The estimated subsidies at each of the three systems are the sums of average instructional and capital costs per student.[3]

The import of this table should be clear. For those people completing a four-year program, a subsidy of more than $7,100 can be received— but only by those students who qualify, on the basis of their high school records, for the University of California. Those who do not qualify can obtain a maximum subsidy of

[1] Little effort seems to have been given to this entire subject. For one interesting and perceptive foray, see Christopher Jencks, "Social Stratification and Mass Higher Education," *Harvard Education Review* (Spring 1968).

[2] We restrict our attention to undergraduate education.

[3] For additional detail and sources see Tables III-1, 2, and 3 in *Higher Education*.

TABLE 1

Public Higher Education Subsidies, by Type of Program and Years of Colleges Completed, 1965

Type of Program		Year of College			
		1	2	3	4
1. University of California–4 Years	Per year cost	$1,460	$1,460	$2,110	$2,110
2.	Cumulative cost	1,460	2,920	5,030	7,140
3. State Colleges–4 Years	Per year cost	1,350	1,350	1,550	1,550
4.	Cumulative cost	1,350	2,700	4,250	5,800
5. Junior Colleges–2 Years	Per year cost	720	720	—	—
6.	Cumulative cost	720	1,440	—	—
Junior College–2 Years, and					
7. University of California–2 Years	Per year cost	$ 720	$ 720	$2,110	$2,110
8.	Cumulative cost	720	1,440	3,550	5,660
State College–2 Years, and					
9. University of California–2 Years	Per year cost	1,350	1,350	2,110	2,110
10.	Cumulative cost	1,350	2,700	4,810	6,920
University of California–2 Years,					
and State College–2 Years					
11.	Per year cost	1,460	1,460	1,550	1,550
12.	Cumulative cost	1,460	2,920	4,470	6,020

SOURCE: Based on Tables III-1, III-2, and III-3, in *Higher Education.*

$5,800 at the State Colleges. And for those eligible only for the Junior Colleges, the maximum is $1,440, on the assumption that they do not later qualify for transfer to the State College system or the University of California. Therefore, depending on a student's "ability" level as determined by high school performance, the maximum amount of subsidy he can receive is fairly well determined.

SUBSIDIES STUDENTS DO RECEIVE

In reality, the matter is even more complex, however, because not all students proceed through an entire four-year course. A sizable number of students drop out at the end of each year, some for academic reasons and others for a variety of personal reasons. Thus, not everyone can or does choose to avail himself of the full amount of the subsidy for which he is potentially qualified. Equally

important, there are others who, through lack of interest in public higher education, receive no subsidy whatsoever. These are people who join the work force immediately, enter military service, decide not to go on to college for other reasons, or enroll in private colleges.

The actual distribution of subsidies received by students entering each of the various segments of higher education in California is rather difficult to determine, given the paucity of data on attrition and transfer patterns. On the basis of fragmentary data, however, the approximate patterns of progression are indicated in Table 2.

It is quite clear that attrition at the Junior College level is by far the highest, reflecting the fact that a number of its programs require only one year of schooling; that for some students Junior College provides a stepping stone to a State College or

TABLE 2

Estimated Progression Patterns Through Public Higher Education Systems in California, 1965

	Percent of Freshmen Entrants in Each System Completing Indicated Year of School								
	UC System			SC System			JC System		
Year of School	Non-transfer	Transfer to		Non-transfer	Transfer to		Non-transfer	Transfer to	
		SC	JC		UC	JC		UC	SC
1	85	—	—	80	—	—	70	—	—
2	70	5	—	60	—	—	30	—	—
3	60	4	—	55	8	—	—	2	8
4	55	3	—·	50	6	—	—	2	6

SOURCE: Based on a variety of published and unpublished data on patterns of student progression and transfer, as well as on oral conversations with experts on this subject. Subsequent to the preparation of this table and the analysis upon which it is based, we came upon some additional data on transfer patterns among systems; see Coordinating Council for Higher Education, *Feasibility and Desirability of Eliminating Lower Division Programs at Selected Campuses of the University of California and the California State Colleges* (mimeo), January 6, 1967 (this is a preliminary version of the report). The difference between the actual and our estimated patterns of transfer appear to be relatively minor and do not affect the general conclusions we have drawn.

TABLE 3
Estimated Distribution of All High School Graduates by Eligibility For Higher Education and by Type of Higher Education They Plan to Obtain

Eligibility	Plans to Attend by Type of Higher Education					
	UC	SC	JC	Other	None	All
University of California	5	4	5	3	2	19
State Colleges	—	2	8	2	4	17
Junior Colleges	—	—	31	4	26	64
All	5	6	44	9	32	100

SOURCE: Based on Coordinating Council for Higher Education, *Financial Assistance Programs*, 67–13 (Revised) October 31, 1967, Tables I-2 and I-3, pp. I-9 and I-10.

University campus; and that for others, Junior Colleges serve an important function of giving young people a chance to survey the opportunities better before rushing into a job choice.

The rate of attrition at the State Colleges is somewhat lower, and attrition at the University of California is the lowest, largely as a result of its greater selectivity in admissions. Its first-year attrition rate—15 percent—seems rather high, but the four-year completion rate of 55 percent is within the range for most other comparable four-year institutions. However, an additional 3 percent of the initial entrants to the University of California completed their work at a State College, and some others undoubtedly graduated from colleges outside the California system of public higher education.

What can we now say about the distribution of the subsidies to students eligible to enter each of the three different systems? The data in Table 3 attempt to answer this question by showing the distribution of all high school graduates by the percent who are eligible and who say they plan to enroll or not enroll at each type of college.

The extent to which students do not avail themselves of the opportunity to go to the "highest quality" (highest subsidy) college or university segment open to them is indicated by reading across each of the rows. Although 19 percent of all students are eligible for the University of California,[4] only 5 percent plan to enroll at a University campus, with 4 percent going to State Colleges, another 5 percent to Junior Colleges, 3 percent to other institutions, and 2 percent not expecting to enroll in any institution of higher education. Of those eligible for the State Colleges, approximately 2 out of 17 percent eligible plan to enroll, with another 8 percent going to the Junior Colleges, and 4 percent not enrolling at all. And, for the Junior Colleges, only half of the 64 percent eligible plan to enroll. Thus, only 55 percent of the total plan to enroll in public higher education.

Whatever their reasons, many high school students enroll at public institutions which are lower in presumed quality than those for which

---

[4] Note that these figures differ somewhat from other data on eligibility, as indicated by the Master Plan, for example.

they are eligible, with a sizable fraction of high school graduates not enrolling in any public institution whatsoever. Of these latter, however, it must be remembered that some go to private institutions in the state or to colleges out of state.

DISTRIBUTION OF AMOUNTS OF SUBSIDIES THROUGH HIGHER EDUCATION

We can now construct a rough distribution of the percentage of an age cohort of high school graduates who will receive different amounts of public subsidies for higher education. This is summarized in Table 4. The rather startling conclusion is that while a small proportion—9 percent—receives rather large subsidies, exceeding $5,000, more than half of California's young people receive under $750 in total subsidy from higher education. And a substantial fraction—41 percent—receives no subsidy at all. This group is divided between those who obtain no higher education whatsoever—

TABLE 4
Estimated Distribution of Public Subsidies for Higher Education Based on Amount Received During Period Enrolled

Amount of Subsidy	Percentage of Persons Receiving
0	41
$1–749	14
$750–1,999	30
$2,000–3,499	3
$3,500–4,999	3
$5,000–6,499	6
$6,500 +	3
	100

SOURCE: Developed from data in Tables 1, 2, and 3.

almost 80 percent—and those who plan to attend private colleges within California or colleges outside the state—about 20 percent.

In short, there is a highly unequal distribution in the amounts of public subsidies actually received, even though California prides itself on the wide access to higher education it provides and on the high enrollment ratios which are presumably a reflection of this. Moreover, there is little reason to believe that the distribution of public subsidies through the system of higher education is less unequal in other states than it is in California. No state has as widely accessible a junior college system as does California; thus, other states have larger proportions of young people who obtain no college education whatsoever.

DISTRIBUTION OF SUBSIDIES BY FAMILY INCOME

What can be said about the distribution of the subsidies provided through higher education in terms of the students' family income levels? While this is a somewhat more difficult question to answer with the available data, we have been able to restructure one set of data to shed light on this question.

It is useful, to begin with, to gain an idea of the patterns of college-going by level of family income. These are presented in Table 5, where columns 3–6 show the family income distributions for all California public college students in 1964, column 2 shows the income distribution for families without children in California public higher education, and column 1 shows the distribution for all California families.

The distributions by family income clearly differ among the groups shown. Median family incomes (see bottom row of table) are highest for parents of University students, followed by State College student families and Junior College student families. Lowest of all is the median for all families without children in the California system. These patterns are about what one might expect and, in general, conform to the patterns shown in other surveys.[5] Thus we conclude that access to subsidies is positively related to levels of family income, with the highest single-year subsidy going to UC students (and their families) who already have the highest (median) family incomes ($12,000).[6]

We can present some crude figures to illustrate the association of family income and subsidies received, by comparing median family incomes

for the groups shown in Table 5 with the amounts of the subsidies going to each of these groups. Table 6 presents this information, where median income of families of various types is shown in line 1, the one-year subsidy received is given in line 2a, and the subsidy as a percentage of family income is presented in line 2b. Because students first enrolling at each type of institution do not remain in college equally long, the average number of years they are enrolled is also shown, in line 3. The total subsidy received is shown in line 4a, and the percentage of family income that the subsidy constitutes is in line 4b. Because students transfer among the three higher education systems, the average subsidy is not simply the product of the average subsidy in a particular system and the average number of years of schooling obtained by students who *begin* their schooling in that system. As indicated by line 2b, the values of the single-year subsidies vary from zero percent of family income for those without children in public colleges and universities (some of these people may have children in private colleges or in public colleges not in California), to 14 percent of family income for those with State College enrollees. Whereas the average overall subsidy is equal to 9 percent of money income for all parents of publicly-enrolled college students (line 2b, column 3), the subsidy climbs to 18 percent of single-year family income when we take account of the number of years that the educational subsidy is received (line 4b, column 3). But because, as noted before, the amount of schooling received differs, the average total subsidies (line 4a) rise far more sharply than the single-

[5] For example, see the Wisconsin data in L. J. Lins, A. P. Abell, and D. R. Stucki, *Costs of Attendance and Income of Madison Campus Students, The University of Wisconsin, 1964–1965 Academic Year*, Office of Institutional Studies, January 1967; I. M. Boyak, A. P. Abell, and L. J. Lins, *Costs of Attendance and Income of University of Wisconsin–Milwaukee Students, 1964–1965 Academic Year*, Office of Institutional Studies, March 1967; and L. J. Lins, A. P. Abell, and R. Hammes, *Costs of Attendance and Income of University of Wisconsin Center Students, 1964–1965 Academic Year*, Office of Institutional Studies, May 1966.

[6] Were we to relate the data shown in Table 5 to the data on subsidies received over the entire college stay, the differences in the subsidies received would be accentuated. The reason is that University of California students are more likely to complete four years than are State College students, and the latter are more likely to complete four years than the vast bulk of the students who begin at Junior Colleges.

TABLE 5
Distributions of Families by Income Level and Type of College or University, California, 1964 (in percents)

Income Class	All Families	Families Without Children in California Public Higher Education	Families with Children in California Public Higher Education			
			Total	JC	SC	UC
	(1)	(2)	(3)	(4)	(5)	(6)
$0–3,999	16.1	17.0	6.6	8.1	4.1	5.0
$4,000–5,999	14.8	14.9	13.0	15.9	10.2	7.5
$6,000–7,999	18.9	19.0	17.6	19.6	17.0	11.1
$8,000–9,999	18.1	18.3	16.4	16.9	17.2	13.1
$10,000–11,999	12.4	12.1	15.8	14.4	19.9	13.3
$12,000–13,999	7.4	7.3	8.8	17.2	10.8	11.3
$14,000–19,999	7.9	7.5	13.0	11.1	13.0	20.3
$20,000–24,999	1.8	1.6	3.4	2.6	3.3	6.6
$25,000 +	2.6	2.3	5.4	4.2	4.5	11.8
Total	100.0%	100.0%	100.0%	100.0%	100.0%	100.0%
Median Income	$8,000	$7,900	$9,560	$8,800	$10,000	$12,000

SOURCE: Col. (1) Letter from Office of Legislative Analyst, California Legislature, in *Tuition for California's Public Institutions of Higher Education*, Joint Committee on Higher Education Hearings, October 13 and 16, 1967; see Tab T, Table 1.
Col. (2) Percentage distribution of Col. (2), calculated by authors.
Col. (3) Weighted average of Cols. (4), (5), and (6).
Col. (4), (5), (6) Edward Sanders and Hans Palmer, *The Financial Barrier to Higher Education in California* (Claremont: Pomona College, 1965), Table M, p. 21, which relates to distribution of parent-supported students only.

TABLE 6

Average Family Incomes and Average Higher Education Subsidies Received by Families, by Type of Institution Children Attend, California, 1964

	All Families	Families Without Children in California Public Higher Education	Families with Children in California Public Higher Education			
			Total	JC	SC	UC
	(1)	(2)	(3)	(4)	(5)	(6)
1. Average family income[a]	8,000	7,900	9,560	8,800	10,000	12,000
2. Average higher education subsidy per year[b]						
a. Amount in dollars	—	0	880	720	1,400	1,700
b. Percent of Line 1	—	0	9	8	14	13
3. Average number of years of higher education completed[c]	n.a.	n.a.	n.a.	1.2	2.6	2.8
4. Average total higher education subsidy[c]						
a. Amount in dollars	—	0	1,700	1,050	3,810	4,870
b. Percent of Line 1	—	0	18	12	31	41

[a] Median incomes from Table 5.

[b] Average subsidies are based on the distribution of enrollment by year of school and on distribution of enrollment by type of institution.

[c] Average number of years and average subsidies are based on the assumption that entering students progress through the various types of institutions shown in Table 2, that students are distributed among the various types of institutions as shown in Table 3, and that the various subsidies are those shown in Table 1. Because students transfer among the three higher education systems, the average subsidy shown in line 4a is not obtained simply by multiplying line 2a by line 3.

TABLE 7

Distribution of High School Graduates by Eligibility for Public
Higher Education in California, by Type of Education
and Family Income (in percents)

	Percentage Distribution of High School Graduates by Eligibility for	
	University of California	University of California and State Colleges
Family Income		
	(1)	(2)
$0–3,999	10.7	28.0
$4,000–5,999	11.5	26.3
$6,000–7,999	11.9	30.5
$8,000–9,999	16.2	33.2
$10,000–12,499	19.4	37.1
$12,500–14,999	22.5	39.8
$15,000–17,499	27.9	45.4
$17,500–19,999	29.5	45.1
$20,000–24,999	33.3	46.1
$25,000 +	40.1	54.3
Not reported	13.3	28.0
All	19.6	36.3

SOURCE: Based on data from CCHE, *Financial Assistance Programs*, 67–13 (Second Revision), October 31, 1967, Table I-2, p. I-9; Table I-3, p. I-10; and Appendix Table B-3.

NOTE: Excluded from the sample of 8,162 were 302 students planning vocational training, 38 nonrespondents on enrollment plans, and 20 for whom eligibility was indeterminate.

year subsidies, as we contrast the families with children enrolled in California Junior Colleges, State Colleges, and University campuses. These patterns of subsidies raise serious questions about the equity of the current system for financing public higher education in California.

At the same time, however, the distributions of students by parental income (as shown by each of the columns in Table 5) are so wide for each type of system—University of California, State College, and Junior College—that any strong conclusions about the "class-serving" nature of the entire system of higher education in California cannot be drawn. While there is a tendency for the

higher subsidy schools to draw a higher-income clientele, the overlap of the distributions is still very substantial.

Some added light can be thrown on the equity issue by a restructuring of recent data presented by the California Coordinating Council for Higher Education.[7] The data from several of its tables have been combined to show how eligibility and plans for higher education enrollment vary systematically with income.

---

[7] Coordinating Council for Higher Education, *Financial Assistance Programs*, 67–13 (Second Revision), October 31, 1967, Table I-2, p. I-9; Table I-3, p. I-10; and Appendix Table B-3.

TABLE 8
College Attendance Plans of California High School Graduates,
by Family Income and Higher Education Segment, 1966

Family Income Level	Percent of UC Eligibles Planning to Attend UC	Percent of UC–SC Eligibles Planning to Attend Either UC or SC	Percent of All California High School Graduates Planning to Enroll in UC, SC, or JC
	(1)	(2)	(3)
$0–3,999	30.4	22.5	53.1
$4,000–5,999	26.1	29.7	56.1
$6,000–7,999	23.4	28.1	56.3
$8,000–9,999	21.5	36.5	60.0
$10,000–12,499	25.3	32.6	62.0
$12,500–14,999	26.2	37.5	64.6
$15,000–17,499	26.9	32.1	63.4
$17,500–19,999	33.3	45.7	64.2
$20,000–24,999	45.4	52.0	68.2
$25,000 +	46.7	47.8	57.8
No response	30.5	30.1	47.9

SOURCE: Same as Table 7.
NOTE: UC (University of California); SC (State Colleges); JC (Junior Colleges).

We show in Table 7 the percentages of all graduating high school seniors eligible to attend the University of California, and the University and the State Colleges. Approximately 80 percent of the high school graduates do not qualify for the substantial University subsidies because of the academic entry requirements. Even more interesting is the fact that the percentage of all students qualifying for the University of California (column 1) rises quite dramatically by family income level—from about 10 percent in the lowest income bracket (under $4,000) to 40 percent in the highest (over $25,000). Thus, the correlation between high school achievement and family income—and all that it reflects—is startling indeed. This pattern persists as we widen our view to include those eligible for both the University and

State Colleges (column 2). But a close examination of the differences between the two columns shows that the percentage of those eligible only for the State College system is roughly constant at all income levels; thus, University eligibility requirements account largely for the unequal distribution of opportunity.

The extent to which family income influences the distribution of those eligible who *plan* to attend each level of higher education emerges from Table 8. For the University (column 1) a larger fraction of upper- than lower-income students plan to attend; the same holds for the combined University–State College system group (column 2); and the pattern continues—though in somewhat muted fashion—when we consider all high school graduates (column 3). Actually, these results

TABLE 9
Estimated Tax Burdens by Income Class, California, 1965

Adjusted Gross Income Class	State Taxes Only Per Family[a]	Effective State Tax Rate[b]	State and Local Taxes Per Family[c]	Effective State and Local Tax Rate[b]
	(1)	(2)	(3)	(4)
$0–3,999	$ 104	5.2	$ 474	23.7
$4,000–5,999	132	2.6	527	10.5
$6,000–7,999	161	2.3	576	8.2
$8,000–9,999	221	2.4	696	7.7
$10,000–11,999	301	2.7	833	7.6
$12,000–13,999	389	3.0	984	7.6
$14,000–19,999	539	3.2	1,228	7.2
$20,000–24,999	865	3.8	1,758	7.8
$25,000 +	2,767	5.5	4,093	8.2

SOURCES: Personal income, sales, cigarette and beverage taxes by income level were obtained from Letter from Office of Legislative Analyst, State of California in *Tuition for California's Public Institutions of Higher Education*, Joint Committee on Higher Education, Hearings, October 13 and 16, 1967; see Tab T, Table 1. State gasoline taxes and local property taxes were based on itemized tax deductions reported on state income tax returns, 1965, and summarized in Franchise Tax Board, *Annual Reports, 1965 and 1966*, Table 13. Local sales taxes were assumed to be distributed in the same manner as state sales taxes above. Since local sales tax revenues in 1965 equaled one-third of state sales tax revenues, this factor was applied to the estimated amount of state sales taxes in each income level.

[a] Personal income, states sales, cigarette, and alcoholic beverage taxes only.

[b] Taxes as a percent of estimated mean income of each income class. The mean of the highest income interval was arbitrarily assumed to be $50,000.

[c] State taxes include personal income, sales, cigarette, alcoholic beverage, and gasoline taxes. Local taxes include local sales and property taxes.

are somewhat deceptive since those eligible for a "higher" system can attend a "lower" system. Indeed, when we compare the percent of University-eligible students planning to attend one of the three public systems, we find that the proportion is fairly constant with respect to family income, at about 70 to 75 percent (these data are not shown in the accompanying tables). Much the same kind of pattern emerges for both the University and State College eligibles who plan to undertake higher education. The point, however, is that enrollment in a lower system—often dictated by family income considerations—implies a reduced level of subsidies.

WHO PAYS THE TAXES?

Having now shown the extent to which families in different income groups are awarded subsidies through the fiscal system by virtue of the provision of higher education, we turn in this section to develop estimates of the state taxes alone, and the combined state and local taxes, that are paid by families at each income level. The objective is to provide a basis for comparing the subsidies received with the tax payments made. Such information is essential in assessing the equity of the current methods of financing higher education in the State of California. Our approach is to estimate the

TABLE 10

Average Family Incomes, Average Higher Education Subsidies Received,
and Average State and Local Taxes Paid by Families, by Type
of Institution Children Attend in California, 1964

	All Families	Families Without Children in California Public Higher Education	Families with Children in California Public Higher Education			
			Total	J. C.	S. C.	U. C.
	(1)	(2)	(3)	(4)	(5)	(6)
1. Average family income[a]	8,000	7,900	9,560	8,800	10,000	12,000
2. Average higher education subsidy per year[b]	—	0	880	720	1,400	1,700
3. Average total state and local taxes paid[c]	620	650	740	680	770	910
4. Net transfer (Line 2—Line 3)	—	−650	+140	+40	+630	+790

[a] From Table 5.

[b] From Table 6.

[c] Total state and local tax rates from Table 9 were applied to the median incomes for families in each column.

incidence of the most important state and local taxes by family income level, so as to note the absolute amount of taxes paid at each income level. We can then compare this amount with the subsidy received and note any differences. But we still have no real way of determining how much of whatever taxes are paid reflect support for higher education, as against the many other services provided by state and local governments.

The average amount of taxes paid at each income level as well as the effective tax rate, for California state taxes alone and for state and local taxes combined, is shown in Table 9. The most important finding is that while the state tax structure (column 2) seems to be somewhat progressive —that is, the effective tax rate rises

with income—except in the lowest income classes, the combined state and local tax structure (column 4) is regressive below $8,000 and is essentially proportional above that level.[8]

We return now to our major task of this section which is to compare the amounts of taxes paid with the subsidies received by families with children enrolled in college, so that we can observe the extent to which broad groups of families do or do not receive net subsidies through higher education. In making such a comparison we once again remind the reader that this involves comparing *all* taxes with benefits received

---

[8] The recent changes in the California state income tax structure have increased, but only slightly, the over-all progressivity of the state tax structure.

from higher education *alone*. As shown by Table 10, the annual value of higher education subsidies (line 2) received by a family with a single child enrolled in a public college exceeds the total amount (line 3) of all state and local taxes they pay, by rather substantial amounts. On an over-all basis the average higher education subsidy is $880 per year (line 2, column 3), in contrast to total state and local taxes paid of $740 (line 3, column 3); this results in an annual net transfer of $140 from all taxpayers to parents of college students. But this average conceals wide differences by type of college. For families with a child at one of the State Colleges or one of the University campuses, the net transfers range from $670 to $810 per year. Meanwhile, however, families without children or with children not enrolled in public institutions of higher education receive no subsidy whatsoever, while they pay an average of $650 in state and local taxes. This is not to suggest that such families should pay no state and local taxes, for some may have benefited in the past, others may benefit in the future, and still others may have opted for more expensive nonpublic California higher education. In any event, as is evident from a comparison of line 4 and line 1, the current method of financing public higher education leads to a redistribution of income from lower to higher income families; indeed, there is very substantial progressivity in the resulting pattern of transfers.

CONCLUSION

The general nature of the redistributive effects of the current method of financing public higher education in California is clear. Some low-income persons have benefited handsomely from the availability of publicly-subsidized higher education. But on the whole, the effect of these subsidies is to promote greater rather than less inequality among people of various social and economic backgrounds, by making available substantial subsidies that lower income families are either not eligible for or cannot make use of because of other conditions and constraints associated with their income position. To overcome the effects of the present system would require a substantial overhaul of the pricing system in public higher education, a realignment of the tax structure, and/or a broadening of the eligibility base for public expenditure programs. With respect to the latter alternative, eligibility for public subsidies to young people might well be expanded so as to embrace all young people—not only those who go on to college but also those who opt for alternative ways of expanding their earning power, such as apprenticeship or on-the-job training, or even investments in businesses. In any case, it is clear that whatever the degree to which our current higher education programs are rooted in the search for equality of opportunity, the results still leave much to be desired.

INVESTING IN HUMAN CAPITAL

Rapid economic growth shown to be dependent on human resources. Health and education programs will boost GNP.

By BURTON A. WEISBROD*

I. INTRODUCTION

This paper is about people. It is also about productivity and growth of an economy. And it is about the proper role of government in a society devoted to using its limited physical and human resources wisely for the economic and social wellbeing of its people.

A nation's output of goods and services, and thus its capacity to raise living standards, is limited by its resources and by the state of technological knowledge regarding how to utilize them. Of the traditional triumvirate of resources—land, labor, and capital—only capital has been thought of generally as subject to significant and appropriate social control. Land is given by nature, while population and hence the labor supply have been considered to be determined by forces outside the economic system.

The state of technological knowledge, too, has been considered to be determined largely outside the economic system, except to the extent that resources were directed toward research and development. More-

over, knowledge is significant largely to the extent that it becomes embodied in resources—in the form of man-made capital.

With society's supply of land and labor and the state of the technological arts being largely beyond its control, society's ability to escape from mass poverty and to achieve wealth depends critically upon its success in accumulating capital—machinery, equipment, plant, and other man-made producers goods. If the stock of capital can be increased sufficiently, output and living standards can rise despite growing pressure of population on the fixed supply of land.

The trouble with this conventional if somewhat caricatured explanation of the economic growth process is that it fails to explain the growth in United States output in this century. Students of U.S. economic development have consistently concluded that increases in the stock of reproducible physical capital account for only half or less of the growth of our per capita output during this century. What accounts for the remainder?

There are a number of possible answers. Economies of scale may have permitted output to rise proportionately more than the increases in resources. *Improvements in the quality of capital goods* may have occurred without being reflected in

* Mr. Weisbrod is Professor of Economics and of Educational Policy Studies at The University of Wisconsin. This paper was originally prepared for the National Conference on Canadian Goals, Fredericton, September 9–12, 1964.

prices. *Improvements in techniques of organizing production,* which increased productive efficiency, may have taken place.

But an alternative and possibly the principal answer may be that the stock of total capital has grown much more rapidly than our conventional measures indicate. Capital may exist in intangible form, as well as in the tangible, traditional forms of factories and machines. Intangible capital may be embodied in people—in labor resources. This would constitute a hybrid class of productive resources—a combination of labor and capital which might be called "human capital." Studies of the sources of economic growth that have measured only changes in the stock of *physical* capital (plant and equipment) have been incomplete; they have neglected the growing investment in *human* capital.

The concept of human capital is actually an old one in which interest has been revived within the last decade. What may have been the first reference to the social value of a person as a special kind of capital asset was made by Sir William Petty in 1687. Concerned about the economic losses from the London plagues,. Petty estimated the value of an Englishman's production, the extra probability of his death if he remained in London, and the cost of transportation from the city. He then concluded that an expenditure to move people—and thereby to save lives—would indeed be a financially wise investment. The return would be eighty-four-fold!

Neither Petty then nor any of us now—even if *no* payoff had been found—would have advocated public disregard of health hazards. Yet the knowledge that an expenditure on relocation would actually be a profitable investment in human resources may reinforce the social resolve to take appropriate action.

Human capital represents resources which man has utilized to augment his personal productivity. Expenditures on information, labor mobility, health, education, and training all are capable of enhancing the productive capacity of a worker —his human capital. I would regard health and education as the two principal forms of expenditures on human capital, and I shall give attention to each. However, the discussion of health expenditures will be abbreviated, so that I can devote primary attention to education. For education is the area of human resource development in which we face today the most pressing issues of public policy, the greatest and most rapidly climbing demands upon the public purse, and the most challenging opportunities for farsighted social leadership.

In sections II and III, I will analyze private and social, monetary and non-monetary benefits from health and educational investments in human capital. Section IV will then draw some implications from the analysis—for over-all public policy with respect to investments in people, and particularly for investments in their education.

II. HEALTH AS AN INVESTMENT

A healthier worker is a more productive worker—absent less from the job and more productive and creative while on it. Substantial resources have been devoted in Canada and in the United States to improvements in health, and these have brought into being—among other benefits—a more effective labor force.

In the United States, total public and private expenditures on health and medical care have nearly doubled in the last eight years—soaring from less than $18 billion in 1955 to $34 billion in 1963. This represented an increase in the share of Gross National Product devoted to health from 4.7 percent to 6.0 percent. The rate of increase in Canada has been even more rapid. Between 1955 and 1961, the latest year for which I have located Canadian data, expenditures on health and medical care rose 90 percent, while in the United States they rose 63 percent. In the short space of those six years, Canada increased spending on health from 3.2 percent to 4.5 percent of its growing gross national product.

Life expectancies continue to inch upward, responding in part to these health expenditures. In Canada, life expectancy at birth is nearly five years greater today than it was only twenty years ago.

Thus, whereas we have traditionally referred to *expenditures* on health, we now must recognize that a substantial fraction of those expenditures are truly *investments*—in increased longevity and lifetime labor productivity, as well as in increased human happiness and decreased suffering. Moreover, *preventive* health expenditures can be doubly valuable investments. Not only may they reduce the incidence and production-cutting effects of disease, but by liberating labor and capital resources that are now devoted to *caring* for the victims of disease, they may permit these resources to add to the production of other goods and services.

Let me illustrate in specific terms the investment character of health expenditures. A half-dozen years ago I estimated the dollar value of productivity losses resulting from polio in the United States; it ran to at least $46 million per year.[1] This included production lost from the victims of the disease, as well as the cost of resources devoted to treating and caring for them. More recently I have estimated the cost of preventing these economic losses by immunizing everyone in the United States under age 35, and then immunizing the newborn each year. This massive attack would cost only some $27 million per year—a small price to pay for an annual return of $46 million.

At the aggregate level, data from the United States National Health Survey permit us to make a crude estimate of the potential production being lost because of ill health, and this loss is the as-yet-unrealized payoff from additional public or private investment in medical research and disease prevention, cure, and treatment. In the year ended June 30, 1962, approximately 400 million workdays were lost by employed people because of illness or injury, or six days per worker. This is a loss of more than 2 percent of total manpower available to the economy. And it takes no account of either premature deaths or the debilitating effects of illness and accidents for those who remain on the job, but with impaired efficiency.

I do not suggest that public policy decisions on whether to embark on health programs should rest solely

---

[1] *Economics of Public Health* (Philadelphia: University of Pennsylvania Press, 1961), p. 84.

TABLE 1
Sources of Funds for Medical and Health-Related Research,
United States, Selected Years, 1940–70

Years	Total, in millions of dollars	Share of Federal Government	
		In millions of dollars	Percentage
1940	45	3	7
1947	88	28	32
1957	397	186	47
1960	715	380	53
1970	2,300	1,610	70

SOURCES: 1940–60 are from U.S. Senate, Committee of Consultants on Medical Research to the Subcommittee on the Departments of Labor and Health, Education, and Welfare of the Committee on Appropriations, *Federal Support of Medical Research* (May 1960), p. 24; 1970 data are from unpublished projections developed for the Rockefeller Foundation Exploratory Study Report of the Ad Hoc Committee to Study Voluntary Health and Welfare Agencies. The federal government estimate of $1.6 billion is consistent with the Bureau of the Budget projections for 1970 expenditures by the National Institutes of Health: low estimate—$1.2 billion; medium—$1.3 billion; high—$2.0 billion. U.S. Bureau of the Budget, Special Study, *Ten-Year Projection of Federal Budget Expenditures* (1961), p. 48.

on their narrow economic "profitability" or contribution to economic growth. They should not. The point to be emphasized is that health programs may contribute handsomely to economic progress, *as well as* to the broader aspects of mankind's welfare. My research indicates that the United States has been paying a price of more than $700 million per year in economic costs of tuberculosis and over $2 billion per year in costs of cancer.[2] Better health often is very good business. The fact that national income accounts show essentially no health services under "investment" indicates the re-thinking of conventional practices that is needed.

While much of the benefit from improved health accrues directly to the persons affected, there are also important benefits to others in society. In the jargon of economists,

there are "external" benefits. Such external effects are particularly clear when contagious diseases are involved, for then the health of one person affects the health of others. They also exist in the form of benefits to employers, for whom a healthier labor force means less absenteeism and enhanced on-the-job productivity. And they exist in the form of benefits to taxpayers generally; for them a healthier population means, among other things, reduced needs for welfare payments to those whose illness has brought poverty. For all these reasons, there is a national stake in medical research too. New methods for disease prevention, and for treatment, cure, and rehabilitation of the ill, will often spread benefits throughout the society.

To some extent, the investment aspect of improved health is reflected through growing governmental support for medical and health-related research (see Table 1). There are,

[2] *Ibid.*, p. 83.

however, many and complex reasons for this support, only one of which is that better health "pays." Yet, when health program policies are being debated at high government levels, the economic aspects of improved health as an investment in human resources is playing an increasingly prominent role—a role which would be still greater, I would judge, if economists had contributed more to an understanding of the magnitudes of benefits from specific health programs. Nevertheless, the mere recognition of an investment component to health expenditures is itself a major step toward rational government decision-making.

III. EDUCATION AS AN INVESTMENT

Better health—resulting from expenditures on research, prevention, and care and from improved diets and more satisfactory housing—has surely contributed to economic growth by creating a more productive stock of human capital. But an even larger contributor has been education. Properly conceived, education produces a labor force that is more skilled, more adaptable to the needs of a changing economy, and more likely to develop the imaginative ideas, techniques, and products which are critical to the processes of economic expansion and social adaptation to change. By doing so—by contributing to worker productivity —the education process qualifies handsomely as a process of investment in human capital.

The increasing level of formal education among the U.S. labor force has been continuous and sizeable. In 1940, the male labor force aged 18–64 averaged (a median of) 7.7 years of schooling. By 1952 it averaged 10.6 years, and by 1962, 12.1 years, somewhat more than a completed high school education.[3] In Canada, the educational investments embodied in the male labor force have also been rising, more modestly, from 7.6 to 7.8 years between 1941 and 1951,[4] but more rapidly, to around 8.5 years or more, between 1951 and 1961.[5]

The value of education, like the value of all forms of investments in people, is far more than financial. Education is a vital segment of the full life. Still, while we attach great significance to the cultural value of education, public policy toward higher education has apparently emphasized more pragmatic aspects of education, at least in the United States. In an excellent recent monograph, Alice M. Rivlin traces the history of federal legislation affecting higher education in the United States.[6] She finds that, in case after case, beginning as long ago as 1785, federal legislation ostensibly designed to aid higher education actually had more practical objectives, such as aid to farmers (land grants for establishing agricultural universities) and reduction of unemployment (college-classroom construction

---

[3] U.S. Department of Labor, "Educational Attainment of Workers, March 1962," Special Labor Force Report No. 30 (1963), p. A–5.

[4] *Statistical Review of Canadian Education, Census* (1951), p. 69.

[5] Estimated from data in the 1961 *Census of Canada, Labour Force*, Bulletin 3.1–13, pp. 19–1, 2.

[6] *The Role of the Federal Government in Financing Higher Education* (Washington: Brookings Institution, 1961).

in the 1930's). Citizens, or at least legislators, seem to have demanded consistently some evidence that the support of higher education is a profitable investment.

The National Defense Education Act—involving substantial loans, grants, and fellowships—may have signaled the beginning of a new era in which higher education *in general*—not merely those parts which have narrowly practical value—is receiving public attention and support. Yet efforts by economists to determine the financial returns from education in general and the contribution of education to economic growth may be interpreted as attempts to discover whether this new attitude toward higher education is justified on narrow financial grounds. The final verdict is not yet in.

But the growth of expenditures on education continues. Public education expenditures in the U.S. climbed above $24 billion in 1963, from $10 billion only a decade earlier.[7] Since 1900, total expenditures on education in the United States have increased four times as rapidly as total expenditures on physical plant and equipment; in 1900, education expenditures were only 9 percent of investment in plant and equipment, but by 1956, they were 34 percent,[8] and now they are 37 percent.

In analyzing the economic value of education, it is useful to view education as an industry—a user of re-

sources and a producer of outputs. An economy has limited resources and cannot produce all the goods and services we would like to have. Therefore, efforts should be expanded to identify and to measure the values of the education industry's outputs, as well as the costs of all the resources it uses. It is not enough to exhort the virtues of education. While some urge that education merits added support, others press for more resources for health, while still others are urging the expansion of efforts to improve diets or housing, or construct more parks or wider and safer highways.

Unhappily, we must make choices. If they are made without recognition of the full benefits and costs of alternative uses of resources, we are not likely to choose wisely. Within this context, the following sections are devoted to what is known, and to what is not known, about the forms and magnitude of benefits from educational investments in human resources. Private and public benefits will be examined.

By "benefits" of education I mean any of three types of effects: those that increase production possibilities, such as increased labor skills; those that reduce costs and thereby make resources available for more productive uses, such as the reduced crime and law enforcement needs that education may bring by enhancing earnings; and those that increase welfare possibilities directly, such as development of public-spiritedness or social consciousness.

Private Benefits from Education

Direct economic gains to individuals from education are sizeable.

[7] U.S. Department of Health, Education, and Welfare, *Health, Education, and Welfare Trends, 1963* (Washington: GPO, 1963), p. 60.

[8] T. W. Schultz, "Capital Formation by Education," *Journal of Political Economy*, LXVIII (December 1960), p. 583.

TABLE 2
Income and Unemployment by Years of Schooling Completed
in the United States

Years of Schooling Completed	Median Income Males, Age 25 and Over 1959	Unemployment Rate March 1962 (percent)
Elementary:		
8 years	$3,892	7.2
High School:		
1-3 years	4,846	8.3
4 years	5,441	5.1
College:		
1-3 years	5,978	3.7
4 years	7,388	1.5

SOURCES: *U.S. Census, 1960;* and U.S. Department of Labor.

TABLE 3
Income and Unemployment by Level of Education in Canada

Level of Educational Attainment	Income Distribution 1959				Unemployment Rate February 1960 (percent)
	Under $3,000	$3,000– 5,000	$5,000– 10,000	$10,000 & over	
Did not finish primary school	43	33	22	2	18.7
Finished primary but not secondary school	24	34	37	5	8.0
Finished secondary school or better	20	23	42	15	2.7

SOURCE: Dominion Bureau of Statistics.

Two measures of these gains are the greater incomes and the smaller unemployment rates which added schooling seems to bring. Data for both the United States and Canada (Tables 2 and 3) present similar and impressive pictures of the favorable relationships between an individual's educational attainment, his subsequent income, and the prospects for his unemployment.

But let me digress with some words of caution. With reference to the income-education relationship, it is probably not true that the high school dropout in the United States, for example, could increase his annual income from around $4,800 to $5,400 (Table 2), if only he would complete high school. We frequently forget the selection process by which some young people complete more schooling than others. In general, those students who do not drop out are more able, more ambitious, more anxious to learn, and come from families with better job "connections"—all of which assist in lifting their incomes. We cannot be sure how much of the additional incomes associated with additional education is attributable to these factors, and how much is attributable to the schooling itself. The monetary returns from investment in education are doubtless noteworthy, but they are probably not as large as the data in Tables 2 and 3 suggest.

Caution is also required in interpreting the dramatic data on unemployment rates in Tables 2 and 3. It is not unusual to find young people being advised not to quit school partly on the ground that their chances of being unemployed would be reduced if they remained. This approach is too simple. If, by the wave of a magic wand, the entire U.S. labor force could have been endowed with a college education, would the over-all unemployment rate of 6.0 percent in March 1962 have been reduced to only 1.5 percent (Table 2)—the rate for college graduates? I think not.

Education alone does not create jobs. It can, however, help cut unemployment by enhancing the matchability of labor-force skills with employer needs. When the task is attaining and maintaining full employment, education is not an adequate substitute for effective government fiscal and monetary policies and high levels of consumer and business demand. However, it is a valuable complement. Let us not expect too much from education, particularly in the short run. Its economic value lies primarily in its contribution to individual's productive *potential*, rather than in its contribution to the economy's success in achieving that potential.

Having digressed to point up the dangers of over-stating gross economic benefits from education, let me also note that there are important costs as well as benefits of education to students and their families. Costs include more than cash pay-

ments. They also include the earnings and production *foregone* because potentially productive people are in school (or in the hospital or physician's office in the case of investments in health), instead of on the job. In fact, a recent estimate for the United States indicates that the costs of high school and college education in the form of foregone income exceed by more than 50 percent the costs incurred directly by the schools.[9]

Still, when *all* costs are considered, and when an allowance is made for the non-educational factors affecting schooling, our best available evidence for the United States is that formal education does pay in the direct form of enhanced employment opportunities and, thus, of greater incomes. Education is an investment which produces at least as great a financial return as does investment in corporate enterprise—around 10 percent for college, and even more for high school and elementary school.[10]

But the profitability of education does not rest alone on its productivity-increasing or money-income-increasing effects. Some of the value of education accrues to the individual in other forms. The fruits of literacy—an output of elementary education—include the value of its non-market use. Thus, to cite an illustration which closely touches many of us, if a man prepares his

[9] *Ibid.*, p. 580.

[10] Estimates by G. S. Becker, as reported in T. W. Schultz, "Education and Economic Growth," in *Social Forces Influencing American Education* (Chicago: National Society for the Study of Education, 1961), p. 78. See also G. S. Becker, *Human Capital* (New York: National Bureau of Economic Research, 1964).

own income tax return, he performs a service made possible by his literacy. Were this service provided through the market, it would be priced and included in national income. Assuming that 50 million of the 60 million personal income tax returns being filed each year in the United States are prepared by the taxpayer himself, at a value of $5 per return, a rough estimate of the annual market value of the tax return services performed by taxpayers for themselves is $250 million. Obviously, this is only one minor form of return from literacy. But it is in addition to the benefits from elementary education which accrue in money form.

Social Benefits from Education

If students were the only beneficiaries of schooling, the broad public support for education would probably wither. But as valuable as education is privately, it is even more valuable publicly. Its benefits take diverse forms which extend well beyond the individuals who receive it.

For one thing, education has an important intergenerational value.[11] When today's students reach adulthood, their children will gain by virtue of the informal education received at home. Much learning takes place at home, where the child's attitude toward school is also largely shaped. Better educated parents are more likely to raise children who recognize the value of education, in terms of job opportunities, as well as in terms of cultural opportunities.

This means that the social value of educating women is not zero, even if they never enter the labor force to utilize the skills developed in school. It is a mistake to say that education has value to society only when additional earnings and *marketable* production result. If we think of an "investment" as involving future as distinguished from current returns, then education has an investment component in the form of these intergeneration benefits.[12]

Another group of beneficiaries from education is employers, who have a financial interest in the education and training of their employees. An employer's job would be much more difficult and expensive if he had to work with an illiterate and untrained labor force or had to educate and train his own workers.

Education also affects taxpayers in general, who pay—directly or indirectly—for the consequences of the lack of education. For example, insofar as lack of education leads to employment difficulties and crime, the costs of crime prevention, law enforcement, and social unrest—with the related welfare costs—will tend to be high.

These costs, however, may not fall upon taxpayers in the community or area having responsibility for the child's education. The migration of poorly educated people whose behavior patterns and educational attainments differ greatly from those prevailing in the areas they migrate to may necessitate additional effort and

---

[11] W. J. Swift and B. A. Weisbrod, "On the Monetary Value of Education's Intergeneration Benefits," *Journal of Political Economy*, LXXIII (December 1965), pp. 643–49.

[12] Tax implications of the existence of intertemporal education returns have been discussed by R. Goode, "Educational Expenditures and the Income Tax," in S. J. Mushkin, ed., *Economics of Higher Education* (Washington: GPO, 1962).

expense to permit the migrants to adjust to the new school conditions,[13] if they are children, or to the new social and economic conditions, if they are adults. Thus, *residents of areas of in-migration have a stake in the education of children in the areas of out-migration.* People in the U.S. North have a stake in education in the South. People in Ontario and British Columbia have a stake in education in the maritime provinces. In general, people who are or may be in the same fiscal unit with an individual have a financial stake in the investment in his human capital.

The nation as a whole reaps a return from education through the process of economic growth. In an important study of *The Sources of Economic Growth in the United States,* Edward Denison estimated that 21 percent of the growth of real national income per person employed between 1929 and 1957 was attributable to the greater education of the labor force, while another 36 percent was attributable to the "advance of knowledge," much of which is associated with educational advance.

BROAD SOCIAL BENEFITS. We have seen that some of the social benefits from education are enjoyed by individuals and groups that are reasonably identifiable. But some of the benefits are distributed so broadly that the nature of specific benefici-

aries is obscure. These general social benefits are not less important by virtue of their pervasiveness.

For example, literacy is of value not only to the individual possessing it and to employers, but to the entire society. Without widespread literacy, the significance of books, newspapers, and similar information media would dwindle; and it seems fair to say that the communication of information is of vital importance to the maintenance of competition and, indeed, to the existence of a market economy, as well as to the maintenance of political democracy.

Education is, after all, much more than a means of raising productivity or otherwise bringing financial returns. It is also a means of inculcating children with standards of socially desirable attitudes and behavior and of introducing children to new opportunities and challenges. In a free society, it helps to develop greater awareness of, and ability to participate effectively in, the democratic process.

No statistics can be marshalled to "prove" that education itself brings about a stronger democracy, but the relationships between people's educational attainments and their participation in activities that help make a democracy strong are striking. For one thing, education appears to develop in people a sense of citizen duty. Measuring attitudes toward the importance of voting on a five-level scale,[14] interviewers from

[13] See, for example, C. F. Schmid, V. A. Miller, and B. Abu-Laban, "Impact of Recent Negro Migration on Seattle Schools," in *International Population Conference Papers* (Vienna: Union International pour l'étude scientifique de la population, 1959), pp. 674–83.

[14] V. O. Key, Jr., *Public Opinion and American Democracy* (New York: Knopf, 1961), pp. 324–25; Angus Campbell, Gerald Gurin, and Warren Miller, *The Voter Decides* (White Plains; Row, Peterson, 1954), pp. 194–99.

TABLE 4
Percentage of the Population Voting for President of the United States in the 1952 and 1956 Elections, by Age, Education, Sex, and Region

Age and Sex	Non-South			South		
	Grade School	High School	College	Grade School	High School	College
Less than 34						
Male	60% (52)	78% (175)	88% (81)	19% (32)	55% (69)	81% (32)
Female	44 (55)	73 (285)	90 (90)	13 (47)	41 (111)	74 (23)
34–54						
Male	80 (156)	87 (222)	96 (103)	55 (87)	80 (54)	88 (33)
Female	71 (170)	85 (312)	91 (85)	22 (97)	56 (86)	82 (38)
55 and over						
Male	87 (179)	93 (96)	100 (31)	63 (72)	71 (21)	82 (11)
Female	71 (173)	91 (126)	93 (30)	31 (75)	58 (33)	86 (22)

SOURCE: A. Campbell, W. Miller, P. Converse, and D. Stokes, *The American Voter* (New York: John Wiley, 1960), Table 17–11, p. 495. See also Table 17–2, p. 478.

NOTE: Sample sizes are in parentheses.

the Survey Research Center of the University of Michigan found that only 25 percent of the grade school graduates were classified in the top level, while 50 percent of the high school graduates and 60 percent of the college graduates achieved it. None of the college graduates was in the bottom level, though 2 percent of the high school graduates and 12 percent of the grade school graduates were.[15] Similarly, favorable effects of education have been found in its relationship with the degree of political participation. Moreover, as Table 4 shows, the percentage of persons who actually do vote increases with educational attainment.

A positive relationship between voter participation and education

was also found in my own analysis.[16] Data on voter participation in the 1952 presidential election for each of the 48 states were correlated with (1) the median years of education of the population 25 years of age and older, for 1950, and (2) the percentage of the state population which was urban. The latter variable was included to isolate the presumably greater difficulty of voting in rural areas. The results indicated that schooling explained 42 percent of the interstate variation in voter participation. And when the percentage of population urbanized was held constant, it was found that 61 percent of the interstate variance not explained by urbanization was explained by schooling.

The brevity of this discussion does an injustice to the important and sometimes subtle ways that educa-

[15] Key, *op. cit.*, Table 13.3, p. 325. These data were compiled from Survey Research Center studies in 1952 and 1956. See Campbell *et al.*, *op. cit.*, Table B.2, p. 197; and A. Campbell, W. Miller, P. Converse, and D. Stokes, *The American Voter* (New York: John Wiley, 1960), Table 17–5, p. 480.

[16] *External Benefits of Public Education* (Princeton: Princeton University, Industrial Relations Section, 1964), pp. 96, 98.

tion strengthens democratic institutions. No attempt has been made here to be thorough in an area where economists probably have little to contribute. Instead, the objective has been simply to recognize the fact that some—and possibly the most important—forms of social benefits from education may defy monetary valuation.

RECAPITULATION. We have found that the social benefits from education take many forms and accrue widely through time and space. Some of the benefits from education —and much of what has been said about education also applies to health and other forms of human investments—are not realized by people in the area which financed the investment. Because the location of gains from some human-resource investments are determined by population movement, the process of migration is a process of spatial shifting of those gains. This produces not only an interstate or interprovincial stake in effective policies of human-resource development, but an international stake as well.

The diversity and complex diffusion of benefits from investments in human capital raise important issues as to how education should be financed and what role government should play generally in the development of human resources.

IV. PUBLIC POLICY FOR EDUCATIONAL INVESTMENT IN HUMAN CAPITAL

The education system produces many forms of benefits. Some interesting issues arise, once we recognize that there are external benefits from education (and better health)—benefits to people other than the immediate recipients. For one principle of financing expenditures is that those who benefit from some expenditure should pay for it. Even a partial use of this taxation principle would call for attempts to identify various groups of direct and indirect beneficiaries from investments in human capital and to assess charges in recognition of the distribution of benefits. I do not mean to suggest that the benefit principle should necessarily prevail in financing investments in human capital. However, since many benefits from education are very broadly dispersed, the application of this principle would, in fact, require broad financial support for education and other such investments.

This paper has underscored the need for social recognition of the process of human-resource investment. The previous pages have developed the views that education and health are not merely consumer-type expenditures, but are investments in human-resource productivity; and that benefits from these investments do not merely accrue just to the persons in whom they are made, but extend to other persons as well. Now it is appropriate to focus attention on the responsibility of government in this area.

To begin with, there would be a significant role for government in the human resource field, even if there were no external benefits— even if all benefits accrued to the individual. One reason is that, with particular respect to education, important decisions are made by young people, who may be poor judges of their long-term interests. Dropping out of high school may seem wise to a youth impatient to increase his earnings, but the wisdom of the decision becomes less obvious with the passage of time.

Of course, additional schooling is of value only to those who have the requisite ability and attitude toward learning. There may be little that society can do about a student's ability, but it may be able to shape his attitude toward schooling. This is the goal of many contemporary programs to prevent high school dropouts, in which well-trained guidance counselors can play an especially vital role. And *government has a responsibility to see that, through counselors and otherwise, people are fully informed about the long-run benefits from education, health, and other forms of investments in people.*

A second reason for public concern about the adequacy of private investment in human resources involves the ability of individuals to finance these investments. In education, a proper student attitude and the necessary intellectual ability are not sufficient; financial ability is also required. The costs of obtaining adequate education and health rations their use among low-income families. With respect to schooling, this would be true even if education, from elementary school through university, were "free." As noted above, much of the real cost of schooling is not the out-of-pocket expense, but the income lost by the student. In a poor family, the immediate pressure upon the youngster to augment family income—foregoing investments in his own human capital, if need be—may be enormous.

To some extent, the financial

hurdles to private investments in human capital by low-income persons can be overcome by borrowing. But one should not forget the real obstacles to obtaining a loan for educational purposes through the private market. The capital market conventionally provides loans for the purchases of tangible assets which, if necessary, can be taken over by the lender. Loans for education and for other forms of investment in human capital have a special characteristic. The fruits they produce are intangible—they are embodied in people. Therefore, the asset cannot be attached by an unsatisfied lender. This fact limits the availability of private loans for financing education or other human capital investments. *Government can help to overcome limitations in the private capital market through programs of direct aid, loans, and guarantees of private loans to facilitate investment in people.*

But government responsibility surpasses the need to improve capital markets and provide counseling. It must help the nation to recognize that the benefits to *society as a whole* which result from investment in human resources exceed the direct benefits to the *individual* in whom the investment is made. It must help the nation to recognize that a society bent on economic growth—on raising living standards and erasing poverty—is a society committed to change; and change requires a creative, adaptable, and efficient labor force capable of creating innovations and adjusting to new, often unforseen, skill requirements. A rigid labor supply is a formidable obstacle to change.

Education can contribute mightily

to economic growth by meeting the needs for flexibility and adaptability. But this implies a greater emphasis on the teaching of *basic* techniques and concepts and on the postponement of a student's specialization until late in the educational process. It also implies that the distinction between "vocational" and "general" education may in reality be a great deal more fuzzy than conventional usage suggests. In a world of changing technology and skill requirements, the training that appears to be "general" today may be extremely and directly useful in the world of work tomorrow. Similarly, education that appears today to be of direct vocational value may not only be obsolete later, but its narrowness may intensify the difficulties of adjusting to future manpower demands.

In recognition of the broad social and economic interest in investment in human capital, particularly through education and health, *it is appropriate and desirable for government policy to encourage individuals to invest more in themselves than they otherwise would, and perhaps in somewhat different ways.* For example, a teen-ager may prefer not to continue in school or take certain health measures, but the rest of society may prefer that he does, since, as we have seen, it will suffer in many ways if his education, training, and health are not satisfactory.

Today, tax laws provide greater incentives for investment in physical assets than for investments in human capital, because the former are more generally depreciable as a business expense than are the latter. *Reconsideration of tax policy so as to redress the imbalance is warranted.* Similarly, the tradition that the cost of a school building or a hospital is a "capital" cost—which can "appropriately" be financed by borrowing —while the cost of salaries for the teachers or medical personnel in that structure is a non-capital expenditure, leads to an unfortunate emphasis on *con*struction relative to *in*struction in the school and elaborate equipment relative to additional personnel in hospitals. Education and health expenditures other than on buildings and equipment also represent investments—less tangible but no less real than the investments in classrooms. *Government should recognize by its words and deeds the breadth of the investment concept and should help lower-level governments and private decision-makers to recognize it also.*

V. CONCLUSION

Some readers may feel that health and education policies are moral issues that should not be subjected to the cold scrutiny of an economist. But surely one need not choose between an economist's view and a philosopher's view of wise public health and education policies. Both are relevant. Indeed, the discussion above has pointed to a number of important though unquantifiable benefits from investing in people. Returns in the form of enhanced productivity are relevant for wise policy-making. But so are non-economic considerations.

Actions taken by society directly influence the creation and the maintenance of human-capital values. Expenditures for education, training, health, and migration may contribute to the value of our human resources. Expenditures on the detection, treatment, and the prevention of accidents and floods and on the provision of adequate housing and diets—all these preserve and enhance the values of our human resources, just as do maintenance and improvement expenditures on physical capital.

Investments in human resources are not alone sufficient to insure rapid economic growth, let alone an effective democracy or a problem-free society. But it now appears that, as a society, we are paying too little attention to our enormously valuable stock of human capital, while we focus great attention on conventional investment. Health and education programs are primary devices for raising productivity and speeding social progress. Government has a critical role to play in promoting an effective human-resource-development program. The challenge is there to be seized.

FEDERAL SUPPORT OF BASIC RESEARCH: SOME ECONOMIC ISSUES

Geographical redistribution of science research funds proposed as useful tool for attacking poverty pockets in U.S.

By HARRY G. JOHNSON

SUMMARY

There is no necessary connection between leadership in basic science and leadership in the applications of science, because scientific progress is a cooperative endeavor and not a competitive game; indeed, there may be a conflict between basic research and applied science. The notion of "a position of leadership" in science raises questions of what leadership consists in and what its value is to the Nation. The two main arguments for government support of science are cultural-social, and economic. The cultural-social argument stresses scientific activity as a form of social consumption of wealth and raises the question of whether other uses of the resources employed would contribute more to the greatness of the society. The economic argument stresses basic scientific research as a form of investment for the future, and raises the questions of what the rate of return on such investment is and whether and to what extent government support is called for. Relevant economic research results bearing on this problem are scarce. Economic theory suggests that competition in the market will supply less than the optimal amount of basic research; but our society substantially supplements the market through private contributions to and government support of science, and the question is whether this supplementation is deficient or excessive. Here difficult problems arise, on which more economic research is needed; one of these concerns the relative merits of government and private support of science. The rule-of-thumb procedures generally recommended for determining the volume and allocation of Government support to basic scientific research generally ignore these problems, and amount to endorsing the present level of Government support or recommending that it be increased. Allocation of Federal support of science should take account of the possibility of stimulating the economic development of poor regions of the country by locating scientific research facilities in them.

INTRODUCTION

The questions put by the House Committee on Science and Astronautics to the ad hoc committee relate to the level of Federal support of basic research necessary to maintain U.S. leadership, and the allocation of that support among the various fields of scientific endeavor. These are questions of the allocation of scarce human and material resources among alternative uses, falling squarely within the scientific specialty of the economist, and it might be expected that an economist could provide definite quantitative answers to them. Unfortunately, the issues involved are so complex, and serious investigations of them by economists of such recent origin, that an attempt to provide quantitative answers at this stage would represent no more than an exercise of personal judgment. This paper makes no such attempt. Instead, it seeks to discuss certain questions of a kind that naturally occur to an economist confronted by the fundamental problems set by the House committee.

In discussing these questions, it is assumed that a meaningful distinction—albeit an imprecise one—can be drawn between "basic" and "applied" research. Basic research is conceived of here as research devoted to the acquisition of knowledge for its own sake, as distinct from research devoted to the elaboration and application of knowledge in the solution of practical problems or for the attainment of tangible results. Conceptually, basic research is concerned with adding to the stock of knowledge, and applied research with turning the stock of knowledge to practical use. The distinguishing characteristics of basic research, and the main source of difficulty in formulating public policy with respect to it, is the extreme uncertainty of both the contribution to knowledge that will result from a particular line of research, and the ultimate practical usefulness of that contribution.

IS LEADERSHIP IN BASIC RESEARCH ESSENTIAL TO LEADERSHIP IN THE APPLICATIONS OF SCIENCE?

It is a truism that the results of basic research must be available before they can be applied, so that basic research must come temporally before (and frequently has come long before) the practical application of its results. This does not, however, imply either that national leadership in applications of science requires leadership in basic scientific research, or that national leadership in basic scientific research will necessarily guarantee leadership in the advancement of technology or in the various applications of science and technology.

Given the international character of science, which makes scientific discoveries in one country available to scientists in all, and the fact that the value of a scientific discovery may not be apparent for a long time and is frequently contingent on other discoveries of an unpredictable nature, there is no reason to assume that leadership in basic scientific research and leadership in technology and applications of science are necessarily connected. A nation could achieve leadership in applications by drawing on knowledge provided by the basic research conducted by the scientists of other countries, confining its own participation in basic science to the minimum required to keep in touch with developments elsewhere and "fill in the holes" where necessary. Conversely, a position of leadership in basic research might benefit a nation almost exclusively in terms of the intangible prestige of scientific accomplishment, the concrete benefits of the application of scientific findings being reaped mainly by other nations. In that case, the expenditure of public money on the support of basic scientific research would serve mainly to save other countries the cost of basic research and enable them to concentrate on development and application; and the "leadership" so obtained might be largely leadership in the eyes of a relatively small group of scientists in other countries, plus those members of the general public who are interested in scientific achievement in the same sort of way as others are interested in international sporting competitions.

To put the same point another way, leadership in basic science is fundamentally different from other kinds of leadership. Scientific progress is not a conflict (like a game or a war) that a nation can win or lose. It is a cooperative endeavor in which the exertions of each benefit the rest, and in which leadership is measured by contribution to the general advance. Thus the nation that spends a comparatively large amount of public funds (relative to other countries) on establishing scientific leadership is spending its money to a significant extent for the benefit of other countries. This raises the obvious question of how far it is worthwhile to tax the citizens of one country in order to establish a position of leadership in an activity the benefits of which accrue to an important extent to other countries.

The cooperative nature of scientific progress, together with the increasing international mobility of scientists, also imposes limits on the extent to which a nation can establish leadership in basic science, and suggests that it would be courting disappointment to define the objective of scientific leadership in across-the-board terms, as some are inclined to do. It is inevitable that scientists of other countries will assume leadership in certain branches of science, and also that U.S. support of scientific research and training will have side-effects in strengthening other countries' scientific progress. Further, U.S. adoption of the objective of maintaining scientific leadership through governmental support of basic science is bound to provoke—

and has already provoked—emulation by other countries desirous of establishing their own claims to world leadership.

The preceding paragraphs have argued that there is no necessary connection between leadership in basic science and leadership in technology. It is even possible that there is some conflict between them. This possibility is suggested by the broad historical generalization that, at least until modern times, human societies have been distinguished by superior attainment either in pure science or in technology, but not in both together [1]. Even now it is frequently argued (for example, in recent discussions of British science policy) that concentration on basic research detracts from technological progress and the development of applications, by depriving applied science of the prestige necessary to attract able and ambitious minds. Others have argued the contrary, that concentration on applied research diverts manpower from basic research to the detriment of the latter in the short run and the former in the long run. This argument is forcefully developed in Professor Fritz Machlup's *Production and Distribution of Knowledge in the United States* [2], though it is questionable how far Professor Machlup's identification of basic research with university teaching and the production of graduate students is a valid approximation.

WHAT IS MEANT BY "A POSITION OF LEADERSHIP" IN SCIENCE?

In view of the looseness of the connection between leadership in basic scientific research and leadership in technology and applications of science just discussed, it is necessary to define clearly what is meant by "a position of leadership" before it becomes possible to discuss Federal support of basic research as a means of achieving it.

In the writer's personal judgment, it would seem that in the past American leadership has rested primarily on two elements: the capacity to put science and technology to work in the service of raising the standard of living of the masses, and the capacity to mobilize science and technology on a massive scale in the development of superior armament. Both entail the capacity to produce to demand, and both reflect the wealth and efficiency of the U.S. economy. It has been the capacity to pay for and organize scientific and technical progress, in other words, that has established the leadership, rather than the scientific leadership that has established the capacity to perform the projects. The glory of the achievements reflects back on the scientists enlisted in them, of course, and on science in general; and it is natural enough for scientists to seek to claim the credit for the achievements, as a means of raising their status in the society and the amount of support they can claim, both from the Government and from private sources. The question, however, is whether scientific leadership would count for much if it were not allied with the economic and political power of the United States in the world, and what the United States acquires by expenditure on "scientific leadership" as such. It is true that the prestige of U.S. pure science has been growing rapidly—as measured for example by Nobel prizes won and memberships in foreign scientific societies conferred—but one suspects that the prestige gained thereby is limited to a small and select audience—scientists themselves, and those members of the public who make a hobby of following scientific developments—and that the largest part of the audience is resident in the United States, so that most of the accomplishment of leadership is self-congratulation. It is often argued by scientists, nevertheless, that scientific leadership of this kind is of great importance in fostering international good will and cooperation through the personal contacts of top-level scientists of the various nations. This argument, however, when used in recommendation of Government support of basic science, raises the question of the value of this kind of good will in relation to the cost of the support of science necessary to generate the requisite number of top-level scientists.

To the extent that the position of leadership of the United States has been a reflection of its wealth and economic dynamism, there would seem to be no special argument for Government support of basic scientific research; rather there would be an argument for the pursuit of governmental policies designed to foster the growth of the American economy, the maintenance of a superior economic performance being sufficient, in this case, to maintain the U.S. position of leadership. To provide a case for Governmental support of basic research, and some standard for assessing how extensively such support should be provided, it is necessary to adduce some cogent reason why expenditure on basic sci-

entific research produces a net benefit for the Nation that would not be enjoyed unless the Government assumed responsibility for such expenditures. Such a reason is necessary, because a free-enterprise economy normally trusts the processes of competition in the market to produce what is socially beneficial.

One alleged reason has already been mentioned—the contribution of contacts between top-level scientists to international amity and understanding; in the writer's opinion this is scarcely a cogent reason for governmental support of basic scientific research on any substantial scale. Two other reasons commonly advanced in current discussions are worth more serious consideration: one is cultural and social, the other economic.

THE "SCIENTIFIC CULTURE"

Much has been made in some quarters, especially among scientists, of the proposition that contemporary society is evolving a "scientific culture," in which the United States is the pioneer and the model for others to emulate. According to this view, it is the obligation or the privilege of the United States to support basic scientific research as a means of exercising leadership in the progress to a higher form of civilization.

The concept of "scientific culture" raises a number of questions, among which the most fundamental is the question whether basic scientific research is—in the economist's terms—to be regarded primarily as a consumption or an investment activity. Every society devotes a portion of its current output to activities that increase its future capacity to produce (investment); but the bulk of its current output goes to supporting itself (consumption). Depending on its capacity to produce a surplus above the minimum needs of subsistence, it can devote more or less of the income not used for investment to activities that have no economic function—sport and recreation, leisure, meditation and scholarship, religious activities—or to the support of institutions and individuals specialized in the performance of those activities—in Thorstein Veblen's terminology, the leisure class [3].

Much of the contemporary "scientific culture" argument for Government support of basic scientific research is such as to put it—intentionally or not—in the class of economically functionless activity. The argument that individuals with a talent for such research should be supported by society, for example, differs little from arguments formerly advanced in support of the rights of the owners of landed property to a leisured existence, and is accompanied by a similar assumption of superior social worth of the privileged individuals over common men. Again, insistence on the obligation of society to support the pursuit of scientific knowledge for its own sake differs little from the historically earlier insistence on the obligation of society to support the pursuit of religious truth, an obligation recompensed by a similarly unspecified and problematical payoff in the distant future [4]. At the more popular level, the interest in scientific accomplishment represents a leisure-time activity, more elevated than following professional sport and less culturally demanding than the appreciation of artistic endeavor, and hence peculiarly appropriate in the affluent mass society.

These comments are directed at clarifying the nature of the "scientific culture" argument. They do not necessarily imply that if basic scientific research is of the character of a leisure activity, it should not be supported by Government funds, or should be supported only to the extent that it promises to be instrumental in the achievement of nonscientific objectives in such areas as defense, public health, and so forth. Clearly, if the public is convinced that a scientific culture is desirable, it is perfectly appropriate for the taxpayers' money to be used to support scientists and scientific research. But to the extent that scientific activity is of the character of a consumption good (in the broad sense outlined above) its claims for public support need to be weighed against other pressing claims on the social surplus, such as the relief of poverty, the mitigation of social problems, the needs of the less-developed countries, or the claims of the average taxpayer to enjoy the personal dispositon of the income he earns. And the weighing obviously cannot be entrusted to scientists, or to any other beneficiary group: it must be the responsibility of Congress.

Insofar as cultural leadership in the world is concerned, there are several obvious areas—such as race relations, poverty, public health, and social security—where the expenditure of public money might well do more to establish America's image as the emerging society of the future than would equal expenditures on the support of science. Moreover, in a number of these areas there is no reason to believe that effective action requires a major preliminary program of basic scientific research: money applied with existing knowledge would suffice, because it is the nature of our political and social attitudes and institutions, not the backwardness of our social scientific knowledge, that is primarily responsible for the problems. With respect to poverty, for example, a major obstacle to more effective policies is not lack of knowledge of what causes poverty, but the belief that poverty is the poor person's own fault and that giving him money will sap his initiative.

BASIC SCIENCE AND ECONOMIC GROWTH

A great deal of stress is laid, in current arguments for Federal support of basic scientific research, on the importance of scientific progress to the improvement of productivity and the standard of living. Since the findings of economists on this question, such as they are, are easily subject to misinterpretation, it seems useful to provide a brief outline of their nature before turning to the economic argument for Government support of basic science [5].

Broadly speaking, economists concerned with economic growth conceive of the total output of the economy as being the resultant of various inputs of productive services into the production process, and seek to explain the measured growth of output by reference to changes in the quantities of inputs over time. The term "measured growth of output" embodies a limitation important in the present connection, since the methods of measurement of output

largely fail to catch improvements in the quality of the goods and services produced, and such improvements are an important part of the contribution of progress in knowledge to human welfare. The procedure involves specifying both the inputs and the value of their contribution to output; any residual growth of output not explained by changes in input quantities is a measure of the contribution of factors not taken into account in the formulation of the relationships assumed to determine output. In the early stages of this type of research there was an unfortunate tendency to describe the residual as the increase in productivity of the inputs, and to identify it positively as the contribution of the advance of knowledge to increases in output—particularly unfortunate as the early studies worked with very simple models of the production process and an extremely crude measure of labor input in terms of labor-hours without reference to skill, and for this reason among others produced residuals that were extremely high in relation to the total growth of input. Subsequently, the residual has come to be regarded as simply "a measure of our ignorance" and to be described as "the residual" rather than as "increase in productivity." Correspondingly, research on economic growth has aimed at improving the model of production and the specification and measurement of the inputs so as to increase the proportion of measured growth explained and reduce the residual.

The most comprehensive study of this kind is Edward F. Denison's *The Sources of Economic Growth in the United States and the Alterna-*

tives Before Us [6], which attempts in particular to estimate the effects of changes in the quality of labor inputs associated with increased education and other changes, and to apportion the residual increase in output per unit of input among various contributing factors. Since it is the most comprehensive, it arrives at one of the lowest figures for the residual that economists have produced. Denison's figures ascribe approximately 20 percent of the growth of real national income from 1909 to 1929, and approximately 32 percent of the growth from 1929–57, to the increase in output per unit of input. For the latter period, somewhat over half of the increase in output per unit of input (just under 30 percent of measured growth) is ascribed to Denison's residual category labeled "Advance of Knowledge." This label is, of course, misleading, since the category is a residual that incorporates both any errors in the estimates of the influence on the growth of real income of changes in the factors explicitly taken into account in Denison's analysis and the influence of all the factors not so taken into account. It is not a direct estimate of the contribution of "advance ·of knowledge," in any concrete sense of the phrase, to measured economic growth. Moreover, as previously mentioned, the measured growth of output fails to catch improvements in the quality of output, to which advances in knowledge make an important contribution. Nevertheless, imprecise in meaning and unreliable magnitude as it is, the residual figure is the most careful estimate available of the portion of past growth that might be attributable to the growth of knowledge.

The growth of knowledge in question is the growth of all knowledge relevant to efficient production, managerial and organizational as well as technological and scientific. Denison further estimates that about one-fifth of the contribution of "advance of knowledge" to growth in the period 1929–57 can be attributed to organized research and development; and he calculates that the social rate of return on organized research and development is about the same as on investment in nonresidential capital. This in turn implies that the contribution of increased expenditure on research and development to measured economic growth would be small, and, more important, that there is no social benefit to be obtained from governmental measures to increase research and development activity. Denison's calculations are, however, no more than educated guesses; they do not include improvements in product quality, to which much of research and development is directed; the calculated rate of return on research and development could be much higher if research and development yielded its contribution only with a substantial lag [7]; and there are reasons, elaborated below, for believing that resources are not allocated to research and development as efficiently as they could be.

Though the importance of the advance of knowledge to improved living standards is difficult to quantify, and the magnitude of the contribution of basic scientific research to the advance of productivity still more obscure, and though both may easily be exaggerated in carelessly formulated argument, there is no disputing that basic research has played a significant part in the growth of the U.S. economy. This fact by itself, however, does not constitute a case for Government support of basic scientific research, though scientists frequently write as if it did; the argument that it does is equivalent to arguing that, because part of the growth of output is attributable to population growth, the Government should subsidize births and immigration. In order to establish a case for Government support, it must be shown that basic research yields a social return over its cost that exceeds the return on alternative types of investment of resources. Alternatively, it must be shown that the amount of basic research that would be carried on in the absence of Government support would be less than what would be economically optimal. It is, incidentally, important to recognize that even without Government support some basic research would be carried on, as in the past—and probably on a much larger scale than in the past, owing both to the growth of interest in science and to the growth of wealth and the capacity to support scientific research through the universities and through privately supported research organizations. It is also important to recognize that Government cannot create additional resources for the economy, with which to support basic research; it can only take resources away from private individuals, who might prefer to use them for some other purpose, but would probably contribute some of them to the support of science if science is deemed socially beneficial. Government support means the difference between more and less, not between all or nothing at all.

From the point of view of economic analysis, research is conceived of as one form of investment of resources, the investment involving the use of human and material resources to acquire knowledge and the return resulting from the application of that knowledge to increase human welfare in one way or another. Normally a free-enterprise economy depends on the exercise of private decisions operating in the marketplace to decide on the total investment of all kinds and its allocation among alternative forms of investment. The market will arrive at a socially efficient allocation of resources provided that the risks undertaken by and the prospective returns open to the private decision-taker coincide with the risks and returns to society as a whole. These conditions are not fulfilled for private investment in research, and particularly for private investment in basic scientific research. The risk to the private investor in the creation of scientific and technological knowledge is greater than the risk to society, because the knowledge that results from the research may be useful to someone else but not useful for him, and the return to the private investor is likely to be less than the return to society as a whole, because the benefits to society cannot be fully appropriated by charging for the use of the knowledge. These divergences of private and social risks and benefits are by definition greater for basic scientific research than for applied scientific research; they are also smaller for the large diversified research organization or industrial corporation than for the small specialized research organization or company.

In consequence, there is good

theoretical reason for expecting that, left to itself, the market would not only tend to allocate too few resources to research in general, but would also tend to bias the allocation against basic scientific research as contrasted with applied scientific research, and toward research in scientific areas related to the technology of industries dominated by large multiproduct corporations. This expectation seems to be substantially confirmed by the facts, especially those on the industrial distribution of research and development expenditure. A further relevant point is that, insofar as private appropriation of the benefits of successful research requires concealing the new knowledge from other potential users, the social gain from research is reduced correspondingly [8].

These defects of the market mechanism with respect to the allocation of resources toward and among investments in research imply that the market needs to be supplemented, and perhaps, with respect to basic scientific research, entirely replaced by social provision and allocation of resources for the support of scientific research. Our society does not, however, in fact depend exclusively on the market mechanism for decision on the amount and allocation of resources to be invested in. Instead, large amounts of money are channeled into basic research through the universities, through local and State governments, through private contributions, and through the Federal budget. The question then becomes, not whether the market system needs supplementation, but whether the degree of supplementation provided through existing nonmarket channels is adequate, too

large, or too small, in relation to the economically optimum, and whether the resulting allocation of resources among rival fields of scientific inquiry is reasonably efficient.

To provide satisfactory answers to these questions, and therefore some firmer basis for answering the House committee's questions, would require calculations of an extremely difficult sort, probably impossible to effect with any reliable degree of accuracy —calculations that have so far not been attempted on any substantial scale [9]. The difficulties are suggested by some of the questions that need to be asked: What have been the social rates of return on past investments in basic scientific research, for particular research projects, and on the average? How likely are particular proposed lines of research to produce new contributions to knowledge, and how valuable to society are these contributions likely to be in relation to their cost? (The assessment of the returns on specific projects requires an estimate of the likelihood of success, as well as of the value of success and the prospective cost.) How likely is it that if a particular project is not undertaken in the United States it will be undertaken somewhere else, and what net loss, if any, would there be to the United States from relying on scientists to carry it out?

These and similar questions relate primarily to the allocation of resources among research fields. With respect to the total allocation of resources to basic scientific research, questions of a different nature arise. One concerns the extent to which increased allocations of scientific personnel and supporting resources to basic scientific research would reduce the quality of the average research product; in other words, how rapidly do returns to research diminish?

The second concerns the relative extent to which increased expenditures on scientific research is reflected on the one hand in increased research effort and on the other hand in higher money costs; in other words, how far does increased expenditure on scientific research increase the quantity of research results produced, and how far does it merely bid up the salaries and raise the operating expenses of research personnel? Economists who have considered these questions (such as Machlup and Denison) seem to believe that the returns from increased expenditure on scientific research diminish fairly sharply for both reasons; more concrete evidence on these economic questions would be extremely useful.

A final question, of considerable relevance to policy-making, concerns the extent to which Government support and private support of basic scientific research are substitutes for one another, in the sense that larger-scale Government support for science tends to reduce the private support forthcoming, and conversely a reduction in Government support would elicit larger-scale private support. It is quite conceivable that the interest of the public (including business firms) in science, and its faith in the ultimate usefulness of contributions to scientific knowledge, together with the competition for excellence among the universities, would furnish the resources required (or a large part of them) on the alternative basis of private donations and fees. (Raising the funds for basic research in this way would, of course,

involve substantial institutional changes.) Moreover, private support of science might have certain advantages over Governmental support, in that it might tend to produce a more flexible adjustment of support to the changing frontiers of scientific advance. That is, in science as in the production of commodities, a decentralized decision-taking process might produce a closer adjustment of supply to changing needs or opportunities.

The foregoing questions illustrate the kind of information that is necessary to judge the adequacy of Federal support of basic scientific research, from the economic point of view. In the absence of hard information or reasonably reliable estimates, any such assessment has to be an exercise in informed judgment and inference from scrappy evidence. In this connection, Richard Nelson has advanced an argument to the effect that the United States is probably not spending as much as it profitably could on basic scientific research [10]. He reasons as follows:

. . . if basic research can be considered as a homogeneous commodity, like potato chips, and hence the public can be assumed to be indifferent between the research results produced in government or in industry laboratories; if the marginal cost of research output is assumed to be no greater in nonprofit laboratories than in profit-oriented laboratories, and if industry laboratories are assumed to operate where marginal revenue equals marginal cost, then the fact that industry laboratories do basic research at all is itself evidence that we should increase our expenditure on basic research.

The key to the argument is the assumption discussed earlier, that the social benefit from industry research exceeds the benefit to the firm conducting it; the assumptions stated imply that the social benefit exceeds the cost in industry research, and that the same situation is true of nonprofit research. Nelson admits that the factual assumptions are extremely shaky, particularly with respect to the comparability of the research output of nonprofit and profit-oriented laboratories; and some doubt is cast on the argument by carrying it to its logical conclusion, which is that Government support of basic research should be extended to the point where no profit-oriented laboratories have any incentive to conduct basic research.

HOW MUCH FEDERAL SUPPORT SHOULD BE PROVIDED FOR BASIC SCIENTIFIC RESEARCH, AND HOW SHOULD IT BE ALLOCATED AMONG FIELDS OF SCIENTIFIC ENDEAVOR?

The discussion of the preceding section has illustrated the difficulty of providing any firm guidance on these questions by drawing on economic analysis. In principle, the "scientific culture" type of argument for Federal support of basic scientific research requires that public opinion, as expressed through Congress, must decide at what point to strike a balance between supporting the scientific culture and using its resources for other desirable forms of expenditure. The economic argument, on the other hand, would require allocating resources among scientific fields so as to equalize the prospective social rates of return from marginal expenditure on each field, and fixing the total of resources allocated

to basic research at the level yielding a marginal rate of return on all investment in basic research comparable to what is earned on other forms of investment, or else equal to the rate of interest at which the community is willing to forego the alternative of consuming the requisite resources [11]. But since the information required to perform these exercises is absent, the principles can serve at best as a way of formulating decisions on the questions.

In the absence of any firm knowledge about the relation between the level and allocation of Federal support for basic science research and the magnitude of the social benefits obtained therefrom, there is a strong temptation to attempt to evade the issue by resorting to rule-of-thumb procedures based on the situation of the present or recent past. One such is the attempt to establish normative percentages tying expenditure on basic research to gross national product or to Government expenditure on major applied-science projects. The difficulties with this procedure are, first, that the percentages are usually derived from some base period, and there is no reason to expect the level in the base period to have been the right level; and second, that there is no reason to expect the correct relationship to be a constant.

An alternative is to ignore the question of benefits, and to approach the question from the science side: This is exemplified by the recommendation that adequate support should be provided for all qualified talent in the category of "little science" research, while political decision on priorities should be taken in the light of prospective cost in the category of "big science" research. This recommendation essentially amounts to taking the consumption view of scientific research: In little science, support everyone who demonstrates talent according to the scientific standards of his fellow scientists, and, in big science, decide how much society can afford to spend.

As regards little science, the approach just outlined evidently trusts the scientific community and the process of educational selection to produce a total and an allocation of expenditure not wildly out of line with governmental capacity to pay and the rough requirements of efficient distribution of scientific effort (efficient, that is, in scientific but not necessarily economic terms). Ultimately, it relies on the self-equilibrating processes of the intellectual market in ideas and the commercial market in scientifically trained labor to prevent serious misallocations. It should also be noted that the approach depends on a particular assumption about the supply of scientific talent: that there is a limited and fairly readily identifiable group in the population that is capable of acceptable scientific performance, and a sharp difference in ability between this group and the rest. This assumption does not make economic sense in any long-run perspective: One would expect the supply of potential scientists, like the supply of any other kind of skilled labor, to vary in response to the income and career opportunities offered. (Even if scientifically talented people were a fixed proportion of population, it would still be possible to increase the number available in the United States through immigration.) Consequently, any attempt to fix the total

level of support on this basis implies a judgment that the present level of scientific activity (or something near it) is the correct one. Alternatively, if the principle is to offer support to everyone of competence who offers himself for a scientific career, the level of scientific activity will be left to be determined by the attractiveness of alternative occupations.

THE GEOGRAPHICAL DISTRIBUTION OF SUPPORT OF BASIC SCIENCE

In conclusion, it seems desirable to draw attention to a facet of policy toward basic science that is important but tends to be overlooked by scientists. This is the implication of the geographical distribution of science support for the pattern of growth of the U.S. economy. The location of scientific research activity in a particular city or region generally constitutes a focal point for the development of science-intensive industries in the surrounding area, and this should be taken into account in deciding on the location of such scientific activity. There is a natural tendency for scientific activity to agglomerate around established centers of scientific accomplishment; and this is probably the most efficient way of conducting scientific research from the point of view of science itself. From the economic and social point of view, however, and perhaps even from the longer run scientific point of view, there is a strong case for encouraging the development of scientific research centers in the more depressed and lower income sections of the country, as a means of raising the economic and social level of the population in those sections. Much of the poverty problem is associated with geographical concentration of high-income industries in certain areas and their absence from others, which makes migration the only feasible route to economic improvement. A deliberate policy of locating scientific research in the backward areas of the country to encourage their industrial development could in the long run provide a socially and economically more attractive attack on the poverty problem than many of the policies now being applied or considered.

This point, it should be emphasized, is independent of whether the Nation is spending too little or too much on the support of basic research, that is, of whether the beneficial effects described are worth their cost. So long as public funds are allocated to the support of basic research, the geographical allocation of the funds should take account of the social effects of their expenditure.

REFERENCES

[1] On this point see the comment by Thomas S. Kuhn on Irving H. Siegel's "Scientfiic Discovery and the Rate of Invention," in Richard R. Nelson (ed.), *The Rate and Direction of Inventive Activity: Economic and Social Factors* (Princeton, N.J.: Princeton University Press, 1962), pp. 450–57.

[2] Princeton, N.J.: Princeton University Press, 1962.

[3] THORSTEIN VEBLEN, *The Theory of the Leisure Class* (London: Macmillan Co., 1899). It should be emphasized that in this context "leisure" does not mean idleness or frivolous activity, but merely time free from the arduous and uninteresting tasks of producing a subsistence and available for the pursuit of nonmaterial interests.

[4] To an important extent, indeed, scientific research has become the secular religion of materialistic society; and it is somewhat paradoxical that a country whose constitution enforces the strict separation of church and state should have contributed so much public money to the establishment and propagation of scientific messianism.

[5] The following summary is only a broad sketch; for a more extensive survey, see Moses Abramovitz, "Economic Growth in the United States," *American Economic Review*, LII, No. 4 (Sept. 1962), pp. 762–82, a review article on the Denison volume referred to below.

[6] New York: Committee for Economic Development, 1962.

[7] Dension relates the contribution to growth to current research and development expenditures; since research and development expenditure has been growing rapidly, the rate of return would be higher if calculated on the basis of earlier (smaller) expenditures. On this point see Abramovitz, *op. cit.*, p. 780, n. 16.

[8] For more elaborate theoretical analyses of the economics of research, see Richard R. Nelson, "The Simple Economics of Base Scientific Research," *Journal of Political Economy*, vol. LXVII, No. 3 (June 1959), pp. 297–309; Kenneth J. Arrow, "Economic Welfare and the Allocation of Resources to Invention," pp. 609–26 in R. R. Nelson (ed.), *op cit.*; Dan Usher, "The Welfare Economics of Invention," *Economica*, N.S. vol. XXXI, No. 123 (August 1964), pp. 279–87.

[9] An outstanding example of the

type of calculation required is Zvi Griliches' estimate of the realized social rate of return on public and private funds invested in hybrid corn research. (Zvi Griliches, "Research Costs and Social Returns: Hybrid Corn and Related Innovations," *Journal of Political Economy*, LXVI, No. 5 (October 1958), pp. 419–43.) Griliches estimates "that at least 700 percent per year was being earned, as of 1955, on the average dollar invested in hybrid corn research" (p. 419). He is, however, careful to point

out that this was a successful research venture, and that the finding does not mean that any amount of expenditure on research is bound to be worthwhile. One of the limitations of economic research in this area is that it has tended to focus on cases of successful scientific research.

[10] *Op. cit.*, pp. 304–5.

[11] These two standards differ substantially, and there is an outstanding debate among economists regarding which is the more appropriate to use in assessing public investment.

HEALTH AND DRUGS

PRICE DISCRIMINATION IN MEDICINE

Price discrimination behind U.S. health woes. AMA, professional societies, medical advertising, discrimination against Jews in medicine all interrelated.

By REUBEN A. KESSEL*

Many distinguished economists have argued that the medical profession constitutes a monopoly, and some have produced evidence of the size of the monopoly gains that accrue to the members of this profession. Price discrimination by doctors, i.e., scaling fees to the income of patients, has been explained as the behavior of a discriminating monopolist. Indeed this has become the standard textbook example of discriminating monopoly. However this explanation of price discrimination has been incomplete. Economists who have subscribed to this hypothesis have never indicated why competition among doctors failed to establish uniform prices for identical services. For any individual doctor, given the existing pattern of price discrimination, income from professional services would be maximized if rates were lowered for affluent patients and increased for poor patients. However, if many doctors engaged in such price policies, a pattern of prices for medical services would be established that would be

independent of the incomes of patients. Yet despite this inconsistency between private interests and the existing pattern or structure of prices based on income differences, this price structure has survived. Is this a contradiction of the law of markets? Why is it possible to observe in a single market the same service sold at different prices?

The primary objective of this paper, which is an essay in positive economics, is to show by empirical evidence that the standard textbook rationalization of what appears to be a contradiction of the law of markets is correct. It will be argued that the discriminating monopoly model is valid for understanding the pricing of medical services, and that each individual buyer of medical services that are produced jointly with hospital care constitutes a unique, separable market. In the process of presenting evidence supporting this thesis, other closely related phenomena will be considered. These are (1), why the AMA favors medical insurance prepayment plans that provide money to be used to buy medical services, but bitterly opposes comparable plans that provide instead of money, the service itself and (2), why the

---

* Deletions in text and footnotes have been made with permission. See original source for complete report.

AMA has opposed free medical care by the Veterans Administration for veterans despite the enormous increase in the quantity of medical services demanded that would result from the reduction to zero of the private costs of medical care for such a large group.

The second half of this paper represents an attempt, by means of an application of the discriminating monopoly model, to further our understanding of many unique characteristics of the medical profession. If the medical profession constitutes a discriminating monopoly, what inferences can be drawn concerning the relationship between this monopoly and other economic, sociological and political aspects of the medical profession? In particular, does the discriminating monopoly model shed any light upon (1) why a higher percentage of doctors belong to professional organizations than is true of other professions, (2) why doctors treat one another and their families free of charge, (3) why doctors, compared with any other professional group, are extremely reluctant to criticize one another before the public, (4) why specialists are over-represented among the hierarchy of organized medicine, (5) why a transfer of membership in good standing from one county society to a second sometimes requires serving a term as a probationary member, (6) why advertising that redounds to the interest of the medical profession as a whole is approved whereas advertising that is designed to benefit particular individuals or groups is strongly opposed, (7) why malpractice insurance is less expensive for members of organized medicine than it is for non-members, and finally (8)

why minority groups, particularly Jews, have been discriminated against in admission to medical schools.

The body of this paper is divided into five sections. These are, in order of presentation, a hypothesis alternative to the price discrimination hypothesis, a history of the development of the powers that enable organized medicine to organize effectively a discriminating monopoly, evidence supporting the validity of the discriminating monopoly model for understanding the pricing of medical services, and lastly an application of the discriminating monopoly model to rationalize many characteristics of the medical profession that have been hitherto thought of as either anomalies or behavior that could best be explained as non-economic phenomena.

I. A HYPOTHESIS ALTERNATIVE TO THE DISCRIMINATING MONOPOLY MODEL

The standard position of the medical profession on price discrimination is in conflict with what might be regarded as the standard position of the economics profession. Economists argue that price discrimination by doctors represents the profit maximizing behavior of a discriminating monopolist; the medical profession takes the contrary position that price discrimination exists because doctors represent a collection agency for medical charities. The income of these charities is derived from a loading charge imposed upon well-to-do patients. This income is used to finance the costs of hiring doctors to provide medical care for the poor who are sick. The doctor who is hired by the medical charity and the medical charity itself are typically the same person. Since the loading charge that is imposed upon non-charity patients to support the activities of medical charities is proportional to income or wealth, discriminatory prices result. The following quotation from an unnamed but highly respected surgeon presents the position of the medical profession.

> I don't feel that I am robbing the rich because I charge them more when I know they can well afford it; the sliding scale is just as democratic as the income tax. I operated today upon two people for the same surgical condition—one a widow whom I charged $50, the other a banker whom I charged $250. I let the widow set her own fee. I charged the banker an amount which he probably carries around in his wallet to entertain his business friends.[1]

It is relevant to inquire, why have we had the development of charities operated by a substantial fraction of the non-salaried practitioners of a profession in medicine alone? Why hasn't a parallel development occurred for such closely related services as nursing and dental care? Why is it possible to observe discrimination by the Mayo Clinic but not the A and P? Clearly food is as much of a "necessity" as medical care. The intellectual foundation for the existence of price discrimination and the operation of medical charities by doctors appears to rest upon the postulate that medicine is in some sense unlike any other commo-

dity or service. More specifically, the state is willing to provide food, clothing, and shelter for the indigent but not medical care. Since medical care is so important, doctors do not refuse to accept patients if they are unable to pay. As a consequence, discrimination in pricing medical services is almost inevitable if doctors themselves are not to finance the costs of operating medical charities.

The foregoing argument in defense of price discrimination in medicine implies that a competitive market for the sale of medical services is inconsistent with the provision of free services to the indigent. This implication is not supported by what can be observed elsewhere in our economy. Clearly there exist a number of competitive markets in which individual practitioners provide free goods or services and price discrimination is absent. Merchants, in their capacity of merchants, give resources to charities yet do not discriminate in pricing their services. Similarly many businesses give huge sums for educational purposes. Charity is consistent with non-discriminatory pricing because the costs of charity can be and are paid for out of the receipts of the donors without recourse to price discrimination.

However the fact that non-discriminatory pricing is consistent with charity work by doctors doesn't imply that discriminatory pricing of medical services is inconsistent with the charity hypothesis. Clearly what can be done without discrimination can, *a fortiori*, be done with discrimination. Therefore, it is pertinent to ask, is there any evidence that bears directly on the validity of the charity interpretation of price discrimination? The maximizing hypothesis of

---

[1] Seham, "Who Pays the Doctor?," 135 New Republic 10, 11 (July 9, 1956).

economics implies that differences in fees can be explained by differences in demand. The charity hypothesis propounded by the medical profession implies that differences in fees result from income differences. The pricing of medical services to those who have medical insurance provides that what might be regarded as a crucial experiment for discriminating between these hypotheses. Whether or not one has medical insurance affects the demand for medical service but does not affect personal income. Consequently if the charity hypothesis is correct, then there should be no difference in fees, for specified services, for those who do and those who do not have medical insurance. On the other hand, if the maximizing hypothesis of economics is correct, then fees for those who have medical insurance ought to be higher than for those who do not have such insurance. Existing evidence indicates that if income and wealth differences are held constant, people who have medical insurance pay more for the same service than people who do not have such insurance. Union leaders have found that the fees charged have risen as a result of the acquisition of medical insurance by their members; fees, particularly for surgery, are higher than they would otherwise be if the union member were not insured. Members of the insurance industry have found that ". . . the greater the benefit provided the higher the surgical bill. . . ."[2] This suggests that the

principle used for the determinations of fees is, as Means pointed out, what the traffic will bear. Obviously fees determined by this principle will be highly correlated with income, although income will have no independent predictive content for fees if the correlation between income and what the traffic will bear is abstracted.[3]

Other departures from the implications of the hypothesis that price discrimination results from the desires of the medical profession to finance the costs of medical care for the indigent exist. These are: (1) Doctors typically do not charge each other for medical care when clearly inter-physician fees ought to be relatively high since doctors have relatively high incomes. (2) The volume of free medical care, particularly in surgery, has declined as a result of the rise in real per capita income in this country in the last twenty years. Yet there has been no change in the extent of price discrimination. As real per capita income rises, price discrimination ought to fade away. There is no evidence that this has been the case. (3) There exists no machinery for matching the receipts and disbursements

---

[2] Lorber in *Hearings Before the House Committee on Interstate and Foreign Commerce on Health Inquiry*, 83d Cong. 2d Sess. pt. 7, p. 1954 (1954); also Joanis "Hospital and Medical Costs," *Proceedings of*

the *Fourth Annual Group Meeting of the Health and Accident Underwriters Conference*, p. 18 (Feb. 19–20, 1952).

[3] The principle of what the traffic will bear and the indemnity principle of insurance are fundamentally incompatibles and in principle make medical care uninsurable. This has been a real problem for the insurance industry and in part accounts for the relative absence from the market of major medical insurance plans. See the unpublished doctoral dissertation of A. Yousri, "Prepayment of Medical and Surgical Care in Wisconsin," p. 438, University of Wisconsin Library (1956).

of medical charities operated by individual doctors. There are no audits of the receipts and the expenditures of medical charities and well-to-do patients are not informed of the magnitude of the loading charges imposed. Moreover one study of medical care and the family budget reported ". . . no relation in the case of the individual doctor between the free services actually rendered and this recoupment, the whole system is haphazard any way you look at it."[4]

II. HISTORY OF THE DEVELOPMENT OF THE MEDICAL MONOPOLY

A necessary condition for maintaining a structure of prices that is inconsistent with the maximization by doctors of individual income is the availability and willingness to use powerful sanctions against potential price cutters. When one examines the problems that have been encountered in maintaining prices that are against the interests of individual members of a cartel composed of less than fifteen members, one cannot help being impressed with the magnitude of the problem confronting a monopoly composed of hundreds of thousands of independent producers. Yet despite the fact that medicine constitutes an industry with an extraordinarily large number of producers, the structure of prices for a large number of medical services nevertheless reflects the existence of discrimination based on income. This implies that very strong sanctions must be available to those

[4] Deardorff and Clark, *op. cit. supra* note 2, pt. 6, p. 1646.

empowered to enforce price discipline. Indeed, *a priori* reasoning suggests that these sanctions must be of an order of magnitude more powerful than anything we have hitherto encountered in industrial cartels. What are the nature of these sanctions? How are they employed? In order to appreciate fully the magnitude of the coercive measures available to organized medicine, it is relevant to examine the history of medicine to understand how these sanctions were acquired.

Medicine, like the profession of economics today, was until the founding of the AMA a relatively competitive industry. With very few exceptions, anyone who wanted to practice was free to hang out a shingle and declare himself available. Medical schools were easy to start, easy to get into, and provided, as might be expected in a free market, a varied menu of medical training that covered the complete quality spectrum. Many medical schools of this time were organized as profit making institutions and had stock outstanding. Some schools were owned by the faculty.

In 1847, the American Medical Association was founded and this organization immediately committed itself to two propositions that were to lead to sharp restrictions upon the freedom of would-be doctors to enter the medical profession and the freedom of patients to choose doctors whom the AMA felt were not adequately qualified to practice medicine. These propositions were (1) that medical students should have acquired a "suitable preliminary education" and (2) that a "uniform elevated standard of requirements for the degree of M.D. should be adopted by all medical schools in the United States."[5]

These objectives were achieved in two stages. During the first stage, the primary concern of the AMA was licensure. In the second, it was accrediting schools of medicine. During the first stage, which began with the founding of the AMA and lasted until the turn of the century, organized medicine was able by lobbying before state legislatures to persuade legislators to license the practice of medicine. Consequently the various states set up boards of medical examiners to administer examinations to determine whether or not applicants were qualified to practice medicine and to grant licenses to those the State Board deemed qualified to practice. Generally speaking, organized medicine was very successful in its campaign to induce states to license physicians.

However, it was not until the second stage that economically effective power over entry was acquired by organized medicine. This stage began with the founding in 1904 of the Council on Medical Education of the AMA. This group dedicated itself to the task of improving the quality of medical education offered by the medical schools of the day. In 1906, this committee undertook an inspection of the 160 medical schools then in existence and fully approved of the training in only 82 schools. Thirty-two were deemed to be completely unacceptable. As might be expected, considerable resentment developed in the medical colleges and elsewhere as a result of this inspection. Consequently the council withheld publication of its findings, although the various colleges were informed of their grades. In order to gain wider acceptance of the results of this study, the Council solicited the aid of the Carnegie Foundation. "If we could obtain the publication and approval of our work by the Carnegie Foundation for the Advancement of Teaching, it would assist materially in securing the results we were attempting to bring about."[6] Subsequently Abraham Flexner, representing the Carnegie Foundation, with the aid of N. P. Colwell, secretary of the Council on Medical Education, repeated the AMA's inspection and grading of medical schools. In 1910, the results of the labors of Flexner and Colwell were published. This report, known as the Flexner report, recommended that a substantial fraction of the existing medical schools be closed, standards be raised in the remainder, and admissions sharply curtailed. Flexner forcefully argued that the country was suffering from an overproduction of doctors and that it was in the public interest to have fewer doctors who were better trained. In effect, Flexner argued that the public should be protected against the consequences of buying medical services from inadequately trained doctors by legislating poor medical schools out of business.[7]

---

[5] A. Flexner, *Medical Education in the U.S. and Canada*, Bull. No. 4, Carnegie Foundation for the Advancement of Teaching, p. 10 (1910).

[6] Bevan, "Cooperation in Medical Education and Medical Service," 90 *Journal of the American Medical Association*, 1175 (1928).

[7] Flexner, *op. cit. supra* note 5, at p. 14. Two errors in economic reasoning are crucial in helping Flexner establish his conclusions. One is an erroneous interpretation

If impact on public policy is the criterion of importance, the Flexner report must be regarded as one of the most important reports ever written. It convinced legislators that only the graduates of first class medical schools ought to be permitted to practice medicine and led to the delegation to the AMA of the task of determining what was and what was not a first class medical school. As a result, standards of acceptability for winning a license to practice medicine were set by statute or by formal rule or informal policy of state medical examining boards, and these statutes or rules provided that boards consider only graduates of schools approved by the AMA and/ or the American Association of Medical Colleges whose lists are identical.

The Flexner report ushered in an era, which lasted until 1944, during which a large number of medical schools were shut down. With its new found power, the AMA vigorously attacked the problem of certification of medical schools. By exercising its power to certify, the AMA reduced the number of medical schools in the United States from 162 in 1906 to 85 in 1920, 76 in 1930 and 69 in 1944. As a result of the regulation of medical schools, the number

of medical students in school in the United States today is 28,500, merely 5,200 more than in 1910 when Flexner published his report.

The AMA, by means of its power to certify what is and what is not a class A medical school, has substantial control over both the number of medical schools in the United States and the rate of production of doctors. While the control by the AMA over such first class schools as, say, Johns Hopkins is relatively weak because it would be ludicrous not to classify this institution a class A school, nevertheless control over the aggregate production rate of doctors is great because of its more substantial power over the output of less distinguished medical schools.

The delegation by the state legislatures to the AMA of the power to regulate the medical industry in the public interest is on a par with giving the American Iron and Steel Institute the power to determine the output of steel. This delegation of power by the states to the AMA, which was actively sought and solicited, placed this organization in a position of having to serve two masters who in part have conflicting interests. On the one hand, the AMA was given the task of providing an adequate supply of properly qualified doctors. On the other hand, the decision with respect to what is adequate training and an adequate number of doctors affects the pocketbooks of those who do the regulating as well as their closest business and personal associates. It is this power that has been given to the AMA that is the cornerstone of the monopoly power that has been imputed by economists to organized medicine.

of Gresham's Law. This law is used to justify legislation to keep low quality doctors out of the medical care market by interpreting it to mean that second-class doctors will drive first-class doctors out of business. The other is that raising the standards of medical education is necessarily in the public interest. Flexner fails to recognize that raising standards implies higher costs of medical care. This argument is on a par with arguing that we should keep all cars of a quality below Cadillacs, Chryslers, and Lincolns off the automobile market.

III. EVIDENCE SUPPORTING THE DISCRIMINATING MONOPOLY MODEL

The preceding analysis tells us nothing about the mechanism for controlling the price policies of individual doctors; it only implies that the rate of return on capital invested in medical training will be greater than the rate of return on capital invested in other classes of professional training. This difference in returns is imputable as a rent on the power of the AMA to control admissions to the profession by means of control over medical education. Here it will be argued that control over the pricing policies of doctors is directly and immediately related to AMA control of medical education. The relationship is that control over medical education is the primary instrumentality for control over individual price policies. More specifically, control over post-graduate medical training—internship and residency, and control over admission to specialty board examinations —is the source of the power over the members of the medical profession by organized medicine.

A. The Control Mechanism

Part of nearly every doctor's medical education consists of internship and for many also a period of hospital service known as residency. Internship is a necessary condition for licensure in most states. This training is administered by hospitals. However, hospitals must be approved by the AMA for intern and residency training, and most non-proprietary, i.e., nonprofit, hospitals in this country are in fact approved for at least intern training. Each approved hospital is allocated a quota of positions that can be filled by interns as part of their training. Hospitals value highly participation in internship and residency training programs. These programs are valued highly because at the prevailing wage for intern services, it is possible to produce hospital care more cheaply with interns than without them. Interns to hospitals are like coke to the steel industry: in both cases, it is perfectly possible to produce the final product without these raw materials; in both cases, the final product can be produced more cheaply by using these particular raw materials.

There exist some grounds for suspecting that the wages of interns are maintained at an artificially low level, i.e., that interns receive compensation that is less than the value of their marginal product: (1) Hospitals are reporting that there is a "shortage" of interns and have been known to send representatives to Europe and Asia to invite doctors to serve as interns. (2) University hospitals are more aggressive bidders for intern services than non-university hospitals. The fraction of the available intern positions that are filled by university hospitals is greater than by non-university hospitals. If controls are exercised over what hospitals can offer in wages to interns, university hospitals are apt to be less vulnerable to the threat of loss of their class A hospital ratings than non-university hospitals. This would be true for the same reason that Johns Hopkins would have a freer hand in determining the size of its freshman class. The status of university hospitals is stronger because these hospitals are likely to be among the better hospitals in the country. Therefore, if controls over intern wages exist then it seems reasonable to suspect they would be relatively weaker over the wages of interns in university hospitals. For this reason, one would expect university hospitals to be more aggressive in bidding for interns.

However, whether or not interns are underpaid, the AMA has control over the supply of a vital, in an economic sense, agent of production for producing hospital care. Revocation of a hospital's Class A rating implies the loss of interns. In turn, the loss of interns implies higher costs of production. Higher costs of production result in a deterioration of the competitive position of any given hospital vis-à-vis other hospitals in the medical care market. This control over hospitals by the AMA has been used to induce hospitals to abide by the Mundt Resolution. This resolution advises hospitals that are certified for intern training that their staff ought to be composed solely of members of local medical societies. As a result of this AMA control over hospitals, membership in local medical societies is a matter of enormous importance to practicing physicians. Lack of membership implies inability to become a member of a hospital staff.

County medical societies are for all practical purposes private clubs with their own rules concerning eligibility for membership and grounds for expulsion. A system of appeals from the rulings of county medical societies with respect to their members is provided. On the other hand, for non-members attempting to obtain membership in county medical societies, there is no provision for appeal. The highest court in the medical judicial system is the Judicial Council of the AMA. Between this council and the county medical societies are state medical societies. Judicial review is bound by findings of fact made at the local level. For doctors dependent upon hospitals in order to carry out their practice, and presumably this constitutes the bulk of the profession, being cut off from access to hospitals constitutes a partial revocation of their license to practice medicine. Consequently, more doctors belong to their county medical associations than is true of lawyers with respect to local bar associations. More significantly, doctors are subject to very severe losses indeed if they should be expelled from their local county medical associations or be refused admission to membership. It is this weapon, expulsion from county medical associations, that is probably the most formidable sanction employed to keep doctors from maximizing their personal incomes by cutting prices to high income patients. "Unethical" doctors, i.e., price cutters, can be in large part removed as a threat to a structure of prices that discriminates in terms of income by the use of this weapon. For potential unethical physicians, it pays not to cut prices if cutting means being cut off from hospitals.

Thus far we have argued that control over the individual price policies of the members of the medical profession has been achieved by the AMA through its control over postgraduate medical education. By means of its power to certify a hospital for intern training, the AMA controls the source of supply of a crucial agent for the production of hospital care. Control over the supply of interns has been used to induce hospitals to admit to their staffs only members of county medical associations. Since membership in the county medical associations is in the control of organized medicine, and membership in a hospital staff is extremely important for the successful practice of most branches of medicine, the individual doctor can be easily manipulated by those who control membership in county medical associations.

Members of the medical profession are also subject to another type of control, derived from AMA control over post-graduate medical education, that is particularly effective over younger members. Membership in a county medical society is a necessary condition for admission to specialty board examinations for a number of specialties, and passing these examinations is a necessary condition for specialty ratings. Non-society members cannot win board membership in these specialties. This is a particularly important form of control over newcomers to the medical profession because newcomers tend to be young doctors who aspire to specialty board ratings. Consequently the AMA has particularly powerful sanctions over those who are most likely to be price cutters. These are young doctors trying to establish a practice.

B. The Evidence

Just as one would expect an all-out war to reveal a country's most powerful weapons, substantial threats to the continued existence of price discrimination ought to reveal the strongest sanctions available to organized medicine. For this reason, the opposition or lack of opposition to prepaid medical plans that provide medical service directly to the patient ought to be illuminating.

Generally speaking, there exist two classes of medical insurance. One is the cash indemnity variety. Blue Cross and Blue Shield plans fall within this class. Under cash indemnity medical insurance, the doctor and patient are able to determine fees jointly at the time medical service is sold just as if there were no insurance. Therefore, this class of medical insurance leaves unaffected the power of doctors to discriminate between differences in demand in setting fees. If anything, doctors welcome insurance since it improves the ability of the patient to pay. On the other hand, for non-indemnity type plans, plans that provide medical services directly as contrasted with plans that provide funds to be used to purchase desired services, payments are typically independent of income. Costs of membership in such prepayment plans are a function of family size, age, coverage, quality of service, etc., but are independent of the income of the subscriber. Consequently, such plans represent a means for massive price cutting to high income patients. For this reason, the reception of these plans by organized medicine constitutes an experiment for testing the validity of the discriminating monopoly model. If no opposition to these plans exists, then the implication of the discriminating monopoly model—that some mechanism must exist for maintaining the structure of prices—is invalid. On the other hand, opposition to these plans by organized medicine constitutes observable phenomena that support this implication. If such opposition exists, then it supports the discriminating monopoly hypothesis in addition to providing evidence of the specific character of the sanctions available to organized medicine.

A number of independent observers have found that a systematic pattern of opposition to prepaid medical service plans, as contrasted with cash indemnity plans, exists. "In many parts of the county, organized medical bodies have been distinctly hostile to group practice. This is particularly true where the group is engaged in any form of prepaid medical care."[8] "Early groups were disparaged as unethical. But within recent years active steps have been taken only against those groups offering a plan for some type of flat-fee payment."[9] "There is reason to believe that the Oregon, the San Diego, and the District of Columbia cases exemplify a nationwide pattern of behavior by the American Medical Association and its state and county subsidiaries. What has come into the open here is working beneath the surface in other states and counties."[10] This systematic pattern of opposition to single price medical plans has taken two distinct courses. These are (1) using sanctions in an effort to terminate the life of prepaid medical plans already in existence and (2) lobbying for legislation that would abort their birth.

There have been a number of dramatic battles for survival by prepaid nonprice discriminatory medical plans resulting from the efforts of organized medicine to destroy them. These struggles have brought into action the most powerful sanctions available to organized medicine for use against price cutters. Consequently, the history of these battles provides valuable evidence of the character of the weapons available to the participants. For this purpose, the experiences of the following organizations are particularly illuminating: Farmers Union Hospital Association of Elk City, Oklahoma, the Kaiser Foundation of San Francisco and Oakland, Group Health of Washington, Group Health Cooperative of Puget Sound, Civic Medical Center of Chicago, Complete Service Bureau of San Diego, and the medical cooperatives in the State of Oregon. These plans are diverse, from the point of view of location, organization, equipment, sponsorship, and objective. However, they all have one crucial unifying characteristic—fees or service charges are independent of income. Similarly, the experiences of Ross-Loos in Los Angeles and the Palo Alto Clinic in California are illuminating because these organizations both operate prepayment single price medical plans and nevertheless continue to stay within the good graces of organized medicine.

The founder and director of the cooperative Farmers Union Hospital in Elk City, Oklahoma, Dr. Michael A. Shadid, was harassed for a num-

---

[8] *Building America's Health*, report to the President by the Commission on the Health Needs of the Nation, V. I, p. 34 (1952).

[9] Hyde and Wolff, "The American Medical Association: Power, Purpose, and Politics in Organized Medicine," 63 *Yale Law Journal* (1954), p. 977.

[10] See *Restrictions on Free Enterprise in Medicine,* pamphlet, Committee on Research in Medical Economics (April 1949), p. 14.

ber of years by his local county medical association as a consequence of founding and operating this price cutting organization. He was ingeniously thrown out of the Beckham County Medical Society; this organization was dissolved and reconstituted apparently for the sole purpose of not inviting Shadid to become a member of the "new" organization. Before founding the cooperative, Shadid had been a member in good standing in his county medical association for over a decade.

The loss of hospital privileges stemming from non-county society membership was not sufficient for the task of putting Shadid out of business, because his organization had its own hospital. Therefore, organized medicine turned to its control over licensure to put the cooperative out of business. Shadid was equal to this challenge. He was shrewd enough to draw members of the politically potent Farmers Union into his organization. Therefore, in the struggle to take away Shadid's license to practice medicine, the farmers were pitted against the doctors. The doctors came out of this political battle the losers because the state governor at the time, Murray, sided with the farmers. However, the Beckham County Medical Society has been powerful enough to keep doctors who were known to be coming to Oklahoma to join Shadid's organization from getting a license to practice, powerful enough to frighten and cause the departure of a doctor who had been associated with Shadid's organization for a substantial period of time, powerful enough to keep Shadid out of a two-week postgraduate course on bone fractures at the Cook County Graduate

School of Medicine (the course was open only to members in good standing of their local county medical societies), and was able to get enough of Shadid's doctors drafted during the war to endanger the life of his organization.[11] In recent years, the tide of battle has turned. The Hospital Association brought suit against the Beckham County Medical Society and its members for conspiracy in restraint of trade. This case was settled out of court. As part of this settlement, the county medical association agreed to accept the staff of the cooperative as members.

The experience of the Kaiser Foundation Plan is parallel to that of the Farmers Union. Both were vigorously opposed by organized medicine. The medical staff in each case could not obtain membership in local county medical societies. In both cases, the plans were able to prosper despite this obstacle, since they operated their own hospitals. In both cases, the doctor draft was used as a tool in an attempt to put these plans out of business.[12]

Control by organized medicine over licensure was used as a weapon in an attempt to kill the Kaiser Plan. Dr. Sidney Garfield, the plan's medical director, was tried by the State Board of Medical Examiners for unprofessional conduct. Garfield's license to practice was suspended for one year and he was

[11] The story of Shadid and his organization may be found in *M. A. Shadid, A Doctor for the People* (1939), and *Doctors of Today and Tomorrow* (1947).

[12] For evidence on this point for the Kaiser Plan, see *Hearings before a Subcommittee of the Senate Committee on Education and Labor,* pt. 1, p. 338 ff., 77th Cong. 2nd Sess. on S. Res. 291 (1942).

placed on probation for five years. However, the suspension was withheld pending good behavior while on probation. This ruling by the State Board of Examiners was not supported in Court. Superior Court Judge Edward P. Murphy ordered the board to rescind all action against Garfield. The judge ruled that the board was arbitrary in denying Garfield a fair trial. Subsequently the appellate court reversed the decision of the trial court on one count but not the second. Nevertheless the judgment of the trial court in rescinding the decision of the board of examiners was upheld. The entire matter was sent back to the board for reconsideration of penalty.

Subsequently, Garfield was tried by the county medical association for unethical practices, namely advertising, and found guilty. However, he came away from this trial with only a reprimand and not the loss of his license. By virtue of having its own hospitals and legal intervention by the courts against the rulings of organized medicine, the Kaiser Foundation has been able to resist the onslaughts of its foes. However, the battle is not over yet. Although Kaiser Foundation doctors are now admitted to the Alameda County Society, the San Francisco County Society still excludes them.

Group Health in Washington was not as fortunate as Kaiser or Farmers Union with respect to hospitals. Unlike these other two organizations, Group Health did not have its own hospital and therefore was dependent upon the existing hospitals in the community. Consequently, when Group Health doctors were ejected from the District Medical Society, Group Health was seriously crippled.

Nearly all the hospitals in the district were coerced into denying staff privileges to Group Health doctors and bed space to their patients. Moreover, many doctors were deterred from becoming members of the Group Health staff because of fear of punitive action by the District Medical Society. Still other doctors who were members of the Group Health medical staff suddenly discovered attractive employment possibilities elsewhere and resigned their Group Health positions.

It was fortunate for Group Health that it was located in Washington, D.C., and therefore under the jurisdiction of federal laws, in particular the Sherman Act. The tactics of the District Medical Society and the AMA came to the attention of the Justice Department. This led to the successful criminal prosecution of organized medicine under the Sherman Act. The opinion of the Supreme Court delivered by Mr. Justice Roberts pinpoints the primary concern of the petitioners, the District Medical Society, and the AMA. "In truth, the petitioners represented physicians who desired that they and all others should practice independently on a fee for service basis, where whatever arrangement for payment each had was a matter that lay between him and his patient in each individual case of service or treatment."[13]

As a result of this victory, consumer sovereignty with respect to Group Health was restored. As might be suspected from the intense opposition of the AMA and the District Medical Society, Group Health has

[13] American Medical Association v. United States, 317 U.S. 519, 536 (1943).

shown unusual survival properties and flourishes in competition with fee-for-service medical care. Since its victory at court, good relations with the District Medical Society have been achieved by the Group Health staff.

IV. IMPLICIATIONS OF THE DISCRIMINATING MONOPOLY MODEL

In the preceding section, this paper has been concerned with establishing the validity of the discriminating monopoly model for understanding the pricing of an important class of medical services—those produced by doctors in hospitals. Evidence of the existence of a pattern of relatively direct and obvious controls was presented. Yet it was argued that maintaining a structure of discriminatory prices for this large number of independent producers represents a fantastically difficult control problem. Does the existence of this difficult control problem shed any light upon other aspects of the medical profession? Our concern is largely with the more subtle or less obvious methods of control over the price policies of individual doctors.

The controls previously discussed are analogous to surgery; the controls to be discussed are analogous to preventive medicine. In particular, we explore the possibilities of a relationship between maintaining a structure of prices based on income differences and: the representation of specialists in power position within organized medicine; discrimination against minority groups in admission to medical schools; the free treatment by doctors of other doctors and their families; the posi-

tion of organized medicine on advertising; the defense of county medical association members against malpractice suits; the *no-criticism rules* that forbid unfavorable comment by one physician of another physician's work before a member of the lay public.

Specialists have more to gain from price discrimination than non-specialists because their work is more likely to be associated with hospitals. The power to withhold hospital facilities from doctors constitutes the strongest weapon for maintaining price discipline within the medical profession. Therefore, discrimination in pricing ordinary office visits as compared with services rendered in a hospital is much less pronounced. In fact, prices charged for office visits ought to be relatively independent of patient's incomes. Office care can be provided by doctors with no hospital connections whatsoever. Consequently, specialists, particularly those who do most of their work in hospitals, have a greater interest in maintaining price discrimination than general practitioners. Therefore, the fact that specialists are over-represented, as measured by the ratio of specialists to all doctors, in the AMA hierarchy is no accident. This is precisely the group that has the greatest economic interest in maintaining price discipline and, for this reason, are "naturals" for the job.

Newcomers, even if they were formerly presidents of county societies elsewhere, are probationary members when they join some county societies. They achieve full membership only after a successful term as probationary members. Relegating newcomers to a probationary status is a means for segregating from the general membership those who have a relatively high probability of being price cutters. Newcomers represent a group whose members are trying to acquire practices and therefore are more likely to be price cutters than society members who have well established practices. Consequently newcomers require both an extraordinary degree of surveillance and a strong indication of the costs of non-compliance. Probationary membership achieves both of these objectives.

The advertisement of medical services is approved by the medical profession if and only if such advertisements redound to the interest of the profession as a whole. Advertisements in this class are, for example, announcements of the availability for sale of Blue Cross type medical plans. These plans allow their subscribers the choice of any licensed practitioner. Organized medicine consequently takes the position that these advertisements are of benefit to the entire profession. On the other hand, advertisements that primarily redound to the interests of a particular group, for example, advertisements by a closed panel medical group, are frowned upon. Advertisements in this class are, by definition, resorted to only by "unethical" doctors. Why this difference in the position of organized medicine with respect to these two classes of advertising? The approved class, insofar as it achieves its objective, tends to increase the aggregate demand for medical care. On the other hand, the disapproved variety will have the effect of reallocating patients from the profession as a whole to those who advertise. Consequently, advertising in this class constitutes com-

petitive behavior and leads to price cutting. It tends to pit one doctor or one group of doctors against the profession as a whole with respect to shares of the medical care market. Active competition for increased shares of the medical care market by doctors would tend to eliminate price discrimination based on income differences.

The significance of advertising as a means for maintaining free entry is revealed by two bits of interrelated evidence. These are the strong opposition of organized medicine to advertising calling the public's attention to the services of a particular group of doctors and the willingness of some prepaid medical plans to incur the wrath of organized medicine by undertaking such advertising. Kaiser, the Civic Medical Center, and the Complete Service Bureau at one time or another advertised. The use of advertising in the face of strong opposition by organized medicine implies that advertising plays a crucial role in enabling these groups to capture part of the medical care market. Consequently the ban on such advertising by organized medicine constitutes a barrier to entry into this market and is a means for keeping doctors from competing with one another and thereby incidentally destroying the structure of prices.

County medical societies play a crucial role in protecting their members against malpractice suits. Physicians charged with malpractice are tried by their associates in the private judicial system of organized medicine. If found innocent, then local society members are available for duty as expert witnesses in the defense of those charged with malpractice. Needless to say, comparable services by society members for plaintiffs in such actions are not equally available. By virtue of this monopoly over the services of expert witnesses and the tacit coalition of the members of a society in the defense of any of their members, the successful prosecution of malpractice suits against society members is extremely difficult.

On the other hand, for doctors who are persona non grata with respect to organized medicine, the shoe is on the other foot. Expert witnesses from the ranks of organized medicine are abundantly available for plaintiffs but not for defendants. Therefore the position of a plaintiff in a suit against a non-society member is of an order of magnitude stronger than it is for a suit against a society member. Consequently it should come as no surprise that the costs of malpractice insurance for non-society members is substantially higher than it is for society members. Apparently some non-society members have experienced difficulty in obtaining malpractice insurance at any price.

This coalition among the members of the medical profession not to testify against one another, like structured prices, puts some doctors in a position of pursuing a policy that does not maximize personal returns. Therefore more than just professional ethics makes this coalition viable. As might be expected, the ability of organized medicine to expel doctors from hospital staffs plays a crucial role in keeping doctors from testifying against one another. Belli reports that a doctor who acted as an expert witness in a malpractice suit he tried was subsequently barred from the staff of every hospital in California.[14] It is because of sanctions of this character that we can find reports of patients with strong prima facie evidence of negligence and yet unable to hire expert witnesses from the ranks of the medical profession.

As a result of this coalition among society members for malpractice defense, two effects are achieved. The more direct and obvious consequence is an increase in the monopoly returns to the members of this profession over what they otherwise would be. The other is the welding together of the medical profession as an ingroup. In this latter role, the coalition for malpractice defense is a force that has the same effect as a reciprocity, that is, the free treatment by doctors of other doctors and their families, and the rule that doctors are not to criticize one another in public. The function of reciprocity and *no-criticism* is to induce the members of the medical profession to behave towards one another as if they were members of an in-group. Doctors are subtly coerced into personal relations with one another. Insofar as these measures bear fruit, doctors view themselves as a large association in which members deal with one another on a personal level. In relation to the general public, i.e., outsiders, the in-group, doctors, are united.

But what does the medical profession achieve by subtly coercing its members into in-group relations with one another? The relationships among members of a family, an

---

[14] M. M. Belli, Ready For the Plaintiff, p. 98 (1956); "The California Malpractice Controversy," 9 *Stanford Law Review*, 731 (1957).

in-group par excellence, reveal the importance of these subtle controls. Members of a family are relatively reluctant to criticize one another before outsiders, tend not to charge each other market prices for services extended to one another, and try to avoid being in direct competition. The essence of in-group behavior is personal relationships among its members. On the other hand, the essential property of market place relationships is impersonality. Consequently insofar as a non-market place attitude can be fostered and maintained within the medical profession, such an attitude constitutes a barrier against doctors thinking of one another as competitors in the medical care market. This in itself constitutes a barrier against such market place activities as cutting prices.

To the extent that the culture of members of an in-group is distinct from that of non-members, this difference reduces the probability that non-members can successfully "join" the in-group. Differences in culture and values constitute a natural barrier to integration. This is particularly important for medicine because it is both a social and an economic club and the returns of the economic club are related to the degree of social cohesion that exists within the social club. Consequently, members of culturally distinct minority groups would be more difficult to assimilate into such an in-group and it is likely that many would never feel that they were completely members under the best of circumstances. This implies that members of such minority groups would be more difficult to control by means of the informal controls characteristic of in-groups.

Being thrown out of a country club is not much of a loss if one is only the janitor; for informal controls to be effective, they must be exercised over those who belong. Insofar as some minority groups are more difficult to assimilate, there exists an *a priori* basis for discrimination. It is to keep out those who have a higher probability of not being willing to go along with the majority. Minority groups whose culture and values are different from those of the majority could rationally be discriminated against in admission to medical schools because they are more difficult to control by informal controls after they are out in medical practice than is characteristic of the population at large.

The discrimination against Jews in admission to medical schools has been explained, by both Jews and non-Jews alike, as a consequence of irrational prejudice. Yet Jews might be regarded as the prototype of a minority group with cultural properties that, given the special problems of maintaining internal discipline within the medical profession, would make them undesirable candidates for admission to this profession. These cultural attributes evolved as a consequence of centuries of unparalleled persecution. This persecution, which by and large was economic, took the form of laws that barred Jews from particular product and labor markets in many of the most important countries in the history of western civilization. Cartels such as guilds followed similar policies. This exclusion policy channelled Jews into highly competitive markets, markets characterized by free entry, and forced them to develop their commercial skills to a higher level than was characteristic of the population at large in order to survive economically. For Jews, a medieval guild type share-the-market attitude was a non-survival property whereas a policy of vigorously competing was a survival property. The process of adaptation by Jews to laws constraining their economic activities led them to develop considerable ingenuity in minimizing the impact of such laws upon their economic well being. Jews developed into robust competitors with little respect for rules, either government or private, that regulated economic activities and with a substantial body of practical experience in implementing this point of view. These attitudes became a part of Jewish cultural tradition and at least in this respect, distinguished Jews from non-Jews. This was particularly true of Jews that came from Czarist Russia and Poland where discrimination against them was particularly strong.

Because of these special cultural properties, which are vestigial in the United States and therefore are in the process of fading away, the discrimination against Jews in admission to medical schools is far from irrational if one is concerned with maintaining price discrimination in medicine. The *a priori* probability of a Jew being a price cutter because of the special attributes developed in an effort to survive in a hostile environment is greater than that for a non-Jew. The Jewish doctor is more likely to have a commercial market place attitude towards other members of his profession than is the non-Jew. From the point of view of the medical profession, as one doctor expressed it, Jews ". . . spoil

everything they go into by turning it into a business."[15]

If, as this analysis implies, admission to medical schools is influenced by the desire to select candidates who will not become price cutters, then it ought to be possible to observe similar policies for postgraduate education. In particular, it should be possible to observe evidence of bias against Jews in surgical relative to non-surgical specialties. Consequently Jews ought to be underrepresented in surgery relative to other fields of specialization. Converse results ought to hold for psychiatry. A study of physicians who were diplomates in various specialties was made for the year 1946 for Jews and non-Jews for the cities of Brooklyn, Newark, Buffalo, and Hartford-Bridgeport. It was found that thirty-two per cent of the surgeons in Brooklyn were Jews, twenty-five percent in Newark, eight in Buffalo, and six in Hartford. Of the ten specialties considered for Brooklyn, the representation of Jews among the surgeons was lowest. For the other three cities, eleven specialties were considered. For all three of these cities, the representation of Jews among specialists was also lowest in surgery (453 Jewish specialists were considered in Brooklyn, the other three cities added 122). On the other hand, for the category neurology-psychiatry, the representation of Jews among the specialists practicing in this field ranked third for Brooklyn. For the other three cities, the rankings were one tie for fourth

---

[15] Hall, "Informal Organization of the Medical Profession," 12 *Canadian Journal of Economics and Political Science* 38 (1946).

place, one first place and one fourth place.

The distinction between psychiatry and surgery is a special case of the general distinction between surgical and non-surgical specialties. Hospital connections are far more important for the practice of surgical than non-surgical specialties. Therefore controls over the members of the medical profession in surgical specialties are stronger. If, as it has been argued, price discrimination is stronger in the surgical specialties, then there should be a significant difference in the frequency of Jews in surgical and non-surgical specialties. Two independent studies provide evidence that is consistent with this implication. For the state of Pennsylvania, one observer found that the frequency of Jews in non-surgical specialties was forty-one percent larger than in surgical specialties. The probability of a sample of this size, 1,175, of which 190 were Jews, being a random sample of a population characterized by an absence of a difference in the frequency of Jews in the surgical and non-surgical specialties is less than one half of one percent. For Brooklyn the frequency of Jews in the non-surgical specialties was thirty percent greater than for the surgical specialties. This difference could occur by chance with a probability of less than one percent if this were a random sample of a population that failed to exhibit this property. Similar results hold for a combination of the other three cities. The hypothesis that there exists a difference between surgical and non-surgical specialties with respect to the admission of Jews is consistent with the quali-

tative observation found in another report. This source observes that "fair play" exists in the admission of Jews to non-Jewish hospitals for training in the non-surgical specialties but not for training in the surgical specialties. Apparently the Jews who do get into medical schools are "dumped" in the non-surgical specialties.

Another piece of evidence consistent with the price cutting explanation of the discrimination against Jews in medicine is the drop in admissions of Jews to medical schools between 1933 and 1938. During that time, there was a decrease in over-all admissions to medical schools of about five percent and a decrease in admission of Jewish students of about thirty percent. Between 1928 and 1933, the prices of medical services dropped sharply and the real income of doctors as a group decreased. The depression produced a reduction in the size of the pie available to the profession. This smaller pie was contended for quite vigorously by the existing members. The Jews as price cutters were probably relatively successful, and in the process the structure of discriminatory prices was jeopardized. As a result, the threat of Jews to the aggregate income of the profession was brought home in a very forceful way at this time. Therefore the sharp curtailment in admission of Jews to medical schools resulted in an effort to reduce the vulnerability of structured prices to destruction by competitive behavior.

The evidence used to support the proposition that discrimination against certain minority groups results from the desire to maintain price discrimination is also consistent with the implications of simple monopoly theory. If medicine is a monopoly, then it follows that the number of candidates that would like to win entry into the medical profession exceeds the number that in fact are permitted to enter. Therefore unless the number of openings in the profession are sold or auctioned off, a practice that has not been unknown in the American labor movement, non-price rationing is inevitable. This leaves those who have the job of rationing available openings the opportunity to indulge in their tastes for the kind of people that they would like to see in the profession without any effective constraints in the form of costs or positions that must be filled. Under these circumstances, as contrasted with the free entry characteristic of competitive markets, nepotism, discrimination against unpopular cultural groups such as Jews and Negroes, and discrimination against those who hold unpopular ideas such as communists, thrives. Therefore discrimination against Jews and others in admission to medical schools can be rationalized as a manifestation of non-price rationing. Since the surgical specialties are presumed to have more monopoly power than the nonsurgical specialties, there is more non-price rationing in the former and as a result, more discrimination. The increase in the tempo of discrimination in the thirties can also be rationalized as a consequence of an increase in the extent of non-price rationing. The demand for medical services is probably highly income elastic and as a result of the depression and admission policies geared to a demand schedule for medical

services that existed in the twenties, the monopoly returns in medicine declined during the early depression years. Therefore admissions were subsequently curtailed in order to redress the effects of too liberal admission policies in the past. Consequently the extent of non-price rationing increased.

CONCLUSION

If different prices for the same service exist, then economic theory implies that there must also exist some means for enjoining producers of this service from acting in their own self interest and thereby establishing uniform prices. Observable phenomena abundantly support this implication. Available evidence suggests that the primary control instrument of organized medicine is the ability to cut off potential price cutters from the use of resources complementary to doctors' services for producing many classes of medical care. However, techniques other than the withdrawal of staff privileges in hospitals are also employed to maintain discipline in the medical profession. These include *no-criticism rules*, professional courtesy or the free treatment by doctors of other doctors and their families, prohibition of advertising that might reallocate market shares among producers, preventing doctors from testifying against one another in malpractice suits, and the selection of candidates for medical schools and post graduate training in the surgical specialties that have a relatively low probability of being price cutters. All of these sanctions can be rationalized as means for maintaining price discrimination. Therefore the use of these sanctions is consistent with the hypothesis that the medical profession constitutes a discriminating monopoly.

If being cut off from the use of a complementary agent of production, hospital services, is the chief means of disciplining the existing members of the medical profession, then there ought to be a difference in the price discipline maintained in the surgical and non-surgical specialties. Consequently there ought to be a significant difference between the surgical and the non-surgical specialties in the frequency of discriminatory pricing. There are no grounds for believing that there is any difference between the surgical and non-surgical specialties with respect to the effectiveness of the more subtle means of control. Therefore as a result of the relatively weaker impact on the non-surgical specialties of the loss of hospital staff privileges, it should be possible to observe that the non-surgical specialties have not only more price cutters in their midst but also are relatively freer in criticizing other members of the profession, serving as expert witnesses, and violating professional courtesy. Similarly this analysis implies that before the turn of the century, price discrimination in medicine was less pervasive, doctors criticized each other more freely, were more willing to act as expert witnesses against one another, did not as readily provide free medical care to other members of the profession, and did not discriminate against potential price cutters in admission to medical training.

The economic interest of the medical profession in maintaining price discrimination has led to opposition directed against new techniques for marketing medical services that offer promise of utilizing the existing stock of physicians more efficiently than heretofore. Consequently the opposition by organized medicine to prepaid service type medical plans probably has resulted in higher economic costs of medical care for the community than would otherwise have been the case. Similarly the incompatibility of the indemnity principle of insurance and the "what the traffic will bear" principle of pricing medical services has inhibited the development of major, medical catastrophe insurance in this country and consequently has limited the ability of individuals to insure themselves against these risks. Insofar as freer criticism by the members of the medical profession of one another before the public is of value to consumers in helping them distinguish between better and poorer practitioners and in raising standards within the profession, the public has obtained a lower quality of medical service than would otherwise have been obtainable at existing costs. And insofar as being a potential price cutter weeds out candidates from medical schools and post graduate training in the surgical specialties who were better potential doctors than those accepted, then the quality of the medical services that could have been achieved at existing costs was reduced.

Economic theory implies that prepaid medical service plans imperil the existence of price discrimination. Consequently theory also implies that in geographical areas where such plans exist, price discrimination ought to be relatively less prevalent. In California, the Kaiser Plan has captured a substantial fraction of the medical care market and is the largest single producer in the state. In an effort to meet this competition, service-type plans have been offered by orthodox members of the medical profession that are non-discriminatory with respect to income. Competition has had the effect of reducing the extent of discriminatory pricing in the area. This has been true in a number of counties in California where the Kaiser Plan is particularly strong. Therefore both economic theory and empirical evidence suggest that if there were more competition among doctors in the sale of medical services, i.e., if doctors were individually freer to pursue their self-interest, there would be less discrimination in the pricing of medical services.

THE ECONOMIC EFFECTS
OF MALARIA ERADICATION

Malaria eradication causes new costs to government via population growth. Need for birth control program may result.

By ROBIN BARLOW*

In this paper a method is presented for measuring the economic effects of malaria eradication, in particular the effects of eradication on per capita income in the long run. The method, which involves specifying a fairly detailed model of the entire economy, has been applied to the case of Ceylon, and some preliminary results are presented on what the course of Ceylonese per capita income would have been after 1947 if the successful eradication campaign of that year had not been undertaken.

These inquiries may be of interest to the economic historians, as providing an understanding of the far-reaching consequences of eradication programs which have been executed in the past. The inquiries may be relevant also to the decision-maker in government who must choose between alternative expenditure proposals in the context of a budget constraint. Considerations of the economic payoff of the alternative projects may properly influence the decisions which are made in those circumstances.

At the outset it should be stressed

* This paper is a preliminary report on a study sponsored by the Bureau of Public Health Economics, School of Public Health, University of Michigan, and financed by the National Institutes of Health and the Pan American Health Organization. The full report will be published in 1967 by the School of Public Health, University of Michigan, under the title, *The Economic Effects of Malaria Eradication*. For efficient handling of computer operations, the author wishes to thank Barbara Moores, of the Research Seminar in Quantitative Economics, University of Michigan.

that in drawing attention to the economic consequences of disease eradication, the economist does not mean to belittle the noneconomic consequences. Many public health officials seem to feel that when the economist points to the possible economic losses resulting from eradication—such as those implied by a population explosion—he is callously arguing that people should be denied the benefits of modern medicine. The fact is that an eradication program, like all other government programs, ought to be judged by the contribution which it makes toward the several national goals. In most countries the growth of per capita income is a national goal which is accorded a fairly high priority, and therefore the effect of eradication on per capita income is a relevant consideration. It may of course be rational to adopt an eradication program even when it is known that per capita income will probably fall as a result. This may be so when the program makes large contributions to other goals, such as the diminution of suffering.

MALARIA AND ITS ERADICATION[1]

Malaria is a parasitic disease transmitted by certain species of the anopheline mosquito. The parasites invade red blood cells and cause them to rupture synchronously, thus producing the attacks of chills, fever, and sweating associated with the disease. These attacks cause temporary

disability and are sometimes fatal. Those victims who survive the febrile attacks are left in a weakened state because of the massive destruction of their blood cells, and hence are more susceptible to death or disability from other diseases. Their debilitation reduces work efficiency. Eventually the blood cells are replaced and the body may develop some temporary immunity against a further infection. In many areas of the world, malaria has been endemic; in others it has appeared spasmodically or in epidemic form because of such factors as extreme instability in the size of the mosquito population. The annual number of cases on a worldwide basis has been reckoned in the hundreds of millions.

After the discovery some seventy years ago of the means whereby the disease was transmitted, the methods of control or eradication have multiplied rapidly. No universal panacea has been found, and one of the chief tasks in an eradication campaign is to choose from among the numerous possibilities that particular set of measures which is best suited to the local environment. The measures available include the use of mosquito netting, the location of dwellings at an adequate distance from the mosquitoes' breeding places, the use of insect repellents, the administration of drugs such as quinine which reduce or eliminate the parasite population in the human body, the installation of new drainage systems, or the removal of vegetation to render the mosquitoes' breeding places unusable, larvicidal techniques such as the oiling of ponds and streams and (often the most effective of all) residual spraying of house interiors with DDT or other insecticides.

[1] For a full treatment of these matters, see one of the standard works on malariology such as Emilio Pampana, *A Textbook of Malaria Eradication* (Oxford University Press: London, 1963) or Paul F. Russell et al., *Practical Malariology*, 2nd ed. (Oxford University Press: London, 1963).

Before the second World War attempts at controlling malaria were mostly localized and unambitious. In the years immediately following the war several campaigns were organized which made use of the new insecticides and antimalarial drugs then becoming available and in many cases virtually complete eradication was achieved over extensive areas. The possibility therefore emerged that the disease could be rendered totally extinct, and in 1955 the World Health Organization formally established worldwide eradication as one of its goals. In the pursuit of that goal the World Health Organization and its affiliates have provided substantial technical and financial assistance to the national eradication campaigns. The proceedings have assumed a note of urgency as more cases of resistance by mosquitoes and parasites have been disclosed, and the possibility now exists that worldwide eradication will be indefinitely postponed unless it is accomplished quickly, before the resistant strains become established.

By 1966 the eradication campaigns have proceeded to the point where the population of territories freed from malaria exceeds the population of territories where malaria still prevails. Since a campaign cannot succeed without money and some organizational resources, it is naturally the poorest and most backward areas of the world which still suffer from the disease. These areas include most of tropical Africa and parts of Central and South America, the Middle East, the Indian subcontinent, and Southeast Asia.

Malaria eradication is a half-finished task. In some countries the disease was virtually eradicated two decades ago or more, and these cases could provide abundant evidence on the economic and social consequences of eradication. Other countries are still malarial and are in a position to benefit from the experiences of the first group when they come to decide upon the timing, scale, and methods of their own eradication programs.

A CLASSIFICATION OF THE ECONOMIC EFFECTS OF ERADICATION

In the public health literature there is a consensus that malaria eradication is economically beneficial. Occasional misgivings are expressed about the implications of a population explosion; but even when these possible disadvantages are admitted, it is invariably said that they are far outweighed by the economic gains from eradication. These sanguine views have not been based on sound evidence. There have been several casual estimates purporting to demonstrate the economic advantages of eradication.[2] Some of these estimates have involved measuring the additional number of man-days of work which eradication has made possible in a particular country through reducing mortality and sickness, and then multiplying this number by an average daily wage. Other estimates have compared the costs of the eradication campaign itself to the extra hospitalization expenses which would have been incurred if malaria had been allowed to persist.

---

[2] For an account which describes many of these estimates, see C.-E. A. Winslow, *The Cost of Sickness and the Price of Health* (World Health Organization Monograph Series, No. 7: Geneva, 1951).

All of the estimates have been incomplete: they have failed to take into account the multiplicity of economic effects.

In providing a more complete analysis, we can begin by stipulating that per capita national income is the economic variable whose fate concerns us. Eradication could affect income per capita by changing either the number of heads or the level of income. The level of income or output could be affected by changes in the quantity and quality of labor inputs, the quantity and quality of capital or nonhuman inputs, and the manner in which these inputs are combined. Hence there are four categories of effects to consider. In our discussion of these effects we shall not dwell on the problems of measurement. These problems will be aired in the next section, where a model is outlined which incorporates the effects discussed below.

EFFECTS ON POPULATION SIZE. Other things being equal, a rise in the rate of population growth will reduce per capita income. There is evidence that malaria eradication produces this result both by lowering death rates and by raising birth rates. The fall in death rates occurs, not only because of a reduction in deaths directly attributable to malaria, but also because the population acquires a greater resistance to other diseases.

The rise in birth rates which has often been observed to follow eradication can probably be explained by the fact that pregnant women attacked by malaria are more liable to suffer miscarriages. There is also the possibility that the rate of conception is lower in malarial conditions because of the reduced vitality of both men and women.

EFFECTS ON LABOR INPUTS. Other things being equal, a rise in the quantity or quality of labor inputs will cause per capita income to rise. Eradication can affect labor inputs by reducing mortality, morbidity, and debility.[3] The reduction in mortality will bring about an immediate increase in the quantity of labor inputs in cases where the fall in death rates occurs among those of working age. A fall in death rates among those in younger age groups will cause an expansion of the labor force after a lag.

A reduction in morbidity, which is defined here as sickness sufficient to cause absence from work, can bring about an immediate increase in the quantity of labor inputs. A reduction in debility, which is defined as affecting the worker's productivity on the job, can cause an increase in the quality of those inputs. A worker freed of the debilitating effects of the disease can improve his performance both physically and mentally; he may complete a given manual task in a shorter time and also undertake activities more imaginative and ambitious than before.

The economic payoff to disease eradication depends not only on the relative incidence of the disease in the labor force and the rest of the population. It depends also on what segments of the labor force are benefited by eradication. In the case of malaria we are dealing with a dis-

[3] These distinctions are discussed in Selma J. Mushkin, "Health as an Investment," *Journal of Political Economy*, Oct., 1962, pp. 129–57.

ease whose greatest impact is upon the low-income, low-productivity segment of the labor force, and the payoff to eradication is therefore less than would be the case with a disease which involved the same number of victims but which was concentrated among the most productive segment. Malaria is a low-income disease mainly because it is avoidable. Persons with higher incomes and higher levels of education are in a stronger position to take advantage of that characteristic: being better informed, they are more likely to avoid exposure, for example by staying away from mosquito-infested places during darkness; being wealthier, they are better able to afford preventive or curative measures, such as the use of quinine or mosquito netting. From the economic viewpoint, malaria therefore contrasts sharply with such diseases as cancer or heart disease, where the opportunities for prophylaxis are distinctly limited and where the incidence tends to be the greatest among the most productive members of the labor force.

EFFECTS ON CAPITAL INPUTS. Other things being equal, the higher the rate of capital formation, the more rapid will be the growth of per capita income in the future. We must therefore examine the effects of disease eradication on the division of total expenditures between consumption goods and capital goods in both the private and public sectors.

In the private sector the larger population which results from eradication is likely to lower the rate of saving (and hence the rate of capital formation) attainable from a given level of disposable income. Moreover, when the population is growing more rapidly, what limited private saving does occur may tend to be invested in housing, which is a relatively unproductive form of capital stock. There will be some offsetting effects on the disposition of private income. After a government program of eradication, private expenditures for the prevention or treatment of the disease become unnecessary. The funds thus released may be devoted in part to saving and capital formation.

In the public sector the allocation of funds between consumption and investment is governed by political priorities which vary from country to country, and it is less easy to generalize about the effects of eradication. For our purposes, public investment should be defined as outlays which add to the stock of "productive" physical capital (like dams, roads, or government factories); all other resource-using governmental expenditures should be defined as public consumption, even when they provide long-lasting real assets (like police stations, schools, or sports stadia). One fairly common situation is for the highest budgetary priorities to be assigned to various traditional forms of public consumption, with any residual revenues being made available for new projects of physical investment. Other things being equal, the larger population resulting from eradication may necessitate an expansion of the traditional services and thus leave a smaller residuum for public capital formation. In this setting the direct expenses of the antimalaria campaign itself cause an equivalent reduction in public investment. At the same time the lessened morbidity may permit the government to reduce its expenditures for medical care and funds would therefore be released for public investment as defined.

It should be recognized that many of the high-priority consumption expenditures of government promote the growth of income through improving the quality of the labor force even though they do not add to the stock of physical capital as defined. It would seem advisable to pay particular attention to the educational sector in assessing the economic effects of malaria eradication. In most countries of the malarial zone, education is a large-scale high-priority government service; the rapid increase which eradication produces in the population of school age therefore means that a large quantity of extra funds must be committed to education. These expenditures create a more productive labor force, but only after a substantial lag. If eradication did not occur, the funds in question could by assumption be invested to bring an immediate pay-off.

OTHER EFFECTS ON OUTPUT. The level of output depends not only on the quantity and quality of human and nonhuman inputs but also on the manner in which those inputs are combined. It is possible for eradication to increase output by inducing a change in input combinations. The effect in question has been recognized and indeed exaggerated in the public health literature. It is said that malaria eradication permits the exploitation of new territories which previously were shunned because of the threat of disease. Very often the gross value of the output from the

newly exploited districts is cited as a measure of the benefits from eradication. It is not acknowledged that the capital equipment and labor used in these districts presumably had some positive opportunity cost, and that the increase in output from the previously malarial districts is obtained at the price of reduced output elsewhere.

Nevertheless, the phenomena in question may involve net gains for the economy. These gains are perhaps best analyzed as stemming from a spatial reallocation of resources which is induced by a localized decline in the disutility of work. Eradication lowers the disutility of work in the previously malarial districts; labor accordingly tends to migrate to those districts; the shift in labor raises the marginal product of capital in those districts relative to its marginal product elsewhere, and in the long run a migration of capital will accompany the migration of labor. If, as seems likely, the marginal product of land in the malarial districts before eradication was higher than its marginal product elsewhere, eradication will have contributed to an expansion of output by causing labor and capital to be relocated in the districts where the marginal product of land was relatively high.

A MODEL FOR MEASURING THE ECONOMIC EFFECTS OF ERADICATION

If we wish to measure the impact of eradication on per capita income while allowing for all the effects discussed in the preceding section, it is clear that we must make use of a fairly detailed model of the entire economy. The relationships which appear to be relevant should be specified in the form of equations. The model should then be used to provide two simulations of the course of per capita income through a period of n years, the first simulation being based on the assumption that eradication occurs at the start of the period, and the second simulation being based on the assumption that no eradication campaign is undertaken during the period. The method could be used retrospectively, measuring the consequences of a completed program, or it could be used to predict the outcome of a proposed program. One particularly successful application of the method is to be seen in the measurement by Coale and Hoover of the economic gains from birth control in India.[4]

In specifying a model of the entire economy, this approach is somewhat more elaborate than that typically used in "benefit-cost" analyses of health programs. The typical analysis in this field has been of a partial nature, a legitimate approach when the program in question causes nothing more than marginal changes in the structure of the economy. But malaria eradication can cause quite marked changes. By using Newman's results concerning the effects of eradication on birth and death rates,[5] it can be estimated that the population of Ceylon in 1977, thirty years after

eradication, will be 16.0 millions, whereas in the absence of eradication the figure would be only 12.6 millions. It is estimated that in 1977, 27 percent of the population will be in the labor force; without eradication the figure would be 29 percent. In 1977, the education budget in Ceylon will be about 700 million rupees; the figure would be about 500 million rupees in the absence of eradication. The methods of partial analysis, which would essentially ignore the indirect repercussions of eradication, would probably yield misleading results in this situation.

A model has therefore been designed which allows for the major economic effects, direct and indirect, of malaria eradication. With some modifications the model would also be useful for evaluating any public health program which had important effects on demographic structure and labor supply, such as programs of birth control, programs causing substantial reductions in infant mortality, or the eradication of widespread debilitating diseases like schistosomiasis. The model may even be useful for evaluating nonmedical programs such as education.

The model has been designed with the case of Ceylon in mind, and is being used to estimate the effect of eradication on Ceylonese per capita income during the thirty-year period following the successful campaign of 1947, a period of this duration having been chosen as allowing for the adequate operation of all lagged effects. If other investigators wished to apply the method to other countries, they might find it desirable to amend one or two of the equations which reflect structural peculiarities of the Ceylonese economy.

[4] Ansley J. Coale and Edgar M. Hoover, *Population Growth and Economic Development in Low-Income Countries* (Princeton University Press, 1958).

[5] Peter K. Newman, *Malaria Eradication and Population Growth, With Special Reference to Ceylon and British Guiana* (Bureau of Public Health Economics, University of Michigan, 1965).

In the first part of the model, age-specific birth and death rates have been used to generate the age-sex composition of the population year by year. No attempt has been made to specify relationships between the vital rates and the various social and economic variables which appear elsewhere in the model: in a more sophisticated system it would be possible to incorporate, for example, the presumably negative relationship between birth rates and the level of educational attainment among females, or the presumably negative relationship between death rates and lagged per capita income. It is assumed that the vital rates are affected by eradication to the extent estimated by Newman, but no other formal relationships involving the vital rates have been specified. From Newman's analysis it appears that eradication had marked effects on fertility and infant mortality and therefore lowered the average age of the population. It can be estimated that in 1977, 50 percent of the Ceylonese population will be aged under twenty; without eradication the figure would be 45 percent. From the population data thus derived, estimates have been made of the population of "equivalent consumers." The index of economic performance can then take the form of income per equivalent consumer instead of income per capita, which is a somewhat less refined measure.

The main part of the model is devoted to the determination of income, defined as real gross national income. The relevant equations are listed in the Appendix to this paper. [Editors' note: See original source for Appendix.] There is not the space here to explain the equations

fully, and we must be content with mentioning a few of their salient features, along with a brief indication of some of the measurement difficulties encountered in estimating the equations for the case of Ceylon:

1. The production function is of the Cobb-Douglas form, a form chosen because of its relative simplicity and because the terms appearing in the function are readily measurable. The function differs, however, from the simplest Cobb-Douglas formulation in two main respects: (a) the labor input is disaggregated into two components, skilled and unskilled, skilled workers being defined as those with some secondary education; (b) each of the three inputs—skilled labor, unskilled labor, and capital—is characterized by a quality index. The purpose of disaggregating the labor input is to allow for the fact that malaria eradication has a differential impact on components of the labor force which differ greatly in their productivity. The introduction of the three quality indexes allows for various other consequences of eradication.

2. The indexes of skilled and unskilled labor quality are increased when malaria is eradicated, because debilitation is thereby reduced. The measurement difficulties here are acute, and an empirical investigation of the economics of debilitation must surely have high priority among future research projects in the area of medical economics.[6] In the present study the effect of eradication on the indexes of labor quality was estimated on the basis of opinions ex-

[6] For several suggestions as to how the effects of debilitation could be measured, see Mushkin, *loc. cit.*, pp. 141–42.

pressed informally by malariologists. Additional simulations are being performed on the assumption that the effects are much more powerful than initially supposed, the objective being to see whether the effects of eradication on income per equivalent consumer are highly sensitive to the extent of debilitation.

3. The index of the quality of the capital stock depends on the relative importance of three components of each year's investment: imported capital goods (assumed to have a high quality or productivity), housing construction (low quality), and other investment (medium quality). The larger population occasioned by eradication causes more investment to take the low-quality form of housing construction, although only after a considerable lag. Imports of capital goods will be subject to a balance-of-payments constraint. In the case of Ceylon, the foreign exchange receipts needed for purchasing imports are assumed to be independent of eradication. In particular, eradication is assumed to have no effect on exports: the acreage suitable for the major Ceylonese export crops (tea, rubber, and coconuts) lies mostly outside the previously malarial zone, and export production has not been limited to an important extent by labor shortages. In this context, eradication may generate a larger volume of investment, but that volume is likely to be of inferior quality because it will contain a relatively small proportion of imports.

4. There is a fourth quality index in the production function, an index of allocative quality. Eradication can affect the level of this index by inducing a spatial reallocation of resources, as discussed above. Guesses are unavoidable in estimating the

values of this variable, the only relevant information available in the case of Ceylon being that which describes the shift in the labor force between previously malarial and previously nonmalarial districts.

5. The exponents in the production function are the elasticities of output with respect to skilled labor, unskilled labor, and capital, respectively. If, as seems reasonable, the sum of the three elasticities is constrained to equal unity, we can conclude on the basis of the Euler theorem that their values are approximated by the shares of the respective factors in total income. Data on the capital share in Ceylon are not available, and in the present study, simulations are to be based on alternative capital-elasticity values of 0.5 and 0.3 (the latter being a normal value for Western economies). Data on the relative shares of skilled labor and unskilled labor are available from the *Surveys of Consumer Finances* undertaken by the Central Bank of Ceylon in 1953 and 1963. The Central Bank *Surveys* are also invaluable in providing data needed elsewhere in the model, such as data on private medical expenditures and on the proportion of each age-sex group who have received secondary education.

6. The quantity of labor inputs depends in part on morbidity rates. The reductions in these rates following the Ceylonese antimalaria campaign can be roughly estimated from data collected by Cullumbine in a household survey of morbidity.[7]

---

[7] H. Cullumbine, "A Survey of Disabling Illness in Ceylon," *Bulletin of the World Health Organization*, VII (1952), pp. 405–29, and "The Health of a Tropical People," *The Lancet*, May-June, 1953, pp. 1090 ff., 1144 ff., 1193 ff., and 1245 ff.

Cullumbine's data suggest that eradication caused significantly greater declines in morbidity among the unskilled than among the skilled.

7. The value of the capital stock in the initial year, along with the value of the constant term in the production function, can be obtained by simultaneous solution of two versions of the production function—one version containing the values for one arbitrarily selected year and the other containing the values for some later year—in which these two terms are the only unknowns. The capital stock grows annually as a result of net investment. Net investment is assumed to be solely dependent on the supply of saving, an assumption which is justifiable for low-income countries although not for high-income countries. Most of the data needed for simulating the growth of saving are to be found in a detailed set of national accounts. In the case of Ceylon these data are obtainable from the Central Bank's *Annual Reports*, the Census Department's *Statistical Abstracts*, the United Nations' *Yearbooks of National Accounts Statistics*, and in particular from a recent study by Snodgrass.[8]

8. Total saving consists of private saving, government saving (the excess of tax receipts over public noninvestment expenditures), and foreign saving (the current-account deficit in the balance of payments). Private saving is held to be a function of private disposable income per equivalent consumer. In the determination of government saving, it is assumed that the budgetary priorities are like those discussed above: the public noninvestment expenditures—educational spending, other forms of public consumption, and transfer payments—are dependent primarily on population size, and public investment is essentially a residual. Eradication causes an expansion of public noninvestment expenditures but does not cause a corresponding increase in tax receipts, at least in the case of Ceylon. On the basis of the administrative realities in underdeveloped countries, it is assumed that tax receipts are a function of the size of the foreign trade sector. Since, according to our earlier argument, eradication has done little to increase the size of the foreign trade sector in Ceylon, it has also done little to increase tax receipts. In Snodgrass' words, "caught between . . . rising service bills and the relative inelasticity of government revenues, capital expenditures suffered."[9]

9. Imports of both capital goods and noncapital goods are assumed to be a function of (a) demand considerations and (b) the size of foreign exchange reserves at the beginning of the year in questions. When reserves become seriously depleted, it is common for the government to curtail imports by imposing tariffs or quotas. It was thought unlikely that the relationship between imports and prior reserves would be linear. To provide a more plausible relationship, the square root of the reserves was therefore used in the import equations.

MODEL DYNAMICS. It will be clear from the preceding discussion that eradication has numerous positive and negative effects on income per equivalent consumer. These effects do not occur all at once but in a

---

[8] Donald R. Snodgrass, *Ceylon: An Export Economy in Transition* (Irwin, 1966).

[9] *Op. cit.*, p. 194.

TABLE 1
Selected Lags in the Effects of Malaria Eradication on
National Income per Equivalent Consumer

Number of Years after Eradication	Positive Effects	Negative Effects
0		Resources are devoted to eradication campaign
1	Quantity and quality of labor inputs are increased due to reduced mortality, morbidity, and debility; private expenditures on medical care are reduced; spatial reallocation of resources begins	Population grows due to reduced mortality
2		Population grows due to increased fertility
6		Part of first cohort of "eradication babies" enters primary school
11		First cohort becomes "equivalent consumers"
15	Part of first cohort enters unskilled component of labor force	Part of first cohort enters secondary school
16		Females in first cohort enter childbearing age bracket
20	Part of first cohort enters skilled component of labor force	Part of first cohort enters institutions of higher education
21		First cohort enters housing market
26		Females in first cohort enter age bracket where fertility at maximum

staggered fashion, and the model therefore involves several lags. Some of the more important of these lags are listed in Table 1. On the positive side it is shown that there are some strong effects occurring in the first year after eradication. The lags in the negative effects can be best seen by following the career of the first cohort of "eradication babies"; that is, those babies who would not be alive one year after the eradication campaign if the campaign had not occurred. One should add that the second cohort is appreciably larger than the first: in the second year after eradication, not only are infant mortality rates at their new lower levels but birth rates begin to rise.

THE MODEL APPLIED
TO CEYLON

The model described in the preceding section and in the Appendix has been used to simulate the course of income per equivalent consumer in Ceylon on the assumption that malaria was not eradicated. Some partial results of the simulation are depicted in Figure 1. At the time of writing, the simulation had proceeded from 1947 through 1955. It

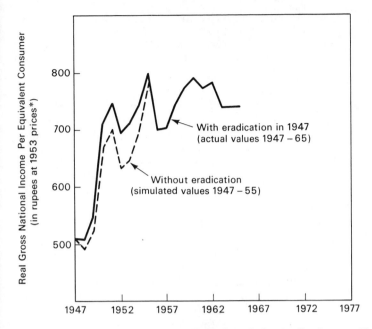

FIGURE 1 **The Net Effect of Malaria Eradication on National Income per Equivalent Consumer in Ceylon**

* In 1953 the official exchange rate was $1.00=Rs. 4.76.

can be seen that at the outset eradication had a strong positive impact on income per equivalent consumer. As the years progressed beyond 1947, the gap widened between the with-eradication values and the without-eradication values of income per equivalent consumer, until by 1953 the income figure with eradication, at Rs. 712, was 10 percent higher than the figure without eradication, at Rs. 646.

Thus in the short run, malaria eradication in Ceylon proved economically beneficial. The explanation for this result can be found most readily by referring to Table 1. Eradication makes an immediate contribution to output by increasing the quantity and quality of labor inputs, primarily through reductions in morbidity and debility, and secondarily through reductions in mortality. In the short run the negative effects of eradication on income per equivalent consumer are weak. The direct expenses of the campaign itself are inconsiderable. During these early years, most of those who are alive because of eradication are infants: not until they are five years old will they begin to impose burdens on the educational sector; not until they are about ten years old will they become fully-fledged "equivalent consumers."

But the negative influences of eradication gather strength as time progresses. Already by 1953 government saving—a major determinant of investment and hence of the future growth of output—was substantially smaller with eradication than without, even though gross national income was 14 percent higher in the former case than in the latter. By that date the extra population resulting from eradication had begun to make demands on the public sector of such a size that government saving amounted to only Rs. 80 millions; without eradication the figure would have been Rs. 170 millions. Both in 1953 and in 1954 actual net investment fell short of the level it would have attained without eradication. As a consequence, by 1955 income per equivalent consumer, at Rs. 802, was a mere 3 percent higher than the figure without eradication, at Rs. 779. It is likely that future results will show the two curves of Figure 1 crossing beyond 1955.

FURTHER ANALYSIS. Besides extending the two curves of Figure 1 to 1977, future calculations will show whether the results are highly sensi-tive to the assumptions made about the values of certain critical coefficients which are difficult to measure. Additional simulations will be based on the assumptions (a) that the capital-elasticity of output is 0.3 instead of 0.5 as assumed in obtaining the results shown in Figure 1 and (b) that the effect of malarial debilitation on labor quality is three times as great as initially supposed.

The main economic disadvantages of eradication are seen to lie in the rapid increase in the population of children resulting from the marked changes in infant mortality and birth rates. A final set of simulations will therefore be performed on the assumption that these disadvantages were avoided in Ceylon through the adoption in 1947 of a twin program of malaria eradication and birth control. It seems likely that the twin program would have made a dramatic contribution to the growth of per capita income.

THE CLANDESTINE DISTRIBUTION OF HEROIN, ITS DISCOVERY AND SUPPRESSION

What are the expected consequences of more energetic enforcement of the laws against the trade in narcotics?

By SIMON ROTTENBERG

Heroin that is illegally consumed in the United States derives, for the most part, from opium produced in Turkey which is converted there or in Lebanon to morphine base and which is, in turn, shipped through Istanbul or Beirut to France. In France it is transformed to heroin in small laboratories and is transported to the United States, either directly or via Italy, Canada, or Mexico (Giorgano, 1966, p. 5; U.S. Senate, Permanent Subcommittee on Investigations, 1964, pp. 881 ff.).

A distribution system in the United States puts the product into the hands of consumers. There are said to be between 45,000 and 100,000 narcotics addicts in this country,[1] about half of whom are in New York City.

The trade is illegal, and various federal agencies (mainly the Bureaus of Customs and Narcotics and the Food and Drug Administration) and state and local law enforcement authorities are charged with the responsibility of the execution of the law.

The prevention of the contraband introduction of narcotics into the country is apparently very difficult because narcotics are easily transported and concealed and have great value relative to their weight and volume (Anslinger and Tompkins, 1953, p. 172). It is estimated that one and one-half tons of heroin are brought into the country illegally each year (President's Advisory Commission on Narcotics and Drug Abuse, 1963, p. 5); only a small fraction of this quantity is intercepted and seized by the authorities.

THE ORGANIZATION OF CLANDESTINE ENTERPRISE

Clandestine enterprises consist of two parts: one that produces the service or good which is the nominal product of the enterprise and another that conceals the activities done in the pursuit of the first object.

Both activities consume resources.

The firm will, in the fulfilment of the second object, choose among alternative strategies for security on optimizing principles. That is to say, it will seek to minimize security costs per unit of concealment achieved, and it will carry the security operations of the enterprise to a scale that will fulfil the condition that the marginal cost of that activity will equal its marginal revenue.

A unit of revenue in the firm's security operations is the magnitude by which the probability of detection diminishes times the "loss" suffered (the costs incurred) if detected. Thus 0.4 probability of detection may be reduced, by incurring additional security or concealment costs, to 0.3 probability. The incremental revenue derived from the additional expenditure would be 0.1 times, say, the negative value put on five years in prison—which might be lost earnings—net of consumption while in prison, plus the negative value put on the state of being shut away from society and being deprived of the freedom to move, both discounted, minus the capitalized value of the income stream produced by schooling in criminal business skills while in prison and by business associations formed there.

The probability of discovery of someone engaged in the narcotics trade is a partial function of the number of transactions in which he engages. Thus one kilo of heroin sold in a single one-kilo transaction is to be preferred by those engaged in the trade to one kilo sold in two half-kilo transactions.

This suggests that the risk of discovery is largest at the point in the chain of distribution where the quantum of heroin transferred in

---

[1] Estimation methods in current use yield approximations that are subject to a large coefficient of error; the true number of addicts is not known (President's Advisory Commission on Narcotics and Drug Abuse, 1963, p. 4).

any given transaction is smallest at the mean and where, therefore, the number of transactions is largest.

Since the mean of the magnitude of transactions becomes successively smaller as heroin makes its way from importing to retailing, and the number of transactions engaged in by any operators becomes larger in the same process, the risks of detection are, other things being equal, smaller for the importer and larger for the retailer.

The narcotics distribution system may be long or short. In principle, the importer can do his own retailing; or his own wholesaling, selling to other retailers; or he may sell to jobbers who, in turn, sell to wholesalers who sell to retailers.

The length of the system will depend, in part, on the extent of the market, since this, in turn, affects the degree of specialization in the trade.

If the organization of the trade is managed—if, that is to say, a central director (say the importer or a factor) determines the number of transaction points—then the length of the system may be greater than that indicated by efficiency criteria. This is because the narcotics trade is illegal, and, therefore, those who engage in it operate clandestinely. A clandestine enterprise can be expected to be organized so as to minimize the probability of discovery of its organizer.

The larger the number of transaction points, the smaller the quantity of information possessed by any participant at any point. By elongating the chain, therefore, a organizer of the trade creates a buffer between himself and any point on the chain. The risk he runs of being discovered is inversely proportional to the number of informants who must be successively broken in order that he be found out.

The narcotics trade in some territory may be that of a single monopoly firm which organizes a chain of dealers of some number, or the trade may be carried on by a number of complementary monopolists (U.S. Senate, Permanent Subcommittee on Investigations, 1964).

If it were a single firm, then the organizer (manager) would determine the magnitude of the difference in prices of heroin between each pair of links in the chain of distribution. This magnitude would be just what is sufficient to attract the relevant number of people to the trade at each link. The compensation of the traders would be determined by the differences between their buying and their selling prices net of the costs of doing business, including the cost of being thought odious by the community and the cost of punishment for engaging in an illegal trade, in a probability sense.

If the trade is carried on by complementary monopolists, the price at each transaction link will be indeterminate, since this would simulate Edgeworth's classic duopoly case; the price would depend upon the relative shrewdness of the monopoly traders, within some range.

The magnitudes of differences in prices of narcotics between successive pairs of transaction points will be primarily affected by differences, between successive pairs of points, in the cost of doing business.[2] In this

---

[2] The U.S. Attorney for the Southern District of New York reported that the wholesale price of heroin rose greatly immediately after the arrest of two wholesale traders (U.S. Senate, Subcommittee to Investigate Juvenile Delinquency, 1963a).

trade, the largest single cost is that associated with discovery, apprehension, conviction, and punishment. The quantity of law enforcement resources and its allocation along the distribution chain would seem to be the primary determinant of the structure of narcotics prices.

Sellers of drugs, when they hold inventories, possess commodities which, if they are discovered, constitute incriminating evidence (Eldridge, 1962, p. 53). There will be a strong incentive to "unload" rapidly and to refrain from holding inventories. As with other stored commodities, inventories may be held in expectation of a price rise; there is an optimal storage policy that takes account of the cost of storage. In the case of an illegal commodity (that is, one whose mere possession, or whose possession with intent to sell, is illegal), the cost of storage is pre-eminently the negative value associated with discovery.

Law enforcement would be advantaged by any change that induced sellers to hold larger inventories and for longer periods. Can enforcement policy be designed to bring this about? Would it be helpful in this connection if possession were not illegal, nor presumptive evidence of illegal activities accepted by the courts? If this induced illegal operators to hold inventories and, in turn, provided information to the authorities about the persons to watch (for *other* kinds of activities than possession—which activities *would* be illegal), would the incidence of discovery rise? But, if possession, even if legal, were found to have secondary adverse consequences, operators would still have an incentive to refrain from storing.

The distribution of opiates is ap-parently done by "organized criminals," and the distribution of LSD and marijuana is done largely by amateurs.[3] Presumably, this is because the rate of return, adjusted for the cost of doing business, is higher in the opiate trade than in the others. This must be because opiate traders are able to enforce a monopoly which produces rents for them. But why do they not also enforce a monopoly in the other drug trades? Is it because (a) opiate distribution is considered to be the more odious trade; therefore, "amateurs" are less willing to engage in it; therefore, "professionals" have a monopoly of "talent," and it is from this that their rents derive?

Or is it because (b) the costs imposed upon discovered and apprehended opiate distributors are higher than the costs put on traders in LSD and marijuana; these costs are differentially valued by different classes of persons; the amateurs believe a five-year prison sentence is a high price to pay for the monetary gains derived from the trade, but the professionals believe the price is not so high. Therefore, only a small number will engage in the trade (if there were no monopoly and given the relative, adjusted earnings in the opiate trade), and the enforcement costs of a monopoly—which must exclude only a small number of aspirants to the trade—will be low. The costs imposed upon LSD and marijuana distributors are lower (the prison sentences are shorter); therefore, for given rewards, more will engage in

_____

[3] The commissioner of the Food and Drug Administration reports that "a crude form of LSD could be produced by a college chemistry laboratory" (Giorgano, 1966, p. 15; Goddard, 1966, p. 4).

these trades; the enforcement of monopolies in these trades would require the exclusion of many disposed to enter; the cost of enforcement of the monopoly would, therefore, be high in them. Presumptively, since we do not observe monopolies in these trades, the cost of making a monopoly effective is high enough so that such an undertaking is not worth while.

What are the expected consequences of more energetic enforcement of the laws against the trade in narcotics?

Crimes are of three classes (1) They may destroy part of the capital stock of society, as murder and arson; (2) they may involve coercive transfer payments, as theft; (3) they may involve the sale and purchase of commodities that society believes reprehensible, as prostitution and narcotics.

Some crimes damage society more than others. Society can affect the product mix of the crime industry by allocating law enforcement resources among crimes, thus determining the distribution among crimes of the costs of criminal activity paid by criminals.

It is assumed that criminals will choose that criminal career which will maximize their net revenues. If, other things being equal, some crimes are made more costly for those who perpetrate them, criminals will, at the margin, move to other crimes. The degree of enforcement of the law against the trade in narcotics will, therefore, enlarge the cost to society from other crimes.

Society's indifference curve between crimes can be assumed to be concave to the origin so that the increment of other crimes than the

trade in narcotics that it is willing to suffer, in exchange for the reduction by one unit of the narcotics trade, will be small, if the narcotics trade is of relatively small volume and other crimes of relatively large volume; and it will be large if the volume of narcotics trade is relatively large and the volume of other crimes is relatively small.

Criminals now diversify their output to some extent. That is to say, they engage in a number of different criminal activities. This is a form of hedging. If one criminal activity is made relatively more costly to engage in, other things being equal, the quantity of that crime tends to shrink, and that activity becomes inferior, as a hedge, to what it had been before the cost change occurred. The failure rate of criminal enterprises will rise as a consequence.

As heroin moves forward toward the consumer in the distribution chain it is successively diluted, usually by milk sugar or quinine hydrochloride (U.S. Senate, Subcommittee to Investigate Juvenile Delinquency, 1963a, p. 3133). The consumer finally buys a combination of heroin and inert materials that may be 1.5–33.0 per cent heroin by weight.

Why does narcotics dilution take place? As with any other commodity, it is not necessary to dilute in order to effect a rise in price. Two alternative hypotheses are suggested: (1) Consumers will offer less resistance to a price rise produced by additional adulteration of the product and will be less likely to search out alternative sources of supply than if the price rise were outright and open. This seems like a questionable hypothesis, since users can apparently tell the intensity of their experience in the consumption of drugs and do adjust by increasing the number of bags used in a single dose when adulteration occurs. On the other hand, adulteration simulates the behavior of, say, the candy manufacturers who kept the price of candy bars constant while shrinking their sizes. (2) Adulteration is a rationing device employed when heroin is in short supply. This hypothesis would explain variance in the degree of dilution but not the apparent secular tendency for dilution to occur.

Another possible hypothesis is that dilution opens options for consumers. It permits users to choose between small (say one bag) doses and large (say three bag) doses. But this hypothesis gives no clue as to why the extent of dilution has increased with time; it suggests only that dilution will always occur in order to provide a lower "quality" product for those whose preference functions make it desirable to ingest small quantities. It is like explaining why Falcon automobiles will be manufactured, as well as Continentals, but would not explain why the fraction of Falcons rises and the fraction of Continentals falls.

THE MARKET FOR THE SERVICE OF POLICE INACTION

An increase in the probability of interception of illegally imported heroin would have the expected effects of raising its price and of shrinking the trade. These effects can also be achieved in other ways. Anything that increases the expected costs of engaging in this trade will have the same results. Thus, if the fraction of illegally imported heroin

that is intercepted does not rise, but if there were an increase in the probability of discovery, apprehension, and/or conviction of smugglers, the trade would also tend to decline. Conversely, of course, anything that diminishes the expected cost of doing business in the trade will diminish the price of its product and enlarge the trade.

The narcotics trade, like many other criminal activities, is probably cartellized (U.S. Senate, Subcommittee to Investigate Juvenile Delinquency, 1963b, p. 3029), and it produces monopoly rents. Those engaged in the trade have earnings which are superior to those they could earn in alternative competitive employments, and they might be disposed to use these differential earnings to buy the "services" of law enforcement officers (Maurer and Vogel, 1954, p. 230). Even if the trade were competitive, the earnings of the traders would be higher than those in alternative employments by some quantity just sufficient to compensate them for the higher risks they run of having fine, imprisonment, deportation, and other costs imposed upon them; these are risks they would not run in legal employments. It would pay them, therefore, to use part of their differential earnings to reduce, in a probability sense, the magnitude of the expected costs for which the differential compensates them. Competitive traders, too, therefore, would be disposed to buy law enforcement officers' services. They will do so only if the price of these services is less than the "value" of the fraction by which the risk of the trader is diminished.

The quantity of discovery and apprehension can be expected to be a function of the quantity of information that comes into the possession of the law enforcement officers charged with the execution of the narcotics laws and of the officers' willingness to use that information to proceed against violators of the law.

The information that comes into the possession of these officers may be suppressed. It is reported that "the importation and distribution at wholesale levels, and frequently at retail levels, is likely to flourish only under some form of police protection" (Maurer and Vogel, 1954, p. 207).

This protection can occur, however, only if the administration of law enforcement activity has the properties of a monopoly industry (Rottenberg, 1960, pp. 5 ff.). Law enforcement officers are employed in something like a competitive labor market. They are paid the market wage for performing the services of their craft. For this wage, they are expected, among other things, to receive information or to search it out, to develop information that will be acceptable in the criminal courts, and to report this information to their relevant superior officers. The officer may, however, be in a position to extract some of the monopoly rents of monopoly illegal traders or to share with them the differential earnings for superior risk of competitive illegal traders. The officer can do this only if he, himself, monopolizes access to the relevant information and the initial "right" to report information. If other officers "compete" with him in the performance of these services and if there are enough of them so that coalitions cannot be formed among them at low cost, then the officer is without monopoly power and has nothing to sell to the illegal trader. For if the trader should buy inaction from one officer, he still runs the risk of discovery and action by another.

This problem can perhaps be solved by contriving arrangements in the administration of the law enforcement function so that administrative monopolies of the kind here suggested do not exist, and administrative competition is substituted for it. Another possible solution is to install incentive-compensation systems for law enforcement officers that will pay off for the delivery of information. There are, of course, problems associated with this form of the solution; the system may generate larger police earnings to patrols which are in crime-prone areas than others; and, if not done with care, it may produce the formation of coalitions of criminals and policemen whose object is the promotion of criminal activities which, in turn, produce incentive earnings.

A nominal rule of police administration is that officers will execute the orders of their superiors and, ultimately, that the police will be administratively responsive to the behavioral implications of the law—that they will do those things which they must do, if the law is to be effectively applied.

The law imposes costs upon criminals in some probability sense, but these costs can be diminished by purchasing inaction from a police officer. To the extent that these costs are reduced, the incidence of crime and the cost of crime borne by the community rises.

The propensity to sell the services of inaction varies among police officers so that some will fail to act (refrain from enforcing the law) if they are given, say, $100, while others would require $1,000 for the same (non)act.

If it were possible to identify the class with respect to which the propensity to be dutiful (to do only those things which are consistent with nominal and relevant rules or, perhaps, to do only those things which the community does not think odious) is high, police recruitment and selection procedures ought to be biased in favor of that class.

Given the magnitude of these propensities in a given police force, it should be possible to organize the activity of the police so as to minimize the quantity of police inaction.

If the probability of buying non-performance at a given price by one officer is 0.1 and by another also 0.1, then the probability of doing so for two independently deciding officers is the product of these probabilities, or 0.01. If these were the magnitudes involved, there would be great advantage in organizing the law enforcement machinery in such a way that inaction, to be effective in a given case (to have value to someone), would require that more than one officer be bought off.

If the individual propensities to sell non-performance were much larger than this, the advantage of such an organization would be much smaller. For example, if the corresponding probabilities were 0.9 for each officer, then the probability of securing inaction from two of them would be reduced to only 0.81, and there may be other costs associated with such an organization of police activity that would cause this arrangement to produce net disbenefits.

On the assumption that the probability numbers are small, the clear advantage associated with an organization such that inaction requires that non-performance be bought from more than one officer will occur, as has been mentioned, only if each officer makes his decision with respect to whether he will sell his (non)services independently of the decisions of other officers.

If the decision of one affects the decision of the other, the factor by which the joint probability is reduced is smaller. The organization of police activity ought, therefore, to take account, also, of joint decision effects. There is an advantage, that is to say, in refraining from establishing regular pairs or teams of officers that encourages the formation of coalitions among them.

Corrupt behavior by a police officer may be either known or not known to his colleagues on the force. If known, others who possess the knowledge may either divulge it to their superiors or they may not. Non-divulgence may imply the imposition of costs upon those who conceal information about the malfeasance of their fellow officers, and these costs may be of different magnitudes rising from the polar case of zero cost. Or divulgence may be rewarded, and the gains may be of different magnitudes. Whatever increases the cost of concealment or increases the gains from non-concealment will increase the quantity of information about corrupt behavior that passes to superior officers.

An increase in the quantity of information on the corrupt behavior of an officer that is transmitted to higher echelons of the force will increase the probability of discovery

and punishment of the corrupt officer. This will increase the price of
corrupt behavior. Corrupt behavior
purchased from the police officer is
an input of a criminal activity. If
the price of this input rises, the cost
of doing criminal business rises, and
the price of the product (narcotics-
selling services) also rises. If there is
any demand elasticity, the quantity
(of narcotics, and narcotics-selling
services) transacted falls.

A bribe paid to a police officer is
different in detail, but similar in
effect, to the payment of an insurance premium. If one insures against
disaster, he does not diminish the
probability that the disaster will
occur but reduces the cost of the
disaster *to him* to the magnitude of
the premium payments. Bribes paid
to officers *do* reduce the probability
of the occurrence of the disaster and,
in doing so, reduce the disaster cost
to the payer of the bribes. If the
probability of occurrence is reduced
to zero, then the disaster cost is the
cost of its avoidance and is equal to
the magnitude of the bribes paid. A
criminal may self-insure by running
the whole risk that disaster will
strike and by bearing the whole cost
associated with it. If he pays the
bribe-premium instead, it is because
his costs are lower this way.

The purchase of police inaction
can be thought of in another context. If the state prohibits the sale of
narcotics and executes, say, a punishment of three years of imprisonment
or a fine of $500 upon offenders, it is
saying, substantially, that the value
of that punishment is the price for a
license to engage in the trade. A
police officer who accepts a private
payment made to him for failing to
charge an offender is selling the

license—the right to enter the trade
—for some other price. The officer's
price must be lower than the state's
or the offender would not consent to
transact the license with him; he
would prefer to purchase it from the
state by paying the state's (punishment) price. The officer's behavior
shifts traders' marginal cost curves to
the right and enlarges the trade.

THE ALLOCATION OF POLICE RESOURCES

Even if corruption tends to be
most common at the lowest level of
police administration—with the man
on the beat—it may be that the more
uncommon cases at higher levels,
when properly weighted, turn out to
be more important in the aggregate.
In any case, detected information
tends to grow by a chain process, and
the suppression of a seemingly trivial
bit of information discovered "on
the street" may forestall the coming
into possession of more important
pieces some links away.

A large fraction of law enforcement activity is that subset of activity which generates information.
Information is of a number of
classes, for example, information
that a crime has been committed,
information about the identity of
the criminal and his whereabouts,
and information of an evidentiary
nature that will pass muster in a
criminal court proceeding.

Information-generating resources
are commanded by the police, and
they are scarce goods that ought to
be economized. The police have
options in the allocation of these
resources along the narcotics distri-
butional chain. This allocation is
optimal when the information out-

puts at every link, which are produced by the final units of information-generating resources employed at each link, are themselves equal. The fulfilment of this condition undoubtedly requires the use of more of the resources at some links than at others. It seems reasonable to suppose that a larger expenditure at middle links than at polar links is appropriate, since the former may produce information which, in turn, produces a second generation of information about occurrences both forward and backward in the chain of distribution, while information produced at the poles can have only unidirectional second-generation consequences.

This is complicated by the fact that the cost of acquiring a bit of information is less at the retail end of the chain than elsewhere along its length; concealment seems to be more difficult at the retail end (Schur, 1962, p. 58; Chein et al., 1964, pp. 17 and 331). This is probably because retailers advertise their wares more than do distributors at other parts of the system.

If a large part of the cost of doing business is the imprisonment cost imposed upon discovered operators, this cost becomes successively larger. Margins between buying and selling prices can be expected to cover the full cost of doing business. This explains why margins become progressively larger as heroin moves toward the consumer (U.S. Senate, Subcommittee to Investigate Juvenile Delinquency, 1963b, pp. 3028–29).[4]

In seeking information that is necessary to law enforcement, it is appropriate that information-collecting resources be employed preferentially at the points (a) where information is concentrated and (b) where the cost of concealment of information is high.

Customs personnel and search resources are not sufficiently large to permit intensive inspection of all entries of persons and cargo (President's Advisory Commission on Narcotics and Drug Abuse, 1963, pp. 37–38; U.S. Senate, Subcommittee to Investigate Juvenile Delinquency, 1963b, p. 2989). If these resources *were* large enough for this purpose, intensive inspection would apparently prolong the time consumed in entry beyond permissible limits. Except for persons and cargo which are suspect because U.S. Customs possess incriminating information about them (all of which should presumably be intensively examined), Customs has the options of extensive examination of all entrants, or intensive examination of a sample of entrants, or some combination of these two. The sample that is examined intensively may be randomly selected. It is not clear whether there would be any advantage in the intensive inspection of a randomly selected sample of the universe of entrants.

Narcotics agents work overseas, infiltrating, producing information, standing at the ready to receive information, and offering payments for information. Is the price paid for information sufficient to draw forth

---

[4] It is reported that, in the spring of 1966, the price of a gram of heroin (at 10 per cent purity) was a little less than $0.05 in Turkey (in the form of illegal opium), $1.40 at the point of importation in New York, $35 at wholesale in Chicago, and $295 at retail in Chicago.

the optimal quantity of it?[5] Information is non-homogeneous with respect to its value in enforcement of the law. Is the structure of rewards or payoffs to informers appropriate from the standpoint of maximizing information (adjusted for quality) received by the law enforcement agencies for given expenditures for this purpose?

The narcotics trade is now apparently a monopoly trade. We assume that, as in other monopoly cases, the net revenue position of the narcotics trader is maximized when the prices he charges are higher and the output he produces is lower than they would be if this were a competitive trade.

The enforcement authorities are in a position to re-enforce the monopoly or to make the trade more competitive. They do the former if they are more energetic in the enforcement of the law against new entrants than against the monopolist incumbent in the trade. They do the latter if they are equally energetic in enforcement against all.

If consumer expenditure for narcotics were of income earned from the performance of services or from the ownership of assets, it would clearly be in the community interest to re-enforce the monopoly on the ground that a smaller noxious industry is preferable to a larger one.

Since it is known, however, that income spent for this purpose is derived largely from clandestine or coercive extraction of unwilling transfer payments from others (that is, from theft), it is not so certain that a smaller industry is always to be preferred. This is because the demand schedule for narcotics, if relatively inelastic, causes a smaller industry to impose higher larcenous transfer payment costs upon the community than would a larger industry.

The optimal allocation of enforcement resources will be affected by the mechanism by which addiction spreads. Two possible hypotheses are: (1) There are constant "returns" to scale, and (2) there are increasing "returns" to scale. If the first of these characterizes the world, one addict will infect x number of non-addicts (causing them to become addicts), and a cluster of ten addicts will infect $10x$ non-addicts. If the second is true, then if one addict will infect x non-addicts, a cluster of ten addicts will infect some number of non-addicts which is larger than $10x$.

If the second hypothesis is correct, it suggests that critical mass of some magnitude is necessary for infection to occur. The process would be analogous to the spread of fire. If a matchstick burns, the probability of neighborhood fires is less than if a house burns. Or if ten houses burn, each of which is separated from any other burning house by ten miles, the probability of disastrous spread of fire is less than if the ten burning houses were in the same neighborhood.

Suppose non-addicts experiment with drugs for a number of reasons, say: (a) they are told by an addict that it produces pleasurable experiences, or, by observing a user, they

---

[5] It is reported that the U.S. Treasury Department pays $500 for information leading to the seizure of a kilo of narcotics; that this is less than the payment for information that leads to other kinds of contraband goods, where the payment is 25 per cent of the value of the contraband recovered and may be as much as $50,000; and that the Treasury's "standing offer" to informers of narcotics smuggling is a weak incentive for disclosure (U.S. Senate, Subcommittee to Investigate Juvenile Delinquency, 1963a, p. 3067).

can see that it produces these experiences; (*b*) they admire another whom they know to be a user because of other qualities he possesses (he is an accomplished playwright, or poet, or musician); and (*c*) they desire to be a member of a community they believe to be congenial, and the consumption of drugs is a necessary condition of entry into this community.

Of this small catalogue of motivations for experimentation, (*a*) and (*b*) would be operative whether the observed addict is isolated or one of a cluster of addicts. However, (*c*) would be operative only when there were clusters. As long as there is one additional incentive associated with a cluster which is absent in the case of the isolated addict, the cluster will be a stronger focus of infection than the individual; and a cluster will have stronger infecting consequences than an equal number of isolated individuals.

This suggests that the quantity of enforcement per addict should be larger where clusters occur than where there are no clusters and addicts are isolated; that clusters should be broken up and their members diffused more thinly in the population and in space; that clusters, where they are not broken, should be isolated; that devices should be employed to cause that segment of the non-addict population which is on the margin of experimentation to believe, given the values they presently hold, that the

addict cluster community is not congenial (this may require either the exposition of the truth, or systematic misrepresentation of fact, or some combination of them); and that devices be employed to alter the values of the sector that is on the margin of experimental drug consumption so that the probability diminishes that experiments occur.

Maximizing individuals seeking euphoric utilities will prefer those instruments for securing it that are cheapest.[6] Can the substitutes for dangerous drugs (either in the form of drugs that are not dangerous or other [non-drug] commodities) be ranked in the order of their goodness as substitutes? If so, policy can perhaps reduce their prices, relative to the prices of dangerous drugs.

The authorities charged with the enforcement of the narcotics laws are faced with a set of alternative strategies among which they exercise options. This paper has touched upon some of the variables that affect optimizing behavior by those authorities.

---

[6] Juveniles arrested in Los Angeles told the police there that they turned from marijuana to barbiturates "because they are cheaper" (U.S. Senate, Subcommittee to Investigate Juvenile Delinquency, 1963*b*, p. 2761). Some price information is available for various illegal drugs. Comparisons are meaningless, however, because the physical units of measure vary among them and because they differ in the properties, intensity, and duration of euphoric experience produced by their consumption.

REFERENCES

[1] H. J. ANSLINGER and W. F. TOMPKINS, *The Traffic in Narcotics*. New York: Funk & Wagnalls, 1953.

[2] ISIDOR CHEIN, *et al.*, *The Road to H.* New York: Basic Books, 1964.

[3] W. B. ELDRIDGE, *Narcotics and the Law*. Chicago: American Bar Foundation, 1962.

[4] H. L. GIORGANO, Statement before the Special Subcommittee on Juve-

nile Delinquency of the Senate Committee on the Judiciary, May 26, 1966 (duplicated).

[5] J. L. GODDARD, Statement before the Special Subcommittee on Juvenile Delinquency of the Senate Committee on the Judiciary, May 23, 1966 (duplicated).

[6] D. W. MAURER and V. H. VOGEL, *Narcotics and Narcotics Addiction.* Springfield, Ill.: Charles C. Thomas, Publisher, 1954.

[7] President's Advisory Commission on Narcotics and Drug Abuse. *Final Report.* Washington: Government Printing Office, 1963.

[8] S. ROTTENBERG, "A Theory of Corruption in Trade Unions," *Series Studies in Social and Economic Sciences.* (National Institute of Social and Behavioral Science, Symposia Studies Series No. 3.) Washington:

National Institute of Social and Behavioral Science, 1960.

[9] E. M. SCHUR, *Narcotics Addiction in Britain and America.* Bloomington: Ind. Univ. Press, 1962.

[10] U.S. Senate, Permanent Subcommittee on Investigations, Committee on Government Operations, 88th Congress. Hearings pursuant to S. Res. 278. Part 4: *Organized Crime and Illicit Traffic in Narcotics.* Washington: Government Printing Office, 1964.

[11] U.S. Senate, Subcommittee To Investigate Juvenile Delinquency, 87th Congress. Hearings pursuant to S. Res. 48. Washington: Government Printing Office, 1963. (a)

[12] U.S. Senate, Subcommittee To Investigate Juvenile Delinquency, 87th Congress. Hearings pursuant to S. Res. 265. Washington: Government Printing Office, 1963. (b)

INTERNATIONAL

THE MARINE FISHERIES:
A PROBLEM IN INTERNATIONAL COOPERATION

Improved economic performance in fishing industry within reach, but sweeping revisions in regulations and international law are called for.

By JAMES CRUTCHFIELD

I

Any discussion of the economics of the high seas fisheries would appear grossly out of place in meetings geared to the theme of efficiency. Among the resource-oriented industries (a group studded with exceptions to general rules about economic maximization) the fisheries stand out as a most recalcitrant performer.

A few examples will illustrate the point. Throughout the North Pacific we find large fleets of vessels, ranging from one-man gill net boats to elaborate factory ships and mothership units, pursuing salmon which, if left to their own devices, will appear in concentrated schools at the mouths of the rivers of their birth, in prime condition, virtually ready to swim into the processing plant. The vessels would be larger and the industry more capital intensive were it not for the quaint custom of reducing excessive fishing pressure by eliminating the more efficient methods of catching salmon. Until the 1950's fishermen in the highly valuable Bristol Bay red salmon operation were still required to use sailboats in the interest of "conservation," and Alaska still forbids the use of any vessel more than fifty feet in length. In the North Sea thousands of subsidized vessels scour the fishery in the face of convincing evidence that a substantial reduction in fishing effort would bring an increase of perhaps 50 percent in physical yield within a fairly short period. This is the only industry, to my knowledge, ever to be subjected to the counsel of an expert hired by a major government agency to reduce its efficiency in the interest of conservation.

The situation has its ludicrous aspects, but the surrounding circumstances are more sobering than comical. Recent controversies over high seas fisheries have put severe strains on major alliances vital to the political and economic stability of the free world. The United States itself is currently involved in running conflicts over marine fisheries with Japan, Canada, the Soviet Union, and several of the Latin-American countries. Thus far no missiles more deadly than codfish have been launched, but the more insidious device of retaliatory restrictions on international trade is being employed with increasing frequency at the bargaining table.

II

What is really at stake? On the one hand, there are platitudes in plenty about the boundless wealth of the sea. To the extent that these rest on any scientific basis, they refer to the yield that might be expected if the organic resources of the sea could be harvested at the points in time and space where the total weight is greatest. It might indeed be possible to produce some millions of tons of protein-rich plankton annually but it could hardly be termed food in an economic sense. At the opposite extreme, estimates based on the physical yields to be expected from extension of present techniques on presently productive grounds directed at presently marketable species suggest a maximum annual output less than twice the present level of about 45 million metric tons [1].

Cast in more appropriate economic terminology, the prospects could be summarized as follows. Supply functions based on present techniques would become relatively inelastic at outputs of perhaps 60 to 70 million tons. On the other hand, the fishing industry is in the throes of technological changes that have shifted supply functions rightward by extending both the geographic mobility of fishing gear and the range within which previously unused species are substitutable for those in limited supply. The potential economic yield appears great enough to warrant considerable concern over the consequences of an unrestricted international scramble to expand the shares of individual nations.

The rationale behind the pressure to expand national fishery operations is more evident in terms of differences in the accessibility of marine resources and in the level and composition of consumer demand in various national economies. For some countries (e.g., Norway, Iceland, Japan, and Peru) exports of fishery products bulk large enough in the balance of payments to warrant real concern. In others, including such diverse nations as Sweden, Norway, Japan, China, and many of the underdeveloped nations of Asia, fishery products make up an important part of the total protein intake.

Consumption of fish appears to be highly elastic to income in underdeveloped areas where population is rising rapidly. Though per capita consumption has been stable or declining in most of Western Europe and North America, aggregate world demand may therefore be expected to increase substantially in the foreseeable future. The present emphasis on the development of high-valued species for export (tuna and shrimp, for example) may give way to a much broader basic pattern of exploitation for domestic consumption as the emerging economies develop more adequate physical and organizational arrangements for utilizing fish products efficiently. The matter is far more complex than a simple matching of available supplies in the sea with areas of critical malnutrition traceable to protein deficiency. Nevertheless, the correspondence is close enough to warrant a serious look at the possibility of devising more adequate solutions to the problems of internationally shared fisheries than are now being considered.

III

The commercial fisheries of the world rest on the productive capacity of a series of organic populations. Like a forest—perhaps the most similar type of useful living resource —a fish population exists in an enormously complex ecological environment. It is impossible, however, to observe directly the size and composition of a specific fish population, nor can environmental conditions be controlled sufficiently to isolate the impact of specific changes known to affect it. In most cases exploratory fishing is prohibitively costly, and we rarely acquire sufficient statistical data to permit even rough approximations of the production possibilities from a given fishery resource until a well-developed commercial fishery is operating on it.

The key variables determining production possibilities from a fish population can be grouped under four headings: rate of entry into the "fishable" age (recruitment); growth rates of individual fish; natural mortality (from disease, old age, and nonhuman predators); and fishing mortality. In the absence of human intervention, any marine population tends toward a maximum aggregate weight, or biomass, at which net increments to stock from recruitment and growth are exactly offset by decrements from natural mortality. Thus, at zero and at maximum population the instantaneous rate of change in the weight of the fishery population is zero. At intermediate levels, the aggregate weight of the stock, in the absence of other disturbances, will tend to rise toward its maximum value, and the instantaneous rate of change in weight will be positive.

Assuming for the moment that recruitment and growth rates are independent of population size, these relationships can be translated into a simple physical production function. As fishing effort (expressed in terms of standard units) is increased from zero level, sustainable yield— that is, the catch equal to the instantaneous rate of change in biomass in the absence of fishing by man— increases at a decreasing rate, while the number and average size of fish will decline continuously. If the selectivity of the gear with respect to fish of different sizes is held constant, the sustainable yield will peak at some level of fishing effort. Further increases in fishing effort will produce an absolute decline in sustained physical yield. The common sense of this is apparent. Assuming a recruitment rate independent of population and a sigmoid growth function, fishing by man will yield a larger net physical product as long as the marginal reduction in weight losses from natural mortality is greater than the marginal weight loss resulting from capture of individual fish before they achieve maximum weight.

The assumption that recruitment is independent of population obviously cannot be of completely general validity. For anadromous fish such as salmon, the relationship is critical. Nature is so profligate in her production of fertilized eggs, however, that the case in which the number of fish surviving to catchable size is independent of the total biomass over relevant ranges is the rule rather than the exception. The other assumptions are less tenable. Growth rates are almost certain to be density-dependent, as are some types of natural mortality, and the production possibilities implicit in the foregoing analysis are not necessarily reversible. As the size of the desired stock is reduced through commercial fishing, permanent shifts in predator-prey relations and in relative numbers of competing food users may occur. Moreover, large and frequent shifts in parameters are inevitable in the ecological setting of the sea.

The economist, however, is clearly in no position to point fingers at other disciplines on the grounds that true variables are impounded in *ceteris paribus*. If we are to make any sense at all out of the concept of optimum utilization of a fishery resource, the delineation of physical production functions must be treated as a problem in partial equilibrium, with at least a pious hope that the functions relating the populations in question to their environment may later be quantified. Analysis of the production possibilities of a fishery population is at best a matter of weighing the gains from more informed guesswork against the extraordinarily high marginal cost of adding to basic statistics. The extreme uncertainty about long- and short-run input-output relations colors every aspect of the high seas fisheries.

The superficial similarity of the yield function in a commercial fishery to that of an agricultural operation conceals substantial differences in concept. As pointed out by Gor-

don [2] the monotonic decline in marginal physical yield is primarily the result of a decline in the size of the "fixed factor" as the level of fishing effect increases. Some elements of Marshallian diminishing returns may also be present; for example, crowding on a particular fishing area may reduce the chance that the gear of each individual unit will contact fish. In general, however, diminishing marginal product is more often a result of a shift in factor proportions resulting from a decline in the number and size of fish in the population exploited than of diminishing returns in the traditional sense.

IV

To the economist, the analytical definition of production functions and the preliminary quantification of these relationships is but a first step in determining optimal output and factor combination in exploiting the resource. It is slightly unnerving, therefore, to discover that performance of most of the world's fisheries, including the few that are actively managed, has been analyzed purely on the basis of these physical relationships. Maximum sustained yield has been equated with optimum yield, despite the insistence by a few fishery biologists that the latter involves "social" considerations not subsumed in the physical relations. Attention has been focused almost entirely on long-run equilibrium relationships, with no basis for recognition of the economic nature of the decisions to invest and disinvest involved in moving from one point to another on these yield-effort functions. Only a few writers have pointed out the repercussions of changes in the size composition of exploited fishery populations where markets in different countries place different values on smaller and larger fish of the same species or on species produced jointly by the gear employed.

The basic elements involved in conversion of physical to economic magnitudes and the subsequent analysis of individual entrepreneurial decisions in the fisheries have been covered fully elsewhere and need only be summarized at this point [3] [4] [5]. In brief, if a fishery were subject to unified control, the conditions for optimal utilization would differ from those in other resource-oriented firms and industries only in the high degree of uncertainty about short- and long-run input-output relationships.

"Ownership," however, in the conventional sense of the word, is almost never possible in marine fisheries except in the extensive molluscan operations. The physical problem of delineating any useful ownership concept, together with an overlay of institutional arrangements and attitudes with respect to freedom of entry, both national and international, have resulted in common property status for most saltwater fishery resources.

The combination of unrestricted entry to a resource regarded as freely available, a high degree of uncertainty about long- and short-run relations between input and output, and the usual nonsymmetric entry and exit conditions result in a peculiarly unfortunate type of economic behavior in the fisheries. In the absence of specific governmental intervention, any economic rent attributable to the resource will always be dissipated by new entry. Fishing effort is not restricted to the range normally regarded as economically relevant in which marginal physical product is positive. Given favorable price-cost ratios, it is perfectly possible for equilibrium to be reached only at levels of fishing effort in which marginal physical product is negative— in some cases markedly so. Moreover, this melancholy situation is couched only in terms of long-run equilibrium, in which factor returns just suffice to prevent further entry or exist at a rate of output consistent with stability in the size and composition of the fish stock. The initial development of the fishery, however, is likely to be marked by a surge of new entry that carries capacity well beyond the levels appropriate for long-run equilibrium. It is not only possible but normal for excess capacity to develop quickly and to persist over long periods of time, accentuated by the traditional immobility of labor in the fisheries and the related ability to maintain capital equipment at little or no real cost.

If catch is restricted to levels at which marginal physical product is positive with no restriction on entry, economic rent will still be dissipated completely in the long run regardless of the regulatory method employed. In more cases than not, the prevention of "overfishing" in the physical sense has been achieved by concentrating on control techniques, the direct or indirect effect of which is to reduce the economic efficiency of individual primary producers.

The basic theory of a high sea fishery, whether exploited by a single nation or by more than one nation, suggests a bleak economic existence, to say the least. Since economists have not concerned themselves generally with performance of various segments of the fishing industries, the empirical evidence regarding economic performance is not extensive. What it lacks in quantity, however, it makes up in uniformity of findings. Examples include: Pontecorvo's study of the lobster fishery [6]; the work of Donald White and other Boston College economists in the ground fish operations of New England [7] [8]; the Crutchfield-Zellner study of the Pacific halibut industry [5]; the study of the Puget Sound salmon fishery by a University of Washington group [9]; and Sinclair's analysis of the fisheries of British Columbia [10]. In every case the record of economic performance is dismal. Each of these fisheries is characterized by heavy excess capacity, chronically low incomes in areas where labor mobility is restricted, and a distressing lack of internal pressure for innovation or even for adaptation of technical improvements developed elsewhere. In those involving relatively high-valued species—the halibut, salmon, and lobster cases—there is substantial evidence that fishing intensity reached levels at which marginal yields were far into the negative region.

This evidence is supported by the work of several marine biologists. Studies by Beverton and Holt [11] indicate that the yield from the heavily fished North Sea grounds is far below maximum sustainable levels, despite heavy increases in fishing effort in recent decades. Schaefer [12] concludes that even the far-ranging yellow-fin tuna fishery of the southeastern Pacific may well have reached the point where marginal physical yields are zero or negative; yet new entrants continue to pour into the operation.

V

The introduction of multinational fishing effort directed toward a single group of fish populations introduces complications but does not alter the formal microeconomic theory of the fisheries in any significant way. The most obvious complications are: (1) factor prices and factor combinations chosen will vary among nations with different economic structures; and (2) variations in incomes, tastes, and preferences and the availability of substitutes will yield significantly different demand patterns in different countries.

It is evident that differences in consumer preferences and costs make it impossible for two or more nations to reach full agreement on optimal rates and techniques of fishing. The seriousness of the resulting conflicts may be illustrated by reference to the present situation in the northeast Pacific. From the standpoint of the Canadian and American fisheries, optimal utilization would require protection of the limited number of highly valuable species that can be marketed profitably by our high-cost industries, all of which are being exploited at levels very close to maximum sustained physical yield. From the Japanese and Russian standpoint, however, the fishery should be organized around the use of highly efficient gear that can harvest at very low cost a wide variety of species that are perfectly acceptable in Japan's domestic and export markets. As recent headlines make clear, these positions are not always compatible. The situation is complicated further by the importance of fishery exports in the Japanese balance of payments and by the mingling of oceanographic research (some of it of military significance) and fishing operations on Soviet vessels.

Clearly, no single set of decisions as to what fish to harvest, what level of fishing effort to maintain, and what types of gear to employ will be optimal for all four nations. Even if cost and preference patterns were identical, there would remain the question of division of the catch. The situation is not eased by the fact that official representatives of each of the countries involved insist on viewing the problem solely in physical terms, apparently on the ground that some basis for general agreement can be found if all pretend that economic effects are nonexistent or unimportant. It is hardly surprising that negotiations among Canada, Japan, and the United States are progressing very slowly; or that the Soviet Union has been—uneasily— excluded from these negotiations.

The frustrating situation in the North Pacific is anything but unique. The same conflicts exist, in greater or lesser degree, in the North Atlantic, the North Sea, the coastal waters of Korea and China, the Gulf of Guinea, and the Pacific coast of South America, to name only the more prominent cases. The growing mobility of the fleets of the advanced nations and the rapid development of offshore fishing capacity in smaller coastal states promise to extend and generalize the pressure.

Any rational system of exploitation must start with the proposition that a net contribution to economic output can be realized from marine resources only by levying a specific charge to limit inputs; or, alternatively, by limiting entry directly, without attempting to divert rent to a public body through a license fee, tax, or other explicit charge.

Assuming that data are adequate to permit some approximation to rent-maximizing fishing methods and levels, there remain vexing problems of allocating the resulting net economic return. Joint maximization policies are not necessarily preferable, from the standpoint of any single participating country, to those yielding a lower aggregate rent with a greater individual share. The allocation of output among participating nations that would minimize aggregate costs is not likely to be satisfactory to all, particularly those with higher costs. Moreover, the ubiquitous tendency to develop excess capacity in the fisheries suggests that maximization of employment in the national industry may be an important political and economic consideration in some countries. Similarly, participants for whom a particular fishery provides an important source of export earnings might not regard maximization of net economic yield, or even of their own share in it, as the governing objective of international management.

A more serious difficulty in developing a reasonably satisfactory shared fishery arises in the treatment of new entrants. Suboptimal arrangements that might be worked out to encompass the ranges of disagreement outlined above require control over new entry from outside the participating group as well as from within. Yet this may not be feasible, not only on political grounds, but in terms of economic maximization. For example, underdeveloped nations adjacent to major fishing grounds may develop capacity for efficient fishing operations as capital and technical skills accumulate and the effectiveness of internal market organization grows. Their plea for entry into managed fisheries may therefore rest not only on some "right" based on geographical location, or "need" based on nutritional deficiencies, but also on economic efficiency.

If we may indulge in the luxury of contemplating alternatives without reference to their political acceptability, the most intriguing possibility would be some type of supranational fishing entity with exclusive rights over a geographic area that encompasses an appropriate ecological unit. There would be no insuperable technical barriers to maximization of rent from the complex of fisheries controlled by such an organization, provided it were free to draw factors from any source and to sell in any market. The allocation of net incomes (and, for that matter, the allocation of employment opportunities) could be handled in a manner which—though something less than an optimum optimorum—would still be incomparably better from the standpoint of economic efficiency than any possible arrangement under free fishing. It should also be possible, under unified control of this sort, to deal equitably with emerging states with valid claims to participating rights.

A second proposal (a long step closer to reality) would contemplate regional agreements on shared fisheries, again encompassing an appropriate geographic and ecological area, under which at least two of the most critical problems—determination of the proper level of effort and types of gear to be employed—could be brought under control. In some respects this would be an expansion of the moderately successful arrangements worked out under existing treaties such as the International Convention for Northwest Atlantic fisheries and the treaties covering the Pacific halibut fishery, the Fraser River salmon fishery, the Pacific fur seal operation, and—with serious reservations—the whaling industry. The allocation of rights to participation would be, of necessity, a matter for hard bargaining. But if the only alternative to acceptance of rough-and-ready compromises as to shares in a reasonably efficient fishery is a wide open competitive struggle, it should be possible to reach agreement.

The experience of the United States and Canada in sharing catches from the halibut and salmon fisheries jointly managed by the two countries is illustrative. There is no rational basis, economic or otherwise, for the apportionment scheme adopted in the salmon fishery, and no formal sharing agreement exists in the halibut convention. Nevertheless, both government and industry in each country have been quite willing to accept the resulting apportionment as long as the aggregate catch is protected. The situation would be less manageable, of course, in instances where factor costs and appropriate factor combinations lead to widely differing preferences as to the level of catch and the proper type of gear to be employed, but even an agreement dictated by any one of the participants would be preferable to unrestricted exploitation.

VI

Space limitations preclude any detailed examination of the legal environment within which internationally shared high seas fisheries must operate. The interested reader will find authoritative discussions in [13] [14] [15] and [16], and an excellent review in Van Cleve and Johnston [17]. The essentials may be summarized briefly. The historic concept of freedom of the seas is clearly incompatible with any program of rational exploitation of marine resources. To the extent that the doctrine has been applied to fisheries, it rests on one complete misconception and another not far removed from total error. The first assumption is that the resources of the sea are inexhaustible, or at least that man's harvest is so small relative to the total stock that it can exert no appreciable effect on marine populations. The second is that appropriation of marine resources is technically impossible.

The first is demonstrably false and the second holds true only if one rules out the possibility of unified management of marine resources under international agreement. From the standpoint of marine resources, the general principle of freedom of the seas has been successively modified from two directions. First, the elaborate body of law relating to territorial waters and the rights of coastal states sets forth a body of exceptions that seems to grow continuously. For purposes of our discussion, only one point need be noted: neither the issues nor the alternatives offered in discussions of territorial waters imply any recognition of economic maximization, properly defined, as a major objective.

Expansion of territorial waters and of special zones for control over fisheries (or for "conservation") obviously have significant repercussions, particularly with respect to the sharing of catch and aggregate employment opportunities. Quite apart from broader considerations of international welfare, however, the fish themselves seem indisposed to accept such solutions. In few of the critical areas would extension of territorial waters or of special fishery control zones actually exclude participation by other nations. It might well make fishing more expensive, but the ability of highly efficient large-scale fishing units to harvest fish outside the limits of territorial waters is sufficiently great to undermine seriously even the conservation argument for extension of control by a single nation.

Second, both the principle of freedom of the seas and concepts of territorial waters have been modified through bilateral and multilateral treaties, some of which have been successful in preventing serious physical depletion of high-valued marine populations. Their extension to other geographical areas and to other groups of fisheries offers real hope for more rational exploitation of the living resources of the sea.

If they are to accomplish anything significant in that direction, however, the treaty approach to multilateral management must be modified in two major respects. First, it is essential that any fishery treaty consider economic maximization as a significant objective. In virtually every existing treaty the objectives are specified only in physical terms, usually in one or another variation of "maximum sustained physical yield." Even this unsatisfactory criterion is further modified in some instances to require the use of fish for food even where other usages would yield higher economic returns. The treaty device, appropriately extended, may well be the vehicle through which real progress can be achieved in obtaining maximum human welfare from marine resources; but it most certainly will not serve that purpose until the significance of net economic yield is clearly recognized as an objective and implemented in substantive provisions of the agreement.

The treaty technique must also be modified to permit both restriction of total fishing effort when necessary and the inclusion, on the basis of some acceptable criteria, of new entrants. If the problem of entry is ignored, there is simply no way to develop a continuing net economic return. At the opposite extreme, the American-Canadian principle of "abstention"—the notion that a fully exploited and scientifically managed fishery should thereafter be closed to all others—however desirable from the standpoint of the original participants, cannot hope to win acceptance as a general rule. It would appear that the key to the entry problem may well lie in the matter of employment opportunities. To the extent that fishing nations are not under heavy pressure to utilize

excess capacity by expanding the range of their fishing operations, a share in the net rent from a multilateral, controlled fishery might be a perfectly acceptable alternative to direct participation. If restrictions on international trade in fishery products could be reduced, the performance achieved under an ideal supranational fishing enterprise might be approached via the regional treaty technique.

VII

It was suggested recently in a national news magazine that international arrangements to deal with the investigation and utilization of Antarctica and outer space should look to the law of the sea for guidance. This may offer hope for penguins and whatever astral beings may exist beyond our globe, but it bodes ill for the long-suffering human race.

There is a very real danger that the pressure to resolve increasingly serious conflicts over high seas fisheries will lead to new concepts of international law that do nothing to meet the pressing need for economic rationality in the harvesting of marine resources. Once established, such principles harden into dogma with alarming speed.

Present biological and economic concepts of the theory and practice of fishing could provide a basis for vastly improved economic performance in the high seas fisheries. Yet nothing short of a sweeping revision of both the objectives and methods of fishery regulation and an equally clear break with the traditional fabric of international law will be required if we are to make more intelligent use of marine resources.

REFERENCES

[1] Food and Agriculture Organization of the United Nations, "International Conference on Fish in Nutrition" (mimeo.) (Rome, 1961), esp. papers by G. L. Kesteven and G. Meseck.

[2] H. Scott Gordon, "On a Misinterpretation of the Law of Diminishing Returns in Marshall's Principles," *Canadian Journal of Economics and Political Science*, Feb., 1952.

[3] ———, "The Economic Theory of a Common Property Resource," *Journal of Political Economy*, April, 1954, 124–42.

[4] A. D. Scott, "The Fishery: The Objective of Sole Ownership," *Journal of Political Economy*, April, 1955, 116–24.

[5] J. A. Crutchfield and Arnold Zellner, *Economic Aspects of the Pacific Halibut Fishery*, Fishery Industrial Research, Vol. 1 (U. S. Department of the Interior, Washington, 1961).

[6] Giulo Pontecorvo, "Regulation in the North American Lobster Fishery," in *The Economics of Fishery Regulation* (FAO Fisheries Report No. 5, Rome, 1962).

[7] Donald J. White, *The New England Fishing Industry* (Cambridge, 1954).

[8] E. J. Lynch, R. M. Doherty, and G. P. Draheim, *The Groundfish Industries of New England and Canada* (U. S. Fish and Wildlife Service Circular 121, Washington, 1961).

[9] W. Royce, D. Bevan, J. Crutchfield, G. Paulik, and R. Fletcher, *Salmon Gear Limitation in Northern Washington Waters* (University of Washington Publications in Fisheries, n.s., Vol. II, No. 1, 1963).

[10] S. Sinclair, *License Limitation—British Columbia: A Method of Economic Fisheries Management* (Ottawa, 1960).

[11] R. J. H. Beverton and S. J. Holt, *On the Dynamics of Exploited Fish Populations* (London, 1957).

[12] Inter-American Tropical Tuna Commission, Annual Report, 1961, Appendix A (La Jolla, 1962).

[13] F. V. Garcia Amador y Rodriquez, *The Exploitation and Conservation of the Resources of the Sea* (Leyden, 1959).

[14] Myres S. McDougal and William U. Burke, *The Public Order of the Oceans: A Contemporary International Law of the Sea* (New Haven, 1962).

[15] Shigeru Oda, *International Control of Sea Resources* (Leyden, 1963).

[16] W. W. Bishop, Jr., "The 1958 Geneva Convention on Fishing and Conservation of the Living Resources of the High Seas," *Columbia Law Review*, 1962, pp. 1206–29.

[17] Richard Van Cleve and Ralph W. Johnson, *Management of the High Seas Fisheries of the Northeastern Pacific* (University of Washington Publications in Fisheries, n.s., Vol. II, No. 2, 1963).

ECONOMICS OF THE BRAIN DRAIN:
AN "INTERNATIONALIST" MODEL

Is "brain drain" a serious economic and cultural problem, or is it a nationalistic boondoggle that obscures the true demand and supply situation?

By HARRY G. JOHNSON*

INTRODUCTION

The concept of "brain drain" is in its origins a nationalistic concept, by which is meant a concept that visualizes economic and cultural welfare in terms of the welfare of the residents of a national state or region, viewed as a totality, and excludes from consideration both the welfare of people born in that region who choose to leave it, and the welfare of the outside world in general. Moreover, though the available statistics are far from adequate on this point, there is generally assumed to be a net flow of trained professional people from the former colonial territories to the ex-imperial European nations, and from Europe and elsewhere to North America and particularly the United States. The concept thus lends itself easily to the expression of anti-colonial sentiments on the one hand, and anti-American sentiments on the other. The expression of such sentiments can be dig-

nified by the presentation of brain drain as a serious economic and cultural problem, by relying on nationalistic sentiments and assumptions and ignoring the principles of economics—especially the principle that in every transaction there is both a demand and a supply—or by elevating certain theoretical economic possibilities into presumed hard facts.

The basic issue that needs to be resolved before discussing the phenomenon of "brain drain" and whether it constitutes a problem, therefore, is whether or not one accepts the nationalistic position. I personally do not; I adopt a cosmopolitan liberal position, and regard nationalism as one of the less pleasant mental vices in which mankind indulges itself, or as one of the characteristics of childish immaturity out of which I hope the people of the world will ultimately grow. (I expect that many educated international migrants would share this position.) Consequently, I start with the assumption that the international circulation of human capital is a beneficial process, since it reflects the free choices of the individuals who choose to migrate, and the presumption that any argument to the contrary needs very careful scrutiny and documentation before it can be accepted. This is especially so because feelings of

---

* This essay builds on my earlier "The Economics of the 'Brain Drain': The Canadian Case," *Minerva*, III, Spring, 1965, pp. 299–311. I have also benefited from a prepublication reading of Brinley Thomas, "The International Circulation of Human Capital," *Minerva* (forthcoming), though I disagree radically with Thomas's arguments and conclusions.

national identity among potential migrants themselves create fairly strong artificial barriers to migration —artificial in the sense that had the individual been born and grown up in another country he would have been culturally conditioned into comparable attachments to that country—so that less migration from low income to high income regions occurs than would be economically optimal, and what migration does occur probably involves substantial gains in world efficiency.

CULTURAL AND ECONOMIC DETERMINANTS OF MIGRATION CIRCUITS

It would be as well at the outset to warn against two sources of optical illusion in the evaluation of the magnitude of international flows of human capital. In both cases, the danger of optical illusion is fostered by the deficiencies of the available statistics on such flows, and by anachronistic concepts of the training and functioning of skilled people. The first is that the education of a professional person in modern times— just like the education of a scholar in medieval times—frequently entails prolonged study abroad, either formally in graduate school or informally in on-the-job training, after which the individual returns to his native country. Such training is not permanent emigration, but is frequently treated as such both statistically and in political discussion. The second is that the trained professional man nowadays typically travels, and is prepared to travel, a great deal in the exercise of his profession; examples are the economist who takes short-term contracts to teach, do research, or advise governments in foreign countries, and the engineer or business executive employed by a large international corporation who works for successive periods of time in different countries. Thus nationality or country of domicile of such individuals is not a reliable indicator of where they do their work. In particular, people who have emigrated may nevertheless perform their professional services to a significant extent in their countries of origin; moreover, the hiring of their services (or those of other non-nationals) when needed may be more efficient for those countries than the attempt to maintain a national stock of all the skills that might be needed from time to time.

Turning to what may be termed "permanent" flows of migration of human capital, one would expect to find, as one does find, certain fairly well demarcated patterns of flow. One such is the flow from ex-colonial territories to their ex-imperial centers, most marked in the case of France and the United Kingdom. The colonial-imperial link means that the cultural barriers to such migration are lower than to other types of migration—the emigrant moves into what he assumes (sometimes wrongly) will be a familiar culture—while the imperial tradition tends to implant the belief that in migrating to the mother country the ex-colonial is moving to a superior and more exciting culture. In addition, the colonial tradition in education policy frequently provides the successful student with an education more useful in the mother country than in his own.

Another pattern is that of general movement through intermediate stages from lower-income to higher-income countries, of which the outstanding features are the position of the United Kingdom as a country of large-scale immigration from the Commonwealth and emigration to the United States and the richer Commonwealth countries, and of Canada as a country of large-scale immigration from Europe and emigration to the United States. This process of migration by stages reflects limitations of the capacity for cultural and economic integration with a higher-level society on the part of the migrant, and also of discrimination in favor of skilled as against unskilled labor on the part of the countries of immigration. It implies that, underlying the particular bilateral flows between pairs of countries or regions, there is a more fundamental mechanism of flow, which may be thought of as the attraction of professionally-trained people towards higher income-earning opportunities, operating in an imperfectly integrated market through a chain of substitutions between groups of people of different "qualities," in terms of educational qualifications and cultural mobility.

It would be over-simple, however, to regard this process as operating in more or less the same way for all types of professional people in all countries, or to conceive of migration of skilled people as being entirely motivated by economic considerations; and this point has an important bearing on the question of whether and in what precise sense the international migration of professional people may be regarded as a problem, even from the nationalistic point of view.

First, much of such emigration from some countries is prompted by aversion to the prevailing political instability, or by the fear of personal victimization by the governing regime. This is particularly the case with certain poor European countries, under-developed countries, and recently-established new nations. It is fatuous in the extreme for sympathizers with the poor nations to assume that these countries necessarily have the political stability and legal protection of individual rights characteristic of the advanced western nations, and to lament as a "brain drain" harmful to their economic development the exodus of political refugees who happen to have the educational qualifications necessary to escape.

Second, for various reasons the higher educational systems of certain countries produce a supply of certain kinds of educated people larger than the economic systems of those countries can absorb; in such cases emigration provides a natural safety-valve rather than constituting a "brain drain."[1] The production of educated people for export in certain countries may or may not involve inefficiency from a cosmopolitan point of view: a country may have a comparative advantage in the production of skills, because it has either specially suitable human raw material, or a superior educational technology (i.e., superior schools), or a low alternative opportunity cost of human time spent in teaching and

---

[1] It is significant in this connection that a foundation-supported enterprise aimed at bringing Indian professional people back to India by undertaking to find them suitable employment had to be closed down due to its inability to find places for its clients.

learning; alternatively, irrationality in educational policy may lead a country to waste resources in subsidizing certain types of education or education in general. From a nationalistic point of view the emigration may be considered a loss, though certain forms of nationalism would prefer emigration to the alternative of restricting the country's educational facilities to the rate of output the country itself could absorb.

Third, the dominating factors in the international migration of different types of professional talent may well be different. In the case of the international migration of medical doctors—traditionally very much a private enterprise profession—important factors have been the success of the monopolistic practices of the American Medical Association in restricting the supply of American-trained doctors and raising doctors' fees, thereby attracting immigrants; and the efforts of the British government to hold down the salaries of the National Health Service doctors in order to keep down the cost of the Service, thereby strengthening the incentives to emigrate. In certain "big" sciences the cost of research equipment is so great that only a few countries can afford to invest in the required resources; people in other countries interested in these kinds of research have to migrate, at least temporarily. In other scientific subjects, the superiority of one or a few research teams at particular locations ("centers of excellence") may have the same migration-inducing effect. In the first case the migration of human capital is a consequence of economies of scale, in the second case of specialization and division of labor. Similar factors, operating

through the economies of scale and of specialization and division of labor made possible by corporate enterprise operating in a large national or international market, influence the international migration of engineers and other scientists who work for private enterprise.

It is important to recognize the influence of scale and specialization, and more generally of complementarities between knowledge and skill embodied in human capital and other inputs into research or production, on incentives to migrate. Otherwise it is too easy to assume, wrongly, that the migrant would have made the same, or a comparable, contribution to research or to national income in the country from which he emigrates as he makes to the country to which he migrates;[2] or to go further and assume that all of these complementary inputs are available in the country of emigration, and that only the wilful departure of the emigrant prevents them from being used effectively.

Two other factors in the international migration of professional people deserve mention, on the grounds that they are in a sense special to this historical period and may prove to be transitory in the longer run. The first is the influence of the massive support of research and development expenditure by the federal government in the United States, and in

---

[2] It is also only too easy to overlook the return flow of benefits that may accrue to the country of emigration from the migration of human capital, in the form of research results available to all countries, improved products obtainable through international trade, etc. For lengthier discussions of these benefits, see my earlier paper, *op. cit.*

particular, the "space race," in attracting an inflow of scientists and engineers. This factor raises some fundamental philosophical questions about how far, if at all, expenditures on armaments can be regarded as a contribution to world output and economic welfare. One might well feel that the resources expended—including the use of the talents of the immigrants attracted to such work—could be better used to promote world welfare. However, there is no possibility that the United States would be deterred from pursuing its military and space programs by cutting off its supplies of immigrant scientists and engineers, and a strong possibility that the scientists and engineers in question would be employed on very similar projects elsewhere if such an embargo were attempted, so that this factor has no obvious implications for the evaluation of the brain drain as a possible problem.

The second factor is the vast and rapid postwar expansion of demand for university education, at both the undergraduate and the graduate level, which has created a corresponding increase in demand for educated people to serve as university teachers, an increased demand which has been satisfied to a significant extent by international migration of qualified people via the intermediary-stages process mentioned earlier. This demand is likely to be abated as current trainees find their way into the market for talented labor.

SOME ECONOMIC ASPECTS OF "BRAIN DRAIN"

From the cosmopolitan liberal point of view adopted here, the international migration of educated people is presumed to be a beneficial process, since it results from the free choices of the individuals concerned, unless for some reason or other the private benefits from migration are obtained at a social cost.

Normally such migrations—like any profit-motivated international movement of factors of production —may be expected to raise total world output, and therefore, in a sense to be elaborated below, to be economically beneficial to the world as a whole.[3] Exceptions may arise when the migrant's private calculation of gain from migration excludes certain social costs that his migration entails. It is important at this stage to notice two points about the exceptional cases. First, such social costs may arise either in the country of emigration, or in the county of immigration, or in both; and in which country they are likely to be incurred is not likely to be closely correlated with whether the migrant is educated or not, though it is conventionally assumed that the migration of poor and unskilled people imposes a social cost on the country of immigration and yields a social benefit to the country of emigration, and that the reverse is true of the migration of skilled and educated people.[4] Second, to demonstrate a

---

[3] The argument will be confined to voluntary migration prompted by the expectation of private gain. The international movement of persons seeking political asylum, such as the recent Cuban exodus to the United States and the earlier westward flight of Hungarians after the 1956 uprising, may impose a heavy net burden on public or private charity in the country of immigration.

[4] As contrary examples, the immigration even of highly educated professional people

net social cost it is not sufficient to demonstrate a loss to those remaining in the country of emigration; such losses, if they occur, must exceed the private gain to the migrant plus any gains or minus any losses to the other residents of his country of immigration.

If this requirement is not satisfied —and there is a general presumption that it will not be, since the evaluation starts from the fact of a positive personal gain to the migrant himself, and most of the valid arguments for the possibility of divergence of social from private cost or gain apply in reverse to the two countries of emigration and immigration—migration may be said to increase potential world welfare, in the technical sense that the gainers from such migration, normally assumed to be the migrant himself and the public of the country of immigration, could compensate the losers, normally assumed to be the public of the country of emigration, and still have something left over. One cannot, however, maintain that the world is actually better off as a result of such migration unless

either there are no (or, pragmatically, negligible) losses to be compensated, or some machinery exists for compensating the losers. While elements of such compensatory mechanisms exist in the world as it is,[5] there is no articulated machinery for compensation; hence it becomes important to determine what, if any, elements of loss there may be, and what sort of compensation might be necessary.[6]

There are thus two questions to be discussed concerning the international migration of educated people: whether and in what circumstances such migration is at all likely to entail an economic loss to the world as a whole, and whether and in what circumstances it is likely to impose an uncompensated loss on the remaining residents of the countries of emigration. In both circumstances it is useful to distinguish between de-

may impose a burden on the health, education, and housing services of the country of immigration (which must be greater than could be financed by the increase in the gross incomes of those people resulting from migration if there is to be a net world loss), while the emigration even of unskilled labor would impose a social cost on the country of emigration if such people had paid taxes in their country of origin greater than the value of the public services they consumed (for this to amount to a net world loss the excess taxes paid must exceed the difference between the gross wages of the emigrants in their country of emigration and their wages net of the cost of the public services they consume in their country of immigration).

[5] Direct elements of compensation exist in the form of private financial remittances by emigrants to their countries of origin, which include both individuals' remittances to their families and collective remittances through charitable institutions; such remittances are frequently quantitatively important, in some cases perhaps large enough to yield a net gain to the country of emigration. Indirect elements of compensation may be found in the provision of education at the expense of countries of net educated immigration to citizens of countries of emigration who eventually return home, and the provision to the less developed of those countries of the trained experts of the developed countries as part of their foreign aid programs.

[6] An alternative to compensation, which nationalists especially find appealing, is to take steps to prevent the emigration from occurring, which might be accomplished by policy action in either the immigration or the emigration country. These alternatives are discussed below.

veloped and underdeveloped countries, and to pay special attention to the latter, though the main lines of the argument are the same for both.

With respect to the question of possible economic loss to the world as a whole, the realization of such a loss requires that the migrant move from a location where his total contribution to social output would be higher to one where it will be lower. If potential migrants are motivated by purely economic considerations, they will migrate in response to differences in the private incomes available to them, where "private income" means the sum of net income after taxation and the value to them of the government services they receive in exchange for their taxes. Hence there can be a world loss from the emigration of educated people only if the relationship between the private incomes available in the countries of emigration and immigration is inverse to the relationship between the alternative contributions to social output in the two locations. This can be possible only in two major types of situations. The first is when, either because the system of public finance—including both the total taxation system and the overall pattern of government expenditure, and allowing for the possibilities of tax avoidance given to the higher-income groups (which educated people may be assumed to be) —is relatively more progressive in the country of emigration than in the country of immigration, or because government policy holds down the incomes of educated people as an extra-budgetary means of redistributing income towards poorer citizens, the ratio of social contribution

to private income is relatively higher in the country of emigration than in the country of immigration. The second is when the activity of the educated person involves what technical economic theory terms an "externality"—that is, it contributes something to the welfare or productivity of others in the country of his residence over and above what the individual is paid for doing and for which he would not be paid in a competitive market for his services, and moreover something which is peculiar to him personally and not in his professional capacity[7]—and that externality is greater in his country of birth than in his country of immigration. Such externalities may include leadership capacity, originality of thought, inventive ability, etc.; but it is necessary to note that many such apparent "externalities" are in fact rewarded through the market, general inspirational qualities and the capacity for making basic scientific discoveries being the main examples of externalities that cannot be "internalized" by market processes.

Externalities also include the effects of the migration of the individual on the proportions in which the various cooperating factors of production are available in the coun-

---

[7] As Grubel and Scott have pointed out, if the externality attaches to the profession rather than to the individual, the emigration of the individual will deprive the country of emigration of the externality only until he is replaced by another member of his profession; see H. G. Grubel and A. D. Scott, "The International Flow of Human Capital," *American Economic Review*, Papers and Proceedings, Vol. 56, No. 3, May 1966, pp. 268–74.

tries of immigration and emigration, insofar as such changes affect the earnings of the other factors of production, and its effects on the sales of production in these two economies, insofar as the productivity of an economy varies with its scale.

In both situations, there is a possibility of world loss; but the actuality requires the inversion of the relationships between private income and social contribution in the two alternative locations. This seems a very unlikely possibility in practice, at least for the migration of educated people among the more developed countries of the western world. While, for example, it is true that English-trained doctors have a distorted incentive to emigrate because they are deliberately underpaid as a national policy, it is not plausible to believe that the true value of their services to the English public would have been greater than the value of their services to the Canadian, Australian, or American public. Again, the professions in the various European countries are well developed and numerous enough, and the systems of financial reward sufficiently sophisticated in compensating individuals for most of the obvious apparent "externalities" they may confer on their fellow-citizens, to make it implausible to assume that the net trend of professional migration towards the United States involves sufficient net loss of externalities (if any) to entail a reduction in world social product. Further, in respect of the externalities specifically associated with basic research, it should be remarked that such externalities are generally available to the whole of the world's popula-

tion, at least insofar as the various countries have enough scientists to remain in communication with the world scientific community, and that for the various reasons given in the previous section (economies of scale, and specialization and division of labor), scientific emigrants to the United States are likely to generate more externalities of this type than they would do if they remained in their countries of origin. Finally, given the sizes of the economies of the advanced countries and the degree of development of their professions, it is extremely implausible that net emigration of educated people from Europe to North America entails any significant loss due to diseconomies of smaller scale or changed factor proportions for the European countries.

The foregoing analysis rests on the assumption that educated migrants are motivated by strictly economic considerations of private income gain; but people are not strictly economic in making choices of this kind, and their departures from economic rationality tend to weaken still further the probability of world economic loss from the international migration of skilled people. First, as mentioned in the introduction, potential migrants generally have a preference for their country of birth which constitutes an artificial barrier to the efficient allocation of their talents among countries, and implies substantial marginal gains from the migration that does occur: typically migrants move only in response to substantial gains in their private incomes. Second, people frequently tend to regard the public finance systems of their country of origin as socially just, and to accept any fiscal redistribution of their incomes towards poorer people that the system may entail, whereas they are not generally either familiar with the government services provided in other countries or convinced of the justice of their tax systems; hence they are likely in effect to compare their gross incomes in their countries of origin with their disposable incomes after taxes in their countries of immigration, which again implies that what migration occurs is likely to produce substantial increases in social output. Third, the educated person is generally aware of the externalities he engenders for others, and a professional education is usually devoted in part to teaching the student to derive satisfaction from the externalities he renders as well as the income he receives for his normal services; thus what may appear to the theorist to be externalities may in fact be internalized in individual satisfaction. Further, the nationalism characteristic of the cultures of most political states is such that the educated person is likely to exaggerate and overvalue the externalities he renders in his country of origin, and to disregard or undervalue the externalities he might render in his country of immigration. The former consideration weakens the likelihood that real externalities exist that might cause international migration to lead to world losses; the latter suggests that positive net externalities are likely to result from migration of educated people, resulting in additional gains of social output above the private gains.

This analysis suggests that international migration of educated professional people, at least among the advanced countries, is extremely unlikely to produce world losses, and is on the contrary likely to produce substantial increases in potential world economic welfare. Does the same analysis apply without qualification to the emigration of educated people from the less developed countries, or is there a substantially strong possibility of world loss in that case?

In one important respect, the argument for a probable world gain from this flow of migration of human capital is much stronger, owing to the much greater size of the income differential between developed and less developed countries than among the developed countries, for people with professional qualifications. This differential is large enough to make it virtually impossible for such migration to result in a world loss as a result of the inversion of relative social and private contributions in the alternative locations by relatively more progressive fiscal systems in the less developed countries, or by the exercise in those countries of more stringent policies of holding down professional incomes for the benefit of the poorer classes of society. (In fact, it is likely on the average that the more progressive fiscal structures and incomes policies are to be found in the developed countries, with the result that the gain in world social product from this type of migration will exceed rather than fall short of the gain in private income.)

Any possibility of world loss must therefore hinge on a loss of externalities to the country of emigration, unmatched by an offsetting gain of externalities to the country of immigration, and quantitatively large enough to outweigh the private income gains to the migrants. Four theoretical possibilities of such loss of externalities may be discovered.[8]

First, individuals who might have made scientific discoveries, or introduced improved methods of production or management, that would have substantially increased the productivity of resources in the less developed countries may be diverted to higher-paid activities of a more routine nature lacking such externally beneficial effects, for example, employment in private industrial research and development. The likelihood that this is a typical and important case must be qualified, however, by recognition that the migrant individual may have taken the probability of his making an important discovery into account in making his decision to emigrate, that the country of emigration may have lacked the resources or failed to provide the social and economic climate necessary to successful innovation, and that in some cases at least the individual migrates because only in a large developed country can he obtain the resources required to solve his research problem or the freedom to experiment with new production and management ideas. In short, emigration may be the only effective means available for the individual to contribute an "externality" to his country of emigration.

Second, the members of a particular profession, or the professional classes in general, may generate externalities in a less developed country that they do not generate in a developed country, by providing informal education through instruction and example to their fellow citizens in the requirement of increased efficiency. If their emigration reduces the stock of educated people performing this function below what it would otherwise be, and if the value of this externality outweighs the increase in the market value of their contribution to world output, there will be a world loss. The likelihood of a world loss on this account is questionable, first because it is debatable how far educated people in the less developed countries perform this sort of educative function, second because the quantitative magnitude of the resulting contribution to world output has not been investigated, and third because it is not obvious that emigration of professional people reduces the quantity of professional people left in residence, as contrasted with increasing the total number of people who undertake professional careers.

Third, the emigration of professional people may involve a significant proportional reduction in their numbers in the less developed countries of emigration, thereby perhaps lowering the incomes (marginal products) of cooperating factors of production, without significantly altering the ratios in which factors of production are available in the developed countries of immigration (this last being a reasonable assumption). This possible source of world loss is also debatable, first because it requires that emigration reduce the number of educated people available, instead of increasing the number prepared to undertake professional education, second because it requires that a change in the relative quanti-

---

[8] These cases were suggested by a reading of the paper by B. Thomas, *op. cit.*, though not identical with those presented in that source.

ties of factors reduce the marginal products of the cooperating factors, and third because it requires that this reduction in the marginal products of the other factors be great enough to offset the income gain to the emigrating factor.

Fourth, the emigration of professional people, by reducing their absolute numbers to a quantitatively significant extent, may reduce the aggregate of resources available in the country of emigration and thus impose on it diseconomies of scale of production, while either not being quantitatively significant enough in the country of immigration to call into play offsetting economies of scale, or not calling such economies of scale into play because they have already been exhausted by the size already achieved by the developed economies. This possibility also depends on the assumption that emigration reduces the stock of trained people, rather than increasing the number prepared to undertake professional training, as well as the assumption that economies of scale are quantitatively important enough to outweigh the income gain to the emigrating factor of production.

In summary, all of these possibilities raise both the qualitative question of whether the externalities posited correspond to the facts of the situation, and the quantitative question of whether their effects are important enough to countervail against the presumption of a world gain from the migration of educated people from less developed to developed countries. In the absence of any very persuasive evidence to the contrary, it would seem reasonable to conclude that there is no significant probability of world loss from the international migration of educated people.

The second question is whether such migration may nevertheless entail uncompensated losses to the countries of emigration. Most of the relevant possibilities are implicit in the argument already presented. To begin with, however, it should be noted that the country of emigration generally obtains some gains from the emigration of educated people, which may provide indirect compensation for any losses incurred. Aside from emigrant remittances, the country will obtain the benefit of basic scientific discoveries made by emigrants; it may also benefit by the availability of better-quality or lower-cost products, produced with the help of the services of the emigrants; and even where it has to pay royalties and license fees to use the product of their research, it may be better off than if it had had to finance the research itself.

The residents of the country of emigration obviously lose from emigration, to the extent that the emigration of educated people deprives them of tax revenue in excess of the cost of governmental services that would have had to be provided to the emigrants had they remained at home. There are two major cases here. The first concerns the redistribution of personal income by governmental taxation and expenditure policies, it being assumed that the emigrant is typically in a higher income-tax bracket than the average of the population; in this case, the emigrant deprives those who remain behind of their tax-mediated share in his income. The second concerns intergenerational transfers of income through the governmental budget:

to the extent that the currently-working generation pays the costs of education of the young through its taxes, and in return expects to be supported in its old age by pensions financed by taxes on the incomes of the presently-young after they have graduated into the currently-working category, emigration of the young after completion of education deprives their elders *pro tanto* of their expected retirement benefits. Precisely the same two cases arise when, instead of the incomes of the educated being taxed especially heavily, the incomes they can earn are reduced by deliberate government policy.

The transfer of taxable capacity from the country of emigration to the country of immigration when the emigrant changes countries has been described in the literature as a gift from one country to the other. The notion of a "gift," however, is ambiguous, in the sense that a voluntary gift entails no real loss to the giver, being recompensed by the satisfaction of having given something of value to a cherished recipient, whereas a gift given in the expectation of a recompense that is not in fact received constitutes a real loss. Thus it makes an important difference to the policy implications of international migration of educated people whether such people are provided with publicly financed education in the expectation that they will remain at home and compensate (or over-compensate) those who have financed their education by paying taxes on the incomes they will subsequently earn, or whether the education is provided as a genuine gift intended to give them a better start in life, regardless of where they subsequently choose to live. Thus it is important to the question of ascertaining whether or not there is a loss from the emigration of educated people to the country of emigration, to determine what the assumptions of its policy of public education are.[9]

There is also an obvious loss to the country of emigration if the emigration of educated people deprives it of externalities that it would otherwise have enjoyed. The question then is one of determining which, if any, theoretically possible externalities are quantitatively significant. Of the four listed above pertaining to the less developed countries, the possible loss of new knowledge or improved methods of production and management is a matter on which *a priori* reasoning can throw no light; the same applies to the question of whether or not professional people perform an unpaid educational function in the less developed countries, though theory does raise the question whether the emigration of educated people reduces the

---

[9] It is relevant also to note the technical point that the value of the gift will be substantially smaller from the point of view of the less developed country than from that of the developed country. The reason is that most of the cost of education is the cost of labor, in the form of tuition, construction of buildings, and foregone student earnings; and the cost of labor is far less in the underdeveloped countries than in the advanced ones. One important consequence is that, when students from less developed countries are trained in and at the expense of a developed country and some of them remain in that country, both countries may enjoy a net increment in their stocks of human capital when the value of human capital is reckoned at the alternative opportunity cost of creating it appropriate to the country in which it finally resides.

locally available supply as distinct from increasing the world supply provided from local sources. The same question arises with respect to the possibility that the emigration of educated people deprives the less developed countries of economies of scale. In addition, theory would suggest that, even if the emigration of educated people does reduce the remaining stock, the effects of this on the scale of the economy are likely to be negligible, because the contribution of educated people to production—as reflected in their share of the total output—is small, and because emigration is typically a small proportion of current additions to the national stock of educated people, and so alters the available total stock only fractionally.

Where economic theory has something to contribute to the analysis of possible loss is with regard to the likelihood that, if emigration alters the relative quantities available of educated people and of co-operant factors of production, this will tend to reduce the incomes of the co-operating factors. According to the familiar analysis in international trade theory of the relation between international trade and factor prices, a country can adjust to changes in the ratios of factors of production available to it, without any change in the prices of the services of the factors themselves, by altering the ratios in which it produces goods that use the available factors with relatively different intensities, while avoiding the losses entailed by consuming the commodities in question in less preferable ratios by exchanging abundant for scarce goods through international trade. This analysis suggests that losses to the

country of emigration through externalities resulting from changes in the ratios of factor availabilities resulting from the emigration of educated people are likely to be negligible.

In addition to the cases of loss discussed above, it is sometimes argued that the country of emigration suffers certain "adjustment costs" of emigration, that is, costs of adjustment to the disturbance arising from the decision of educated persons to emigrate. Such adjustment costs are obviously associated with changes in the rate of emigration, not with the fact of emigration itself, since the economy becomes adjusted to whatever the normal rate of emigration is. Moreover, the costs of adjustment to a change in the rate of emigration can easily be exaggerated, because the normal terms of employment of professional people are customarily designed to minimize the costs of disturbance arising from the termination of the employment contract by either party. In general, the avoidance of, or the provision of compensation for, adjustment costs consequent on migration may safely be left to the market in private contracts among those concerned.

The foregoing discussion of possible losses to the country of emigration has been both quite general, and rather skeptical about the likelihood of significant losses. There is, on the contrary, a natural tendency for those who sympathize with the development aspirations of the underdeveloped countries to assume that the emigration of some of their educated people must impose great losses on them. This assumption, however, usually derives from a logical fallacy based on telescoping the nature and results of the development process. It is true that if and when these countries become fully developed, they will need and be able to employ much larger numbers of educated people; but this does not imply that in their present circumstances additional educated people would necessarily contribute significantly to their development. Development is an integrated process both of accumulating capital in the broad sense—material, human, and intellectual—and of evolving a culture that promotes the efficient use of such capital and the habit of constantly seeking to improve the efficiency of use. It is not likely to be promoted by concentrating attention and economic policy on the accumulation of one type of capital on the assumption that all else will follow. This has been shown by the unsatisfactory results of past development efforts, which have concentrated on the accumulation of material capital. It would be unfortunate if development theory and policy were to resurrect the myth that there is a simple and quick road to development by substituting human capital for material capital as the crucial element in the process.

IMPLICATIONS FOR MIGRATION POLICY

As argued in the preceding section, it is extremely unlikely that the migration of educated people among the advanced countries leads to a loss of world economic welfare, while the possibility of world loss from the migration of educated people from less developed to developed countries is highly questionable. The problem for policy, then, is how to compensate the countries that may lose from international flows of human capital for the losses they may incur; the establishment of institutional arrangements for such compensation would automatically prevent the occurrence of flows that entail a loss of world economic welfare, since the gainers would not be able to compensate the losers in this case without ending up worse off as a result.

Of the cases of loss to the country of emigration previously discussed, that associated with the "gift" element in the international transfer of taxable capacity is the most easily disposed of in principle. All that is required is a binding contractual arrangement by which either the individual whose education is publicly financed on the assumption that he will remain in the country of his origin, or his employer or the government in his country of immigration is legally obliged to repay the cost of his education to the country that educated him, or perhaps to repay that cost plus an estimate of the amount of his income projected in the future in his own country of origin, which he would have been obliged to redistribute via excess taxation to his fellow citizens.

Such an obligation might be imposed on students by their government in the countries of emigration; in that case a more efficient and acceptable solution might be to finance student education, at least at the university level, by loans rather than grants, allowing interest on the loans as a deduction from income for tax purposes; if the educated individual is regarded as owing the society a tax contribution over and above interest on the cost of his education, including in the interest charge a surcharge designed to fulfill this obligation. An alternative solution, which has already been applied to some extent in certain countries, is to oblige the recipient of a publicly-financed education to remain in or return to the country for a specified number of years. This is a less efficient alternative, since it deprives the educated individual of the freedom to decide whether personal service or cash repayment is a preferable alternative, and also fails to recognize the foregone-earnings element in the cost of education, which is bound to differ among individuals.

The other possibility would be for the employer or the government in the country of immigration to pay a bounty to the country of emigration per immigrant received. This also would be an inefficient solution, owing to the difficulty of fixing a bounty that would correspond either to the loss of the country of emigration or the gain to the country of immigration; but it might be less open to evasion and breach of contract than an obligation imposed on the migrant by his own government.

The remaining possibilities of loss to the country of emigration are much more difficult to prescribe for, owing to the difficulty of quantitative estimate of the magnitude of potential losses. In view of the uncertainty attaching to these possible losses, it might be wisest to ignore them, and to concentrate policy measures on recouping for the country of emigration the costs incurred in training the migrants, on one of the alternative lines discussed above.

Where there are clear cases of loss from the various cases cited, there would seem to be a *prima facie* case for the countries of emigration to develop policies of subsidizing the presence of their educated personnel; there would seem to be no reason why the countries of immigration should pay a subsidy to the countries of emigration in return for the privilege of offering the educated citizen of the latter an opportunity to escape from a situation in which their incomes fall short of their true social value.

This last proposition, however, ignores one important element in the structure of the world economy as presently constituted—the discrimination against the international migration of unskilled labor embodied in present immigration laws. If educated people can migrate but uneducated people cannot, the justice of advising countries with predominantly unskilled labor to pay the price of keeping their skilled labor at home is open to serious question. On the other hand, given the present lack of effective population control practices in the less developed countries, it is extremely doubtful whether the effect of relaxation of prevailing barriers to the immigration of unskilled labor into the developed countries would do anything in the long run to improve the lot of unskilled labor in the less developed countries. It therefore appears that existing barriers to the immigration of unskilled labor into the developed countries have some justification and that the recommendation to the less developed countries to subsidize their resources of educated people is indirectly a recommendation to them to do something about solving their population problem. This is an endeavor to which the developed countries might well be asked to contribute, on the grounds that the welcome they accord to educated immigrants helps to perpetuate the population problems of the less developed countries by providing a safety-valve means of escape for people who might otherwise insist on the need for effective population control.

The alternatives to the recommendation of compensation to the less developed countries for losses entailed in the emigration of educated labor is an embargo on the international migration of such labor. This would seem to be very much an inferior alternative, both because it would deprive the educated citizens of the less developed countries of their present opportunities of bettering their economic lot by emigration, and because the deprivation of freedom might induce these people to refuse to render to their countries of origin the externalities that constitute the main argument for depriving them of their freedom to migrate. In addition, it would be extremely difficult to devise a system of embargo that would prevent emigration or immigration while preserving the benefits of foreign study and work experience.

SOME BROADER DYNAMIC CONSIDERATIONS

The preceding sections have been concerned with the economic aspects of international flows of educated people, from a rather narrowly technical theoretical point of view. In the broader historical perspective of world economic evolution, the phenomena underlying current worries about "brain drain" are simply one

aspect of a far more pervasive trend, the trend towards closer integration of the world economy, which has been proceeding rapidly since World War II. Other aspects of it are the reduction of barriers to international trade, the increasing integration of the national capital markets of the advanced countries into a world capital market, the growth of direct foreign investment by the large international corporations, the rapid spread of modern technology from country to country, and the modernization of traditional class- and status-oriented societies into less personal, more mobile, and flexible modes of interpersonal relationship conducive to economic efficiency. Many of the manifestations of this trend towards world economic integration are bound to be distasteful to traditionalists and to nationalists, especially as these manifestations can be readily associated with American influences; fears and hatreds are aroused not only by "brain drain" but by "American control of our economy" and "Americanization of our way of life" ("American cultural penetration," in the Freudian phrase used to describe it in Canada). Nevertheless, the trend towards closer world economic integration is a powerful force operating to raise world living standards, by disseminating techniques, practices, and products that increase human productivity and satisfaction throughout the world.

One important consequence of increasing world economic integration is that the market for educated professional people, like the market for commodities, is becoming increasingly an international rather than a national market, with corresponding economic pressures towards the equalization of prices for professional work throughout the international economy, manifest in the phenomena of "brain drain." These pressures, reinforced by the increase in demand for educated people as professionals and as university teachers associated with the advance of technology and the increase in demand for education as living standards rise, imply a sharp increase in the scarcity value of educated people in most countries, sharper the lower the average level of income in the particular country. This in turn implies serious economic and social disturbance, because not only are the national economic, educational, health, and other productive systems built on traditional assumptions about the relative value and cost of educated labor as compared with ordinary labor and capital, but the social fabric is built on the assumption that economic power and social status derive ultimately from the ownership of property, rather than the possession of educated talent.

Rather than resist these pressures by attempting to eliminate one of their symptoms, "brain drain," policy in the countries affected should aim at adjusting the use of educated people to the new prevailing situation of increased relative scarcity, by recognizing the higher value of such people in contemporary circumstances, paying them accordingly, and seeking at the same time to economize on their use. In particular, industrial and governmental employers of educated people should abandon the notion of a "just price," conformable to past social relationships based on the dominance of property owners, for the services of such people, and revise methods of combining the services of the educated with other factors of production based on the assumption that the cost of these services is that "just price." The effect of the competitive pressures referred to will in any case inevitably be to force such adjustments; the question is only whether policy will be dictated by foresight or by hindsight.

In general, as already suggested, the effects of these competitive pressures in the market for educated labor should be to promote economic growth. They should also, in the longer run, promote a more desirable society, by undermining the dominance of property ownership as a source of wealth and social status. These effects should prove beneficial in the developed and less developed countries alike, in the long run. In the near term, however, they may conceivably aggravate the problem of promoting economic development in the less developed countries. But in the broad perspective of world economic development, "brain drain" is a trivial factor in the problem of developing the underdeveloped regions of the world; and doing something about "brain drain" is far less important than increasing the flow of development assistance and the efficiency with which it is applied in development programs, and expanding the opportunities for the less developed countries to participate in world economic growth through international trade. It would also be worth considering whether the developed countries could not contribute more to the relief of poverty in the underdeveloped countries by lowering their barriers to the immigration of unskilled labor, thereby allowing poor people more direct and immediate access to the high living standards of the developed countries than is afforded by present policies of supporting development programs in their own countries, designed to bring them in the very long run to the standard of living that the poor in the developed countries already enjoy.